MICROECONOMICS

MICROECONOMICS

The Analysis of Prices and Markets

Donald Dewey

Columbia University

New York

OXFORD UNIVERSITY PRESS

London 1975 Toronto

Library of Congress Catalogue Card Number: 74-79620
Printed in the United States of America
Copyright © 1975 by Oxford University Press, Inc.

Preface

To put first things first, this book was written for students. However, since teachers sometimes read prefaces while students almost never do, this preface is written mainly for teachers. My hope in writing this book was that it might make some contribution to improving both the content and the pedagogy of the course in microeconomics (also called microeconomic theory, price theory, theory of the firm, and sometimes merely economic theory) that lies—or should lie—at the center of every undergraduate program in economics. That microeconomics lies at the center of every graduate program in economics can be taken as self-evident.

While microeconomics may be the foundation course in the undergraduate economics program, in my experience neither students nor teachers are especially happy with it. And I believe that the dissatisfactions of both parties to the educational process have a common source, even though their complaints are voiced in different ways. By my reading, the main trouble is that the course in microeconomics has been rendered increasingly unsatisfactory by its failure to adjust to changes in other parts of the economics curriculum. The intellectual content of the Principles course has, of course, greatly changed in the last twenty years. This change has been mostly for the better though, as economists know well enough, all change has its costs. Indeed much of what constituted the microeconomics course of twenty years ago has now been moved down into the Principles course. Today it is safe to assume that most students enroll in the microeconomics course after having spent a full year wrestling with a demanding Principles text (most probably Samuelson). All too often students who come to microeconomics with this background are simply bored with what they are offered.

Teachers of the micro course, for their part, are conscious that too few of the interesting advances and innovations of the subject in recent years are being discussed. For better or worse, the reward structure of the academic profession does not encourage a rapid movement of ideas from journal articles, monographs, and treatises, into the books that students read. There is small professional glory (and no research support) to be had by translating another man's original work into clear English and compact mathematics.

The result is that all too often the micro course is made to serve one or both of two suspect purposes. It is made into an intensive but unexciting review of certain topics the student has already met in his first course in economics. Or it is used as a half-hearted introduction to mathematical economics, where he learns that a number of simple propositions already encountered in economics can be given a mathematical formulation. This last approach is no doubt a useful drill for students who go on to graduate work in economics (though it also means that materials which could be covered in undergraduate microeconomics get postponed to the graduate level). This approach does very little for the majority of undergraduates in economics who do not go on to graduate work.

This book assumes that students in microeconomics should be encouraged and, if need be, chivied into going considerably beyond the ideas encountered in the first course. For with all due respect to the many fine Principles texts in print, there are many important ideas that receive at best a perfunctory treatment in their crowded chapters. I can see no good reason why the materials of the micro course cannot be upgraded and modernized. It is sometimes held that undergraduates do not have the mathematics needed for more advanced microeconomics. This objection strikes me as having little merit. If the representative student in the micro course is not a mathematical sophisticate, neither is he a mathematical illiterate. He comes with previous university work in calculus and linear algebra and often statistics as well. Moreover, there is no good reason why students should be expected to contend without pedagogical help with the original constructions of economic research. Many important research results were given their first convoluted (and perhaps not wholly correct) formulations in language that the beginning economist cannot easily follow. Such results can be—and should be—restated in more intelligible fashion.

I will close with two cautions. The topics emphasized in this book are those that I believe most deserving of attention in a microeconomics course. A glance at the table of contents will indicate that my preference is for treating the theory of the firm as the heart of microeconomics. Accordingly, this book offers an unusually detailed treatment of competition, monopoly, "natural" monopoly, limit pricing, oligopoly, and price discrimination, with particular attention to the multiplant firm. (If this book can be said to have a "message" it is that microeconomics should be restructured to give prominent place to the multiplant firm that has approximately constant average total cost over a wide range of output. The tyranny of the U-shaped ATC curve has endured for too long.) Since most students are interested in the applications of economic theory to economic policy (and rightly so), certain problems of welfare economics are examined at length. Chapter 11 is witness to my conviction that the compleat microeconomics book must somewhere introduce the reader to the ubiquitous operations of capitalization and discount.

My final caution is that while this book aspires to plain English and compact mathematics, it involves no conscious effort to sugar-coat either the methodology or subject matter of modern microeconomics. Too many years in the classroom have brought me to the sad conclusion that many otherwise sensible and able students become acutely unresponsive whenever the instructor begins, "Now let us assume that . . ." The task of reaching this worthy, turned-off minority—or explaining why it is so hostile to even minimal abstraction—I leave to others. This book is for that other minority of students who already like formal, self-conscious abstraction in economics—and for the majority of students who are capable of giving it a sympathetic hearing.

This book was made possible by an accumulation of personal and professional debts too numerous to list. However, my obligations to the following critics should be acknowledged. They kindly read and commented upon parts of the manuscript in its various stages of unreadiness and tried to save me from obscurantism, error, and affronts to the English language. I would especially like to thank: Richard Brief, David Colander, Robert Eagly, Ronald Findlay, Gerald Meier, Norman Mintz, Anwar Shaikh, William Geoffrey Shepherd, Olive Vaughan, and William Vickrey. My thanks go also to Luigi Pasinetti for the many goads and invitations to fresh thinking provided during his time as visiting professor at Columbia.

The generosity of critics should never be allowed to leave them open to a charge of guilt by association. The defects of a book are properly and exclusively charged against him who presumes to write it.

D. D.

New York City
August 1974

Contents

MICROECONOMICS

1
Scope and Method

A rapid review

Since you have been able to enroll in this course, you have almost certainly taken some previous work in economics and mastered it to your examiner's satisfaction. Therefore, we shall proceed directly to business, skipping the preliminaries and homilies appropriate to a first course in economics. ("What is economics?" "Is economics a science?" Etc.) We know that any economic system—capitalist, socialist, or mixed—must contend with the brute fact of scarcity. It must decide:

1. which wants are to be fulfilled, that is, it must set the "goals of production";
2. how scarce resources are to be allocated so as to realize these production goals as fully as possible;
3. how the results of production ("goods and services") are to be distributed among the population;
4. what provision (if any) is to be made for economic progress, that is, the system must allocate some resources for the creation of additional capital goods (including workers) and for research and development.

Finally, we know that these four tasks of an economic system will not be eliminated if we shoot all capitalists or, alternatively, convert the rulers of the Soviet economy to the free market philosophy of the American Manufacturers' Association. So long as human beings retain their capacity to be envious, ambitious for themselves or their children, or otherwise discontented, the economic system will have to face up to scarcity.

Economic anthropologists tell us that the above four problems have been solved within a great number of different social frameworks—that many different economic systems have existed in the world. Economic historians emphasize that every economic system regardless of the label applied to it has undergone continual change. Whatever it is, American capitalism of the 1970's is not the American capitalism of the 1890's; and Soviet communism of the 1970's is not the Soviet communism of the 1920's.

Since economics is the study of how an economic system copes with scarcity, and since there are many ways of coping, many different kinds of economics are possible. Most of us, however, have only a minuscule interest in the economic organization of the Greenland Eskimos in the early nineteenth century; or in the extreme forms of communism of certain modern religious groups. We are mainly interested (perhaps myopically) in how technically advanced economic systems operate. All such systems have one important feature in common—extensive reliance upon markets ("the price system") to solve the four problems rooted in scarcity.

In the case of the American economy of the nineteenth century, the leading role of markets is perfectly obvious. Virtually all economic decisions were then left to markets, the role of government being largely confined to internal improvements, national defense, rudimentary education, and a postal service. (As late as 1929 in the United States over one-half of all federal employees worked in the Post Office, and the tariff was the greatest federal revenue source.) In the present century many decisions formerly entrusted to the market in the American economy have been transferred to the political process. But most have not. Government policy now has a considerable influence on the level of aggregate economic activity, notably on the rate of unemployment and the rate of inflation. Yet even today government policy has little to do with determining how many barber shops will operate, the price of haircuts, and the take-home pay of barbers. Or with how many steel mills will operate, the prices of one thousand and one different steel products, or the wages paid to fifty different categories of steel workers.

Economists may differ over how much success the federal government has enjoyed in its effort to use direct price controls to slow the rate at which prices have increased in recent years. But the policy was not intended to determine the set of relative prices in the economy (e.g. the price of bread in relation to the price of a bottle of Scotch whisky); and it has comparatively little impact on these relative prices.

Nor is the widespread use of markets confined to capitalist and so-called "mixed" economic systems. The Yugoslavia of Marshal Tito openly proclaims its dedication to "socialist pricing," and there is a wealth of evidence to suggest that in the Soviet Union, co-operatives and state-owned firms deal with consumers, and with one another, in more-or-less organized markets. Indeed, no technically advanced economic system has yet managed to function (even in wartime) without the extensive use of markets. We have good reason to believe that none ever will. In a modern industrial economy an enormous number of decisions must be made every day. It is difficult to believe that they can be made without the aid of the millions of buyer-seller transactions that constitute the price system.

Economic theory as the study of markets

Since markets have played so great a role in all technically advanced economic systems—and since the discipline of economics grew up, so to speak, with these systems—modern economics is mainly the study of one kind of economic system: the price system. What is called economic theory or economic analysis is the study of the price system by the method of formal, self-conscious abstraction. (This method is also called model building.) As you have learned somewhere in your college career, all thought involves abstraction; hence a linguistic purist may properly question that there can be such a thing as a non-theoretical course in economics or, for that matter, a non-theoretical course in anything else. This is true. Nevertheless, in much of economics the practitioner feels under no obligation to make clear, either to himself or others, the nature of his model. It remains implicit in his work. For example, when you read a book on labor movements in nineteenth-century America by an economic historian, you can usually tell whether he viewed a particular labor market as highly competitive, reasonably competitive, or hardly competitive at all. But he does not feel it worthwhile to treat you to a long digression on the meaning of competition and/or monopoly in the labor market, or to a critique of the assumptions that underlie his implicit definitions of these terms.

In contrast to the economic historian, the economic theorist is an intellectual child of Euclid (the geometer) to whom assumptions are all-important. They must be clearly stated—which, in practice, means that they must be briefly stated. They must be checked against one another for consistency; and conclusions must be derived from assumptions according to the accepted canons of logic. Above all, the assumptions used by the economic theorist must be useful. They must allow him to construct a model that allows him to predict, with a tolerable degree of accuracy, economic developments in the real world. And what is a tolerable degree of accuracy? Simply one which is thought to be justified by the costs that must be incurred to achieve it. Thus, while weather forecasting is certainly not an exact science, its economic benefits almost certainly exceed its modest economic costs (mainly the salaries of a few meteorologists in the federal civil service).

Contrary to one popular impression, it does not matter greatly whether the assumptions of economic theory are "realistic" or not. As Milton Friedman has noted:

> Truly important and significant hypotheses will be found to have "assumptions" that are wildly inaccurate descriptive representatives of reality and, in general, the more significant the theory, the more unrealistic the assumptions. . . . The reason is simple. A hypothesis is important if it "explains" much by little, that is, if it abstracts the common and crucial elements from the mass of complex and detailed circumstances surrounding the phenomenon to be explained and permits valid predictions on the basis of them alone. To be important, therefore, a hypothesis must be descriptively false in its assumptions; it takes account of, and accounts for, none of the many other attendant circumstances, since its very success shows them to be irrelevant for the phenomenon to be explained.[1]

Or again:

> A theory or its "assumptions" cannot possibly be thoroughly "realistic" in the immediate descriptive sense so often assigned to this term. A completely "realistic" theory of the wheat market would have to include not only the conditions directly underlying the supply and demand for wheat but also the kind of coins or credit instruments used to make exchanges; the personal characteristics of wheat-traders such as the color of each trader's hair and eyes, his antecedents and education, the number of members of his family, their characteristics, antecedents, and education, etc.; the kind of soil on which the wheat was grown, its physical and chemical characteristics, the weather prevailing during the growing season; the personal characteristics of the farmers growing the wheat and of the consumers who will ultimately use it; and so on indefinitely. Any attempt to move very far in achieving this kind of "realism" is certain to render a theory utterly useless.[2]

1. Milton Friedman, *Essays in Positive Economics* (Chicago, 1953), pp. 14-15.
2. *Ibid.*, p. 32.

In the study of markets by the method of formal, self-conscious abstraction, a great deal is left out. Nothing is said about the laws governing the inheritance of property, the legal remedies that a creditor has against debtors who default, or the justice of income distribution. The possibility of fraud in commercial transactions is ruled out with the assumption that buyers and sellers have complete information about the commodity in which they trade. Economists speak of the "firm" but do not usually bother to specify whether it is owned by private stockholders, workers, or the state.

Is "too much" left out in the study of markets by the method of formal, self-conscious abstraction? Is it reasonable to assume that there is some standard body of economic theory that can be usefully applied to the study of price making in the laissez-faire economy of nineteenth-century America, the centralized planning of the Soviet economy in the 1930's, and the mixed economy of present-day Sweden? Economic theorists believe that such a body of economic theory does exist; it has been their experience that "little explains much" in the study of markets with widely different institutional frameworks. At the end of your college work in economics (when you finish your work in economic theory you should, of course, take additional economics courses with a policy orientation to try out your newly acquired set of tools) you may share this view. Then again you may not. In the marketplace of ideas, there is no shortage of substitute products.

Three kinds of economic models

We can divide the models of economic theory into three sorts. We have first "static" models wherein all participants are presumed to have complete information relevant to the decision that they must make. In static analysis, nobody ever makes a mistake. Second, we have risk models. Here an economic decision can have more than one outcome; however, the number of outcomes is known in advance and so, also, is the probability coefficient that attaches to each. Finally, we have uncertainty (or "incomplete information") models wherein the possible outcomes of a decision and/or their probability coefficients are not completely known in advance.

The crucial differences among these three types of models can be illustrated by their treatment of the idea of "demand." The demand curve of the firm that produces a product as set forth in all basic economics books belongs to a static model. Given the conventional demand curve, the firm

TABLE 1.1

Price	possible demand (units of output)	probability coefficient
$5.	100	0.4
	80	0.6
$4.	115	0.3
	95	0.7

does not have to guess the quantity of its output that consumers will demand at a given price. The firm *knows;* this information is a given condition of the problem.

In a risk model there is, strictly speaking, no such thing as a demand curve. Rather quantity demanded is what statisticians misleadingly call a random variable. Consider table 1.1. It indicates when a price of $5 (per unit of output per unit of time) is charged, the firm may sell either 100 units or 80 units. (Sales may depend upon whether the weather is "good" or "not good.") The probability that the firm will sell 100 units at a $5 price is 0.4. The probability that it will sell 80 units at a $5 price is 0.6. Likewise, when a price of $4 is charged, the firm may sell either 115 units or 95 units. The probability that it will sell 115 at a $4 price is 0.3; the probability that it will sell 95 units at a $4 price is 0.7.

In an uncertainty model, the notion of demand becomes even more difficult to formulate. The simplest way to convert a risk model into an uncertainty model is by specifying that both possible sales at a given price and their probability coefficients are subjectively estimated by the decision maker. Thus if the numbers in table 1.1 are assumed to describe demand in an uncertainty model, they represent only the best guesses of the firm's decision maker who may, of course, be either a single individual or a committee. In an uncertainty model, these guesses may well prove to be wrong. For example, the firm may decide to charge a price of $5 and wind up selling 200 units. When this happens, the decision maker presumably learns from experience and revises the probability coefficients that he assigns to the possible outcomes of a similar decision that he may make in the future.

The case for static models

For the most part, economic theorists do their work with static models. This is because static models, being vastly easier to construct and alter, have proved to be more useful. There are only a very few situations in which it is worthwhile to employ a risk model. For once we are prepared to assume that we have complete information about the possible outcomes of an economic "move," and the probability that each outcome will come to pass, we might as well go all the way. That is, we might just as well specify that an economic move has only one possible outcome. The principal defect of uncertainty models (aside from the fact that they are even more complicated than risk models) is that they have—and can have—only limited predictive value. After all, uncertainty exists, by definition, to the extent that accurate prediction is impossible. The only parts of economic reality where economic theorists have attained the power to predict with reasonable accuracy are those parts that can be handled with the aid of static models.

Two fundamental assumptions

Since the conclusions that we shall draw with the aid of our models (mainly static) depend on the assumptions we shall employ, the more important of these assumptions will be explicitly set down. So also will be the most important conclusions (theorems) that we shall derive. It would, of course, be impossible to list all of the assumptions that will be used or to explicitly set down all of the conclusions that they make possible. We shall introduce assumptions and theorems "as needed" throughout this book. However, two assumptions are so important and pervasive in our work that we shall introduce and comment on them here. They are:

A1.1 All decision makers—consumers, entrepreneurs, and factor suppliers—are income maximizers.

A1.2 All decisions are taken upon the basis of complete information: the prices of factors and commodities are universally known, and every consumer "knows what he likes."

Are the above assumptions "realistic"? Of course not. Decision makers are presumably human; up to a point they will forgo earning additional income in order to do other things—watch television, play with the kids, more carefully spend income already earned, etc. And obviously nobody has complete information relevant to the decisions that he must make.

Are the above two assumptions useful? The utility of assumption A1.1 is not likely to be challenged by even the most suspicious and severe critic of formal abstraction in economics.[3] The used car salesman may give what from the automobile trade's standpoint is an irrationally good deal to his favorite aunt. But most of his transactions will be with non-kinsmen whom he regards as fair game for "all that the traffic will bear." We do not really believe that, in the real world, prices are kept down by the benevolence of entrepreneurs, consumers, and workers. Nor do we really believe that they are raised by the crazy malice of these groups. We quite reasonably believe that the assumption of income maximization allows us to predict with a high degree of accuracy how people behave in the real world.

We might note that it does not greatly matter whether or not decision makers really are income maximizers—it is enough that they behave "as if" they were. For example, it is quite likely that many college professors, if compelled to, would forgo X amount of income in order to obtain Y amount of status. But to the extent that there is a positive correlation between income and status in the teaching profession (and there most certainly is), we can explain the movement of professors between universities on the assumption that they are income maximizers.

Assumption A1.2, which says that decisions are taken on the basis of complete information, is harder for most of us to accept. Perhaps the utility of A1.2 can best be appreciated by considering the alternative. If the decision maker does not have complete information, then how much information does he have out of the total amount that is available in the universe—15, 50, 90 percent? And what is he doing to increase his fund of information? Or, for that matter, how do we measure his "amount of information"? The assumption that decision makers have complete information simply saves an enormous amount of time and expense in economic theory.

The limits of economic theory

The principal merit of the study of markets by the method of formal, self-conscious abstraction is its generality. But generality, like most things in

3. A few writers, however, contend that decision making in the large corporation is now so bureaucratized that its behavior can no longer be adequately explained by assuming that its goal is income maximization. As yet nobody has come up with an assumption about corporate behavior that gives better predictions. In a period of high prosperity when corporations are making (well-publicized) contributions to charity and local symphony orchestras and their executives are on the banquet circuit proclaiming a dedication to the social responsibility of business, the depreciating of the income maximizing assumption has a certain plausibility. In a period of severe recession when workers are being laid off, dividends skipped, research and developments slashed, and corporate good works drastically curtailed, criticism of the income maximization assumption is less frequent and less persuasive.

this world, can only be obtained at a price. In the case of this type of economic theory (which is now what most economists mean by the term "economic theory") the price that must be paid is the loss of applicability to specific situations. For example, suppose that we wish to calculate the additional revenue that will flow into the treasury of New York State if the tax on a pack of cigarettes is raised from 20 cents to 25 cents. Economic theory merely allows us to say that *if* the supply and demand functions of cigarettes are of a certain form, the tax rise will bring in a certain sum. Likewise, if they are of a different form, then New York State will realize a different sum from the tax rise.

In order to make a sensible prediction about the probable impact of the tax change, we have to decide what numbers to plug into our supply and demand equations. Economic theory has little to say about which of all possible sets of numbers that we can choose is the "best." Only empirical observation of the cigarette market can suggest which set is best. The numbers obtained can be estimated by casually observing the cigarette-buying habits of our friends. Or they can be obtained by spending one million dollars on marketing research directed by a corps of statisticians with Ph.D.'s. Economic theory can tell us what information we need to have in order to make a sensible prediction of the impact of the tax rise on state revenue. It cannot supply the necessary information.

The domain of microeconomics

In this course we shall limit our attention to those topics that form the core of what, in recent years, has come to be called "microeconomics." All classification being arbitrary, the exact location of the boundary between "micro" and "macro" in economics is properly a matter of argument. By common practice, the activities of the household, the firm, the labor union, and the industry are now assigned to the micro category while the forces that affect the important aggregates of the economic system—income, consumption, investment, and over-all economic growth are placed in the macro category. The best argument for respecting this division of labor is that a generation of economists has found it to be useful. That "macro" considerations affect the decisions of households, firms, labor unions, and industries, is clear enough, e.g. in recent years labor contract negotiations have usually been conducted with an eye of possibility of more inflation and government wage-price controls. Still, it seems best to leave the exploration of the complicated interface between micro- and macroeconomics until later. Before considering their interconnections we should first make the acquaintance of each branch of economics in its simple form.

Alleged bias in economic theory

In conclusion, it seems advisable to say something about the charge repeated by each generation of sociologists, political reformers, and economists with an aversion to formal, self-conscious abstraction, that economic theory contains an ideological bias. Most commonly the charge is that the subject is biased in favor of laissez-faire capitalism. Occasionally (especially in recent years) the bias is alleged to be toward market socialism. By now it is a terribly tired cliché of its defenders that economic theory *per se* is merely a tool of analysis; that bias can only be sought in the minds of people who employ the tool. This answer is just a little too slick. Obviously economic theory *per se* is ideologically neutral. The same cannot be said for economic theorists. (This observation, as will soon become apparent, is not meant as a criticism of economic theorists.)

The truth is that virtually all economic theorists—hard-core free market men with Ph.D.'s from the University of Chicago, with-it advocates of the mixed economy from the Ivy League, and avowed Marxists—alike have a healthy respect for the price system. This respect has two main foundations.

First, most economists believe in the kind of political liberty represented by free elections and civil liberties. So, of course, do millions of other people. But many economists, rightly or wrongly, believe that there is an essential connection between political liberty and the dispersion of power and decision making that characterizes the price system. In its most simplistic formulation, this view asserts that there can be no political freedom unless a large number of people are in a position to tell bureaucrats to go to hell and still be able to earn a living. In its more sophisticated formulation, this view holds that the only alternative to economic decision-making by markets is economic decision-making by politics; that a democratic politics is possible only when there exists a consensus on fundamental values in the society; and that this essential consensus is jeopardized to the extent that the number of decisions required of the political process is increased. In the words of one writer:

> Political determination of relative prices, of relative returns from investment in different industries, and of relative wages in different occupations implies settlement by peaceful negotiation of conflicts too bitter and irreconcilable for deliberate adjudication and compromise. The petty warfare

of competition within groups can be kept on such a level that it protects and actually promotes the general welfare. The warfare among organized economic groups, on the other hand, is unlikely to be more controllable or less destructive than warfare among nations. Indeed, democratic government would have hardly so good a chance of arbitrating these conflicts tolerably as have the League of Nations and World Court in their field.[4]

Put bluntly, the fear of many economists is that the democratic political process will break down if it is required to decide the "just" price for a ton of steel, the "fair" wage for a plumber, etc. Economists and others who see a tie between political freedom and the price system do not argue that markets will ensure the emergence of political freedom—only that markets are a necessary condition.

Second, most economists, whatever their politics, believe that the price system is a more efficient way of solving economic problems than its critics commonly concede. Whatever its shortcomings, a price system does generate a set of up-to-date data, i.e. transaction prices, on which hundreds of thousands of economic decisions are made every day.

If economic decisions are not to be based upon transaction prices, what basis are they to have? To say that an economy should give first priority to producing those commodities which are "needed" rather than those commodities which are "profitable" is a nice-sounding bit of rhetoric. But it begs the important question: how do we measure a "need" and calculate the cost of satisfying it? In fact, any sort of rational economic calculation requires the use of prices. So-called "planning" merely involves the substitution of "accounting" or "shadow" prices for market prices as, for example, when one department in a large firm charges another department an accounting price for a service rendered. Rightly or wrongly, most economists believe that a market-determined price is usually a better measure of "alternatives sacrificed" than an accounting price set by bureaucratic command. Indeed, the most useful accounting prices are regarded as those which can be easily checked against corresponding market prices.

A final caution

In the study of the price system there is probably no way that you can escape the biases of your instructors in favor of markets. But you need not accept these biases or even feign holding them yourself in order to

4. Henry Simons, *Economic Policy for a Free Society* (Chicago, 1948), p. 44.

pass examinations. Economic theory, after all, is mainly a matter of getting from assumptions to conclusions according to the accepted rules of logic.

In any event, there is not much point in being for or against markets in the abstract. There is no reason why one cannot favor a freer market for gold in the United States while, at the same time, favoring a less free market for the sale of barbiturates. Or why one cannot advocate more state control over the employment of children and less state control over the employment of adults. Many of the most important problems of economic policy on which, as a citizen, you can be expected to have an opinion, will involve judgments about the proper mixture of political action and pricing. You have been learning about politics since kindergarten. The time has come to consider what the price system can—and cannot—do.

REFERENCES

Friedman, Milton, "The Methodology of Positive Economics," *Essays in Positive Economics* (Chicago, 1953), pp. 3-43.

Koopmans, T. C., *Three Essays on the State of Economic Science* (New York, 1957), pp. 129-49.

Knight, F. H., "The Limitations of Scientific Method in Economics" in *The Ethics of Competition and Other Essays* (New York, 1953), pp. 105-47.

Kuhn, T. S., *The Structure of Scientific Revolutions* (Chicago, 2d ed., 1970).

Meek, R. L., "Value Judgments in Economics," *British Journal for the Philosophy of Science,* 15 (1964), 89-96.

Popper, K. R., *The Logic of Scientific Discovery* (New York, 1959), Chapters 1 and 2.

Robbins, Lionel, *An Essay on the Nature and Significance of Economic Science* (London, rev. ed., 1946).

Stigler, G. J., "The Politics of Political Economists" in *Essays in the History of Economics* (Chicago, 1965), pp. 51-65.

2

Consumer Behavior

Five fundamental assumptions

In our study of microeconomic theory we must begin somewhere. Therefore let us start with the basic building block in microeconomics—the single consumer who has an income and the opportunity to spend it on different goods and services. For convenience we shall henceforth use the term "commodity" to designate a good or service that is available to the consumer. Specifically, we assume

    A2.1 Every consumer has a set of tastes for the commodities that he can buy in the market; and these tastes are "given" in the sense that they are not affected by a change in his income or a change in the price of any commodity.

    The assumption of given tastes is absolutely fundamental in microeconomic theory because it is necessary to ensure the predictability of the consumer's behavior. As we shall presently see, if we also know (i) the commodities that he can buy and (ii) his money income and (iii) commodity prices, then we can deduce how he will divide his expenditures among them. Note that assumption A2.1 does not assert that the amount of commodity that the consumer will buy is unaffected by a change in his money income or a change in the price of any commodity. As we shall soon see, quite the contrary is true. But A2.1 does say that the consumer "knows his own mind." He will not be moved to experiment by sampling new commodities or substituting one commodity for another on a trial basis merely because his income and the prices of commodities change.

    A2.2 Every consumer always prefers more of a commodity to less of it.

Some economists would rather say instead: a consumer never prefers less of a commodity to more of it. By this awkward choice of words they allow for the possibility that at some point a consumer can have so much of a commodity that he is sated with it. In the real world, however, he will never become sated with a commodity unless it is a free good; and, while a few such goods do exist, e.g. air, and in some places water, they form an inconsequential fraction of national income. We shall ignore free goods and say simply that "more is always preferred to less."

A2.3 The commodity preferences of every consumer are consistently ordered. If he prefers one dozen eggs to one loaf of bread, and one loaf of bread to a quart of milk, then he also prefers one dozen eggs to one quart of milk.

A2.4 If the consumer spends his income on two commodities, say commodities A and B, he will willingly give up some quantity of commodity A in exchange for some additional amount of commodity B. That is, commodity preferences are "weakly ordered."

The principal implication of assumption of A2.4 is this. If some quantity of commodity A is taken away from the consumer, there is always some additional amount of commodity B that he is prepared to accept as compensation for the loss of commodity A. Perhaps the meaning of "weak ordering" can best be made clear with an example of its opposite—the strong ordering of consumer preferences. One hoary example of the latter is the consumer's preference for left and right shoes. Obviously, if he is deprived of one left shoe, no number of additional right shoes will adequately compensate him for his loss.

A2.5 Let successive units of commodity A be taken away from the consumer. Then he will require ever greater quantities of commodity B to compensate him for his loss of commodity A.

In the terminology of microeconomics, this assumption says that the marginal rate of substitution of commodity B for commodity A increases as the ratio of B to A increases in the consumer's budget.

If you think hard enough you can imagine situations in which the above assumptions do not accurately describe the real-world behavior of individual consumers. For example, assumption A2.1 obviously does not apply when a new product is offered on the market for the first time. Faced with something novel and unfamiliar, the consumer's behavior is likely to be exploratory. He may spend part of his income on the new product in order to discover whether or not he wants to revise his set of tastes to include it. Again, assumption A2.1 is unrealistic in that it implies that a fixed and immutable set of tastes is somehow implanted in the consumer before he leaves the womb. In the real world, consumer behavior is learned behavior. Learning necessarily involves experimentation. And any change in the consumer's income or in prices of the commodities on which he spends his income will probably trigger a new round of experimentation.

Each of the five assumptions set down above is in some sense "unrealistic." But since to explain is to abstract—and hence to distort and simplify —the charge of unreality could be brought against any set of assumptions that we might employ to study consumer behavior. One way to underscore the utility of our assumptions is to consider the results that would follow if we assert the converse of each of them. (We will perform this exercise only for assumption A2.1.) No doubt we will sometimes go wrong by assuming that the consumer acts upon the basis of tastes that are "given." To say the obvious, if consumer tastes in the real world were completely fixed and immutable, advertising would be a total waste of the advertiser's expenditure since it could have no effect on consumer behavior. But we will make far more serious mistakes if we try to analyze the consumer's behavior on the assumption that having no known tastes for anything, he spends his income at random on whatever set of commodities that the market makes available to him.

Constructing indifference curves

Once our five fundamental assumptions about consumer behavior are accepted, we can construct for the consumer the very useful set of indifference curves. These in turn will allow us to fashion the indispensable tool of microeconomic theory—the demand curve for the commodity. For convenience, let us assume that all of the commodities which the consumer can buy with his income can be divided into two groups. The first group consists of one item only—call it commodity A. The second group consists of all commodities which are not commodity A. We shall treat all items in this second group as a composite commodity B.

Now suppose that our consumer is given an initial endowment of income consisting of 20 units of commodity A and 10 units of commodity B. In a series of successive moves, we deprive him each time of two units of commodity A. According to assumption A2.4, his tastes for commodities A and B are weakly ordered. Hence, there is some additional amount of commodity B that he will accept as full compensation for his loss of two units of commodity A. According to assumption A2.4, as the con-

TABLE 2.1

combination	units of commodity A	units of commodity B	S_{BA}*
1.1	20	10	—
1.2	18	11	0.5
1.3	16	13	1.0
1.4	14	16	1.5
1.5	12	20	2.0
1.6	10	25	2.5

* S_{BA} denotes the marginal rate of substitution of commodity B for commodity A, that is, $S_{BA} = \dfrac{\Delta B}{\Delta A}$.

sumer loses successive amounts of commodity A, he will demand even greater amounts of commodity B in order to ensure that he suffers no loss of economic welfare.

The terms on which the consumer can be persuaded to exchange commodity A for additional amounts of commodity B are given in table 2.1. Six possible exchanges are given here. The number of possible exchanges could, of course, be expanded ad infinitum.

The significance of table 2.1 is easily conveyed. If we ask the consumer to choose one of the six combinations of commodity A and commodity B described in the table, the choice will be a matter of indifference to him. Every one of the six combinations would provide him with the same level of economic welfare. Therefore, he is "indifferent" among them. For example, 20 units of commodity A plus 10 units of commodity B (combination 1.1) would give him as much "satisfaction," to use the flat-footed term favored by some economists, as 16 units of commodity A plus 13 units of commodity B (combination 1.3).

Our consumer is presumed to have an original income endowment of combination 1.1 in table 2.1. That is, initially he has 20 units of commodity A and 10 units of commodity B. If we deprive him of two units of commodity A, we can fully compensate him for this loss by giving him one more unit of commodity B; so that he has 18 units of A and 11 units of B (combination 1.2).

Let us continue. We deprive the consumer of another two units of commodity A. Now (thanks to assumption A2.5) we can only compensate him fully for his loss by giving him two more units of commodity B; so that he has 16 units of A and 13 units of B (combination 1.3).

TABLE 2.2

combination	units of commodity A	units of commodity B	S_{BA}*
2.1	25	15	—
2.2	23	16	0.5
2.3	21	18	1.0
2.4	19	21	1.5
2.5	17	25	2.0
2.6	15	30	2.5

* S_{BA} denotes the marginal rate of substitution of commodity B for commodity A, that is, $S_{BA} = \frac{\Delta B}{\Delta A}$.

One more time. We take another two units of commodity A away from the consumer and pay full compensation by giving him three additional units of commodity B; so that he has 14 units of A and 16 units of B (combination 1.4).

Now let us open a new confiscation game. This time we give our consumer an initial endowment of 25 units of commodity A and 15 units of commodity B. Again in a series of five moves we take two units of commodity A away from him on each move. Again, we pay him full compensation for his loss by increasing his stock of commodity B. The results of this second confiscation game are set forth in table 2.2.

Here too if we were to allow the consumer to choose one of the six combinations of commodities A and B described in table 2.2, the choice would be a matter of indifference to him. Each of these combinations represents the same level of economic welfare. For example, 25 units of commodity A plus 15 units of commodity B (combination 2.1) satisfies as well as 15 units of commodity A plus 30 units of commodity B (combination 2.6).

Compare tables 2.1 and 2.2. Combination 2.1 (25A, 15B) in table 2.2 contains more of both commodity A and commodity B than does combination 1.1 (20A, 10B) in table 2.1. By assumption A2.2, the consumer always prefers more of a commodity to less of it. Therefore, he must prefer combination 2.1 to combination 1.1.

We can generalize further. By assumption A2.3 consumer preferences are consistently ordered. The consumer prefers the combination 2.1 in table 2.2 to combination 1.1 in table 2.1. He is indifferent as regards the six combinations of table 2.1. Therefore, assumption A2.3 ensures that

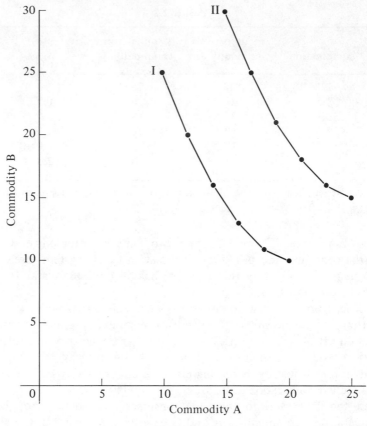

FIGURE 2.1

the combination 2.1 in table 2.2 is preferred to every one of the six combinations in table 2.1. Using this same line of reasoning, we can show that every combination of commodities A and B described in table 2.2 is preferred to every combination of commodities A and B described in table 2.1.

The information contained in tables 2.1 and 2.2 can also be conveyed with the aid of simple geometry. Every combination of commodities A and B described in these two tables can be represented by a point on a two-dimensional diagram. This is done in figure 2.1.

The six combinations represented by table 2.1 are connected by curve I in figure 2.1. The six combinations represented by table 2.2 are connected by curve II.

If we assume that both commodities can be divided into any number of parts, there is no limit to the number of points which can be located on each indifference curve. Hence the indifference curve—the curve which, to say the obvious, shows the set of combinations of commodities A and B among which the consumer is indifferent—is usually drawn as a smooth curve. We shall respect this tradition. Henceforth, all of our indifference curves will be smooth. Note also that since, by assumption A2.2, the consumer always prefers more of a commodity to less of it, there is no limit to the number of indifference curves that can be constructed for him.

Two properties of indifference curves

Two important properties of indifference curves should now be noted and, hopefully, committed to memory. (i) Every indifference curve is *convex to* the origin (or, if you prefer, *concave from* the origin). This property is dictated by assumption A2.5 which says that, as successive units of commodity A are taken away from the consumer, he will demand as compensation ever greater quantities of commodity B. (ii) No matter how many indifference curves are constructed for the consumer, no two indifference curves can ever intersect. This property is dictated by assumption A2.3

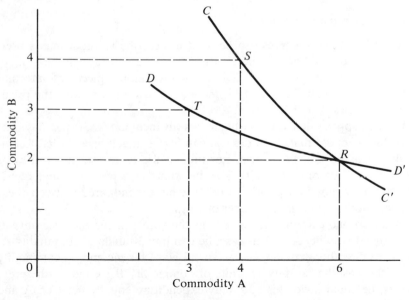

FIGURE 2.2

which states that the consumer's preferences are consistently ordered; and by assumption A2.2 which states that the consumer always prefers more of a commodity to less of it.

If you are momentarily puzzled by the assertion that two indifference curves can never cross, do not despair. This absurdity is depicted in figure 2.2. Here two curves *CC'* and *DD'* do intersect. Consider why they cannot be indifference curves.

In figure 2.2 point *R* lies on both curve *CC'* and *DD'*. It represents a combination of 6 units of commodity A and 2 units of commodity B. Point *S* lies on curve *CC'* only. It represents a combination of 4 units of commodity A and 4 units of commodity B. Presumably the consumer is indifferent between combinations *R* and *S*.

Point *T* lies on curve *DD'* only. It represents a combination of 3 units of commodity A and 3 units of commodity B. Presumably the consumer is indifferent between combinations *R* and *T*. If so, is he indifferent between combinations *S* and *T*? Clearly, this cannot be the case. By choosing combination *S* over combination *T* in figure 2.2 the consumer can have both more of A and more of B. In short, two indifference curves which crossed would contradict the postulate that "more is always preferred to less." Figure 2.2 is, to repeat, an economic absurdity.

Maximizing economic welfare

A set of indifference curves can be used to describe the consumer's preferences for commodities A and B. But before we can say anything about his actual consumption we must have two additional pieces of information. We must know the size of his income. And we must know the prices of commodities A and B.

Let us suppose that the consumer has an income of $30 per day. Let us further suppose that, each day, he can buy as much or as little of commodity A as he wants at a price per unit of $1. Likewise, he can buy as much or as little of commodity B as he wants at a price per unit of $2. Clearly, he is now in a position to divide his expenditures between these two commodities in a great number of ways.

Going to one extreme, he can spend the whole of his $30 per day income on commodity A. In this case, he can buy 30 units of commodity A. Going to the other extreme, he can spend all of his income on commodity B. In this case he can buy 15 units of commodity B. Avoiding these extremes, he could divide his $30 daily expenditure equally between A and B. If he were to do this, he would buy 15 units of commodity A and 7.5

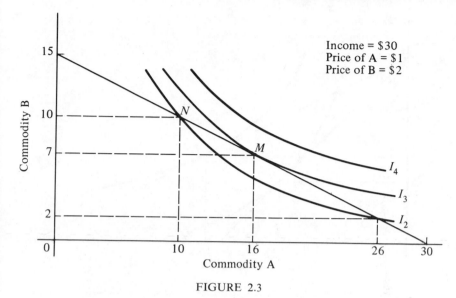

FIGURE 2.3

units of commodity B. We have described but three of many possibilities. But precisely how will the consumer divide his expenditures between the two commodities? The answer can readily be deduced from figure 2.3.

Curves I_2, I_3, and I_4 are three curves in the consumer's set of indifference curves. The straight line which intersects the vertical axis at 15 units and the horizontal axis at 30 units is the so-called *budget constraint*. It shows the combinations of commodity A and commodity B that the consumer could buy each day given (i) an income of $30 and (ii) a price of $1 per unit for commodity A and (iii) a price of $2 per unit for commodity B.

Admittedly the consumer would prefer any combination of A and B represented by a point of curve I_4 to any combination that he can buy with his $30 income at the given prices. Since he is subject to these price and income constraints, he must settle for a combination which lies on the budget line. Three such combinations are L, M, and N. Which will he choose?

Examine figure 2.3 carefully. Obviously the consumer will choose combination M because it lies on curve I_3—his highest *attainable* indifference curve. Combination M consists of 16 units of commodity A and 7 units of commodity B. Thus each day he spends $16 on A and $14 on B. Combinations N and L are not purchased since both lie on the lower indifference curve I_2.

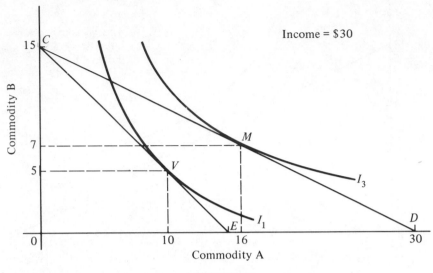

FIGURE 2.4

According to assumption A2.5 ("increasing marginal rate of substitution of B for A") every indifference curve is convex to the origin. When the consumer's income and the prices of commodities A and B are given, the budget constraint is necessarily a straight line. Hence, only one indifference curve can be tangent to this line. And only one combination of commodities A and B is preferred by the consumer to all other combinations of these two commodities *that he can buy with his present income at present prices.* He would, of course, prefer to have more income and lower prices.

Suppose now that we *reduce* the consumer's real income. This we do by raising the price of commodity A from $1 to $2 per unit. The price of commodity B remains unchanged at $2 per unit; and the consumer's money income stays at $30 per day. The increase in the price of commodity A creates a new budget constraint for the consumer. In figure 2.4, the old budget constraint is represented by the line *CD*. The new budget constraint—that which applies after the increase in the price of commodity A from $1 to $2—is represented by the line *CE*.

The old budget constraint *CD* was tangent to indifference curve I_3 at point *M*. The new budget constraint *CE* is tangent to curve I_1 at point *V*. Thus as the price of commodity A rises from $1 to $2 (the consumer's income and the price of commodity B remaining unchanged) we note two results. The consumer's purchase of A falls from 16 to 10 units. His purchase of B falls from 7 to 5 units. Note that the rise in the price of A causes him to buy less of B because he chooses to spend a greater fraction of his income on commodity A. That is, his demand for commodity A is price "inelastic" in the interval from $1 to $2.

As a consequence of the rise in the price of commodity A, the consumer is clearly worse off. We show this loss of economic welfare by moving him down to the lower indifference curve I_1.

We do not rule out the possibility that the consumer's loss of economic welfare may have improved his health and/or his morals. But we leave the investigation of this possibility to other social scientists and philosophers.

Generating a demand curve

We know that when the consumer has an income of $30 per day, the price of commodity A is $1 and the price of commodity B is $2, then his daily purchase of commodity A is 16 units. When his income and the price of commodity B remain unchanged while the price of commodity A rises from $1 to $2, his purchase of commodity A will fall. Specifically, it will fall from 16 units to 10 units. In short, we now know the coordinates of two points on the customer's demand curve for commodity A. For ready reference, we plot these two points in figure 2.5.

A second look at figure 2.4 suggests a technique by which we can plot as many points on the consumer's demand curve for commodity A as we wish. Note that we found our two points by, in effect, rotating the budget constraint clockwise in figure 2.4 from line *CD* to line *CE*. This rotation,

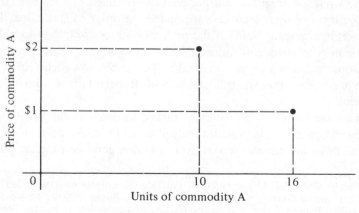

FIGURE 2.5

of course, registers the rise in the price of commodity A from $1 to $2.

Assume that there is no limit to the number of parts into which a given amount of commodities A and B can be divided. Then we can draw any number of indifference curves between curves I_1 and I_3 in figure 2.4. And by drawing a budget constraint tangent to each new indifference curve and radiating from point C in figure 2.4 we obtain the coordinates for another point on the consumer's demand curve for commodity A.

We shall not pursue this exercise in draftsmanship further. Our object was only to show that indifference curve analysis can be used to generate the demand curve that you met in your first course in economics. For this purpose, two points on the demand curve are as good as two hundred.

The Giffen paradox

In figures 2.3 and 2.4 the location and shape of the indifference curves dictate that as the price of commodity A rises the amount purchased by our consumer must decrease; hence his demand curve for commodity A must have a negative slope. Nobody in his right mind will question the "realism" of the indifference curves which produce this result. In the real world, after all, a merchant who wishes to close out an inventory of any commodity does so by cutting price—not by raising it.

In the musty cellar containing unused bits of economic analysis, however, there is a curious relic called the Giffen good, for which the demand curve is upward sloping. No such commodity has ever been positively identified in the real world, although it was once conjectured that, in nineteenth-century Ireland, potatoes satisfied the definition. It was assumed that the wretched Irish (a) did not particularly like potatoes but (b) had to spend most of their incomes on potatoes in order to stay alive. Therefore (so the argument went) if the price of potatoes fell, they would have more money to spend on more expensive foods and, craving variety in diet, would cut down on potato intake. This is the so-called Giffen paradox named after the English statistician Robert Giffen who allegedly propounded it.[1]

Since large numbers of Irishmen starved to death in the middle of the nineteenth century, it is most unlikely that a fall in the price of potatoes ever led them to consume fewer. Still, a Giffen good is a logical possibil-

1. The possibility of an upward sloping demand curve for a commodity was first attributed to Giffen by Alfred Marshall but later investigations have failed to find the idea in any of Giffen's published work. See G. J. Stigler, "Notes on the History of the Giffen Paradox" in *Essays in the History of Economics* (Chicago, 1965), pp. 374-84.

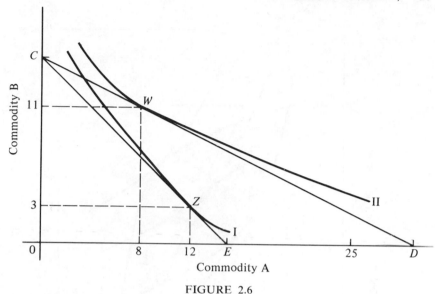

FIGURE 2.6

ity. Its existence does not contradict any of our five fundamental assumptions about consumer behavior.

If commodity A really is a Giffen good, we can use the following geometry. Once more we assume that the price of commodity B is $2 per unit; that the consumer's income is $30 per day; and that the price of commodity A is initially $1 per unit. In figure 2.6, line *CD* is again the budget constraint that is imposed upon the consumer by these assumptions. He reaches his highest attainable indifference curve (which is curve II in figure 2.6) by purchasing combination *W*. This consists of 8 units of A and 11 units of B.

Let the price of commodity A rise from $1 to $2 per unit, the price of commodity B and the consumer's money income remaining unchanged. In figure 2.6 the budget constraint is now line *CE;* and the consumer reaches his highest indifference curve (which has become curve *I* in figure 2.6) by purchasing combination Z. This consists of 12 units of A and 3 units of B. Thus, as the price of commodity A rises from $1 to $2, his purchase of A rises from 8 to 12 units.

Note again that the Giffen paradox does not contradict any of our five assumptions that give the consumer a set of indifference curves that are convex to the origin. But, of course, for the Giffen paradox to occur, the consumer must be spending a very large fraction of his income on a single commodity.

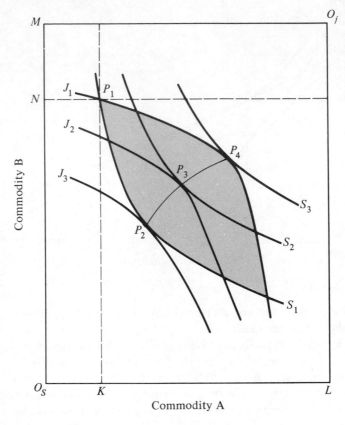

FIGURE 2.7

The case for free exchange

In microeconomic theory, consumer indifference curves have one other important use. They can be employed to show that "free exchange is not robbery"—that the economic welfare of individuals can almost invariably be increased by allowing them to exchange commodities among themselves. This we do with the aid of figure 2.7—the venerable Edgeworth box diagram.

Let us assume that our economic model consists of two consumers, say Smith and Jones, and two commodities, A and B. In figure 2.7 the "width of the box," which is equal to the horizontal distance O_sL, gives the total amount of commodity A that is owned by both Smith and Jones. The "height of the box," which is equal to the vertical distance O_sM, gives the total amount of commodity B that is owned by both Smith and Jones. Note that $O_sL = O_jM$ and $O_sM = O_jL$.

The amount of commodity A that Smith alone owns is measured horizontally from the origin O_s at the lower left corner of the box. The amount of commodity B that Smith alone owns is measured vertically from the origin O_s. Therefore, any interior point in the Edgeworth box diagram indicates a possible combination of commodities A and B in Smith's possession. Consider point P_1 in figure 2.7. It indicates that Smith owns O_sK units of commodity A and O_sN units of commodity B.

Now consider Jones's position. The amount of commodity A that Jones alone owns is given by the horizontal distance to the left of point O_j on the box diagram. The amount of commodity B that he owns is measured by the vertical distance downward from point O_j. Therefore, any interior point in the box diagram also indicates a possible combination of commodities A and B in Jones's possession. Look at point P_1 again. It indicates that Jones has $(O_jM - O_sK)$ units of commodity A and $(O_jL - O_sN)$ units of commodity B. This must be true since Smith owns O_sK units of A and O_sN units of B.

In figure 2.7 let point P_1 represent the division of commodities A and B between Smith and Jones before they are permitted to trade with each other. When trade is allowed, will it actually take place between them? If so, why? And on what terms?

To answer these questions we must first supply Smith and Jones with a set of consumer indifference curves. Three of Smith's indifference curves are given in figure 2.7. They are S_1, S_2, and S_3. Three of Jones's indifference curves are also given. They are J_1, J_2, and J_3. If the indifference curves of Jones look peculiar, turn diagram 2.7 upside down. Remember that the amount of commodity A owned by Jones is measured horizontally to the left of point O_j; while the amount of commodity B owned by Jones is measured vertically and downward from point O_j.

In general, Smith's economic welfare will increase as he moves from points close to O_s upward and to the right toward point O_j. Likewise Jones's economic welfare will increase as he moves from points close to O_j downward and to the left toward point O_s.

Given the initial division of the two commodities between them (point P_1), Smith is on indifference curve S_1. And Jones is on indifference curve J_1. If the two consumers are free to trade with each other, trade will obviously make both better off, i.e. move each to a "higher" indifference curve. In figure 2.7, for Jones "lower is higher" since we have turned his set of indifference curves upside down. Smith will gain by giving up some part of his stock of commodity B in exchange for some part of Jones's stock of commodity A. Jones becomes better off by parting with some part of his stock of commodity A in order to get part of Smith's stock of commodity B.

How much trade will take place between Smith and Jones? We cannot predict the precise amount from figure 2.7. We can say, however, that the point at which they will wind up after exchanging will be an interior point in the shaded area. Why? Simply because any interior point in the shaded area of figure 2.7 puts both consumers on a higher indifference curve.

If exchange moves the division of the commodities between them from point P_1 to P_4, only Smith is better off. He has moved to the higher indifference curve S_3 while Jones stays on his original indifference curve J_1. Conversely, if exchange moves the division of the commodities from point P_1 to point P_2 only Jones is better off. Jones is now on curve J_3 while Smith remains on his original curve S_1. However, if we move to any interior point in the shaded area of figure 2.7, both Smith and Jones are better off, i.e. on higher indifference curves.

In figure 2.7, the curve connecting points P_2 and P_4 can be thought of as connecting all points at which an indifference curve of Smith is tangent to an indifference curve of Jones within the shaded area. It is the so-called *contract curve*. Without too much trouble, we can demonstrate that if Smith and Jones are off this curve, they can each be better off by moving to a point on it by the process of exchange.

Once Smith and Jones have moved to a point on the contract curve P_2P_4, they have exhausted the possibilities of a mutual gain from exchange. Further trade will only serve to make one consumer better off by making the other worse off. As we move upward along the contract curve from P_2 to P_4 in figure 2.7, Smith's economic welfare increases while Jones's economic welfare decreases. As we moved downward along the contract curve from P_4 to P_2 the results are reversed. Jones's economic welfare increases while Smith's decreases.

We now see that after trade between Smith and Jones has opened up, the final division of commodities A and B between them will be at a point on the contract curve. One possible point is P_3. We cannot be more specific. The final outcome will depend in part on the bargaining skill of the two consumers. If Smith is extremely adept at bargaining while Jones is incompetent, the final division will lie close to point P_4. If the opposite is true, then the final division will lie close to P_2. If Smith and Jones are approximately equal in bargaining skill, the final division will lie close to P_3 in figure 2.7.

Summary

In this chapter we made the acquaintance of "the theory of consumer be-havior." We assumed a consumer who has an income, a set of commodity tastes which are given, and the chance to buy different amounts of com-modities. We invoked assumptions which gave the consumer a set of convex indifference curves. Our analysis was conducted in terms of two "commodities," A and B. Commodity B was defined as the set of all com-modities that are not A. We found that the consumer would maximize his economic welfare by dividing his expenditures in such a way that he would reach his highest attainable indifference curve.

It was conceded that this "static" analysis of consumer behavior is unrealistic in one important respect. It assumes that the consumer has complete information on the characteristics of the commodities that he buys; so that he does not have to spend part of his income to try out new commodities or refresh his memories about old ones. In defense of static analysis we noted that all analysis—static or otherwise—must rest upon assumptions which are, in one way or another, unrealistic. It is never possible to completely describe any feature of the real world, be it animal, vegetable, or mineral; and the multiplication of factual details soon carries one into diminishing intellectual returns. (Who cares that some male con-sumers carry their wallets in their right hip pockets and others in their left hip pockets?) It is sufficient to recognize that consumers do not spend their incomes at random when confronted with a set of commodities. Even the proverbial drunken sailor who recklessly throws his earnings about is assumed to have a marked preference for liquor and certain forms of entertainment. Finally, we do not want to spend the whole course on consumer behavior. Therefore, since the typical consumer of the real world has a great deal of information about the characteristics of the com-modities that he can buy and has highly stable commodity tastes, we find it useful to cut short qualification and pass to the limit. We make our analysis static (and manageable) by giving the consumer in microeco-nomic theory complete information about commodities and unchanging tastes for them.

While indifference curve analysis is mainly employed in microeconom-ics to show how a consumer will allocate his expenditures among differ-ent commodities, it has other uses as well. We saw, for example, that it allows us to deduce the consumer's demand curve for each commodity which is available to him at a price. We also used consumer indifference curves to show how and why the economic welfare of all consumers is increased when they are allowed to exchange commodities with one another. In addition, consumer indifference curves can be used to show the effect of an income change on consumer purchases. This possibility is examined in the appendix to this chapter.

REFERENCES

Ferguson, C. E., *Microeconomic Theory* (Homewood, Ill., 3rd ed., 1972), chapters 2, 3, and 4.
Hicks, J. R., *Value and Capital* (Oxford, 2nd ed., 1946), chapters 1, 2, and 3.
Liebhafsky, H. H., *The Nature of Price Theory* (Homewood, Ill., rev. ed., 1968), chapter 5.
Little, I. M. D., *A Critique of Welfare Economics* (Oxford, 2nd ed., 1957).
Mansfield, Edwin, *Microeconomics: Theory and Applications* (New York, 1970), chapters 2 and 3.
Robertson, D. H., *Utility and All That* (London, 1952).
Slutsky, E. E. "On the Theory of the Budget of the Consumer," *Giornale degli Economisti* LI (1915) pp. 1-26, translated from the Italian and reprinted in American Economic Association, *Readings in Price Theory* (Chicago, 1952), pp. 27-56.

APPENDIX TO CHAPTER 2
INCOME VERSUS SUBSTITUTION EFFECT

For the vast majority of commodities of the real world, it is reasonable to assume that quantity demand decreases as price increases. However, two distinct forces are at work to reduce, say, the quantity demanded of commodity A as its price rises.

1. When the price of commodity A rises—and nothing else changes—the consumer *must* buy less of commodity A if he continues to buy the same amounts of other commodities. This necessity we call the *income effect*. We ought perhaps to be more precise and call it the *real income effect*. The consumer's money income, after all, is not altered by the rise in the price of commodity A.

2. When the price of commodity A rises—and nothing else changes—commodity A becomes less attractive to the consumer relative to other commodities. He will prefer to reduce the burden of the price increase on himself by buying less

of commodity A in order that he can buy more of other commodities. This reaction we call the *substitution effect*.

With the aid of indifference curves, we can precisely identify the income
and substitution effects resulting from a price change. Let us again give
the consumer an income of $30 per day. Let us specify that he spends all
of this income on commodities A and B. (Recall that it is permissible to
define commodity B to be the set of commodities that are "not commodity
A.") Let the initial price of commodity A be $0.50 and the initial price of
commodity B be $1.

Thus in figure 2.8, the consumer's initial budget line is the straight
line *XZ*. It indicates, for example, that should he choose to spend all of
his $30 on commodity B, he could buy 30 units. Should he wish to spend
all of his $30 on commodity A, he could buy 60 units. The convex (to-
ward the origin) curves I and II are two of the consumer's indifference
curves. As we know, many more such curves could be drawn for him in
figure 2.8. Two are all that we need.

As figure 2.8 shows, given the consumer's income of $30 and the
specified pair of prices, he reaches his highest attainable indifference

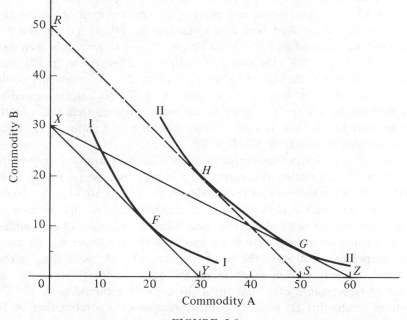

FIGURE 2.8

curve ("maximizes economic welfare") when he buys 50 units of commodity A and 5 units of commodity B. That is, he initially spends $25 on commodity A and $5 on commodity B. This combination of commodities A and B is represented by point *G* in figure 2.8.

Let point *G* denote the initial equilibrium of our consumer. Now let the price of commodity B remain at $1 while the price of commodity A rises from $0.50 to $1. The consumer's money income remains unchanged at $30. Geometrically, this rise in the price of commodity A is shown by rotating line *XZ* clockwise about point *X* until it coincides with line *XY* in figure 2.8.

At the new pair of prices, the consumer attains his highest indifference curve (maximizes economic welfare) when he uses his $30 to buy 20 units of commodity A and 10 units of commodity B. This combination of commodities A and B is represented by point *F* in figure 2.8. But point *F* lies on a lower indifference curve than does point *G*. Therefore, as is inevitable, the rise in the price of commodity A has made the consumer worse off (reduced his economic welfare). And he has minimized the economic welfare loss resulting from this price increase by (a) reducing his consumption of commodity A from 50 units to 20 units and (b) increasing his consumption of commodity B from 5 units to 10 units.

How much of this 30-unit reduction in the consumption of commodity A is income effect? And how much substitution effect? To answer this question, we proceed as follows. In figure 2.8, we draw the broken line *RS* parallel to line *XY* (the new budget line) and tangent to indifference curve II (formerly the highest indifference curve that the consumer could attain with a $30 income). The construction of line *RS* can be viewed as the decision to give the consumer a new money income than will exactly compensate for the loss in real income that he would suffer if the price of commodity A rises from $0.50 to $1.

Figure 2.8 indicates that the payment of full compensation (but nothing more) requires that the consumer's money income be raised from $30 to $50 when the price of commodity A rises from $0.50 to $1. Note, however, that even if the consumer is compensated by this increase in money income, he will still elect to reduce his consumption of commodity A. By raising his money income we can keep the consumer on the same indifference curve II when the price of commodity A rises. But, in this instance, he moves from point *G* on the curve to imaginary point *H*. Point *H* represents a combination of 30 units of commodity A and 20 units of commodity B; whereas point *G* represents a combination of 50 units of commodity A and 5 units of commodity B.

The construction of line *RS* allows us to measure the substitution effect that results when the price of commodity A goes from $0.50 to $1. When the price of commodity A is $1 and the price of commodity B is $1, *RS* represents a money income of $50. If we simultaneously (a) raised the price of commodity A from $0.50 to $1 and (b) raised the consumer's money income from $30 to $50, he would suffer no loss of real income (economic welfare). Therefore, the consumer's decision to move from point *G* to point *H* on curve II would be pure substitution effect. He substitutes consumption of commodity B for commodity A not because he has to but because, at the new pair of prices, he wants to.

What of the real income effect of the price rise? It is, so to speak, a residual. Any fall in the consumption of commodity A that cannot be traced to the substitution effect (i.e. identified with the aid of line *RS* in figure 2.8) is perforce an income effect. In figure 2.8 this real income effect is a fall in the consumption of commodity A of 10 units. The substitution effect is movement from point *G* to point *H*. The real income effect is movement from point *H* to point *F*.

Reprise

To sum up. We first give our consumer an income of $30 per day. We assume that all of this income is spent on commodities A and B. We give him the indifference curves I and II in figure 2.8. We raise the price of commodity A from $0.50 to $1 while leaving the price of commodity B unchanged at $1.

As a result of this price change, the consumer's daily purchase of commodity A falls from 50 units to 20 units. The net decrease in the purchase of commodity A is thus 30 units. Of this decrease, 20 units is the substitution effect of the price rise; 10 units is the real income effect of the price rise. We isolated the substitution effect by asking: how much of commodities A and B would the consumer buy if we increased money income by an amount that would exactly compensate him for the loss of economic welfare that he must otherwise suffer when the price of commodity A goes from $0.50 to $1?

3
The Theory of Demand

Arbitrage and the perfect market

In the preceding chapter we saw how indifference curve analysis could be employed to derive a single consumer's demand curve for a commodity. In this chapter we shall be concerned with certain important properties of the market (aggregate) demand curve for the output of an "industry." We define this industry to be the set of all firms that produce something called commodity X for the same market. Once again we assume that all units of commodity X produced by different firms are indistinguishable from one another. That is, commodity X is assumed to be a "homogeneous" product.

We shall discuss the properties of the market (aggregate) demand curve in two radically different contexts. In the first we assume:

A3.1 Commodity X is sold in a perfect market.

And what is a perfect market? For one thing, it *is not necessarily* the perfectly competitive market that you learned about in your first course in economics.

As you will recall, a perfectly competitive market is one in which no buyer or seller is important enough to affect the price of the commodity that he buys or sells. For reasons that we shall take notice of in a little while, a perfectly competitive market is always a perfect market. But the converse is not true. In fact, we may have a monopolist selling his output in a perfect market. Rather a perfect market is defined as one in which arbitrage is perfect. And what is arbitrage?

Basically, arbitrage is merely the operation of buying a commodity at a price and selling it at a higher price. And one important truth about arbitrage is nearly self-evident. If we can get rid of such complications as incomplete information about the market among buyers and sellers, transportation costs, storage costs, and government controls on buyer-seller transactions, then all units of commodity X offered on the market at any moment in time must sell for the same price. Otherwise, a shrewd operator—known appropriately enough as an arbitrager—would buy commodity X at a low price, resell it at a higher price, and pocket the difference as profit. But when information about price is complete and is freely available to all buyers and sellers, what one man can do all men can do. Therefore, any price differences on different units of commodity X would, if they should ever appear, immediately disappear.

In the real world, market information is never complete and freely available—we must always incur a cost even before we enter into a business transaction; so that a perfect market cannot really exist. However, in many markets of the real world (notably in wheat, cotton, and financial securities) the activities of arbitragers keep price differences within such narrow margins that they can be usefully ignored. Therefore, we need have no qualms about employing a model in which the market for commodity X is assumed to be perfect in the sense that arbitrage is so effective that, at any moment, all units of commodity X sell for the same price. Older economists sometimes defined a perfect market as one that is subject to the "law of one price." Note that there is nothing in the definition of a perfect market that rules out the possibility that the price of commodity X will change over time. The uniform price in the market made perfect by arbitrage can be (and, in the real world, always is) a fluctuating price.

Before we discuss the properties of the market (aggregate) demand curve for commodity X, we must construct such a curve from the demand curves for commodity X of different consumers. This is easily done.

Suppose we have three consumers whom, for ready reference, we label *A, B,* and *C.* Suppose that the demand for commodity X for each of these consumers is given by the appropriately labeled curve in figure 3.1. For example, the curve labeled *A* conveys that when the price of commodity X is $5 or higher, consumer *A* will buy none of it; whereas, should the price fall to zero, he will "demand" 8 units of it.

To obtain the market demand curve for commodity X in our market composed of these three consumers, we laterally sum up the demand curves of the three individual consumers. When this is done, the market demand curve is given by *DD'* in figure 3.1. Note that when the price of commodity X is $10 or higher, none of our three consumers are "in" the

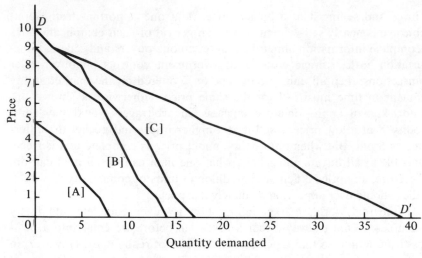

FIGURE 3.1

market. When price is $9, only consumer *C* is in the market. When price is $8, both consumer *B* and *C* are buying. And when price is $4 or lower, consumers *A, B,* and *C* all buy some of the commodity X.

In figure 3.1 the market demand curve *DD′* is full of kinks. This is because we have information on the quantity demanded by consumers A, B, and C only for multiples of $1. If we had additional market information (e.g. information on quantity demanded when price is $7.99) we could, of course, derive a smoother market demand curve for commodity X. In economic analysis smooth demand curves are easier to work with than kinked demand curves (if only because they are easier to draw). And since there is no reason for not using them, all of our demand curves in the future will be smooth.[1]

When the market demand curve for commodity X is defined in the context of its sale in a perfect market, one property of demand is immediately clear. The demand curve provides information on the amount of commodity X that can be sold in the market at different prices. In the

1. There are two main reasons why smooth demand curves are easier to work with than kinked curves. (1) Many smooth demand curves (including all linear demand curves) are graphs of easily discovered algebraic functions which allow us to abandon geometry for algebra whenever (as often happens) the switch will economize on time and energy. (2) Even when a smooth curve cannot be represented by an algebraic function, it implies a smooth marginal revenue curve; whereas a kinked demand curve implies a discontinuity ("break") in the marginal revenue curve at every point where a kink occurs.

TABLE 3.1
Commodity Z

(a) quantity demanded	(b) price	(c) total revenue	(d) marginal revenue	(e) price elasticity
0	$15.00	$ 0.00	—	—
1	14.50	14.50	$14.50	−29.00
2	14.00	28.00	13.50	−14.00
3	13.50	40.50	12.50	−9.00
4	13.00	52.00	11.50	−6.50
5	12.50	62.50	10.50	−5.00
6	12.00	72.00	9.50	−4.00
7	11.50	80.50	8.50	−3.29
8	11.00	88.00	7.50	−2.75
9	10.50	94.50	6.50	−2.33
10	10.00	100.00	5.50	−2.00
11	9.50	104.50	4.50	−1.73
12	9.00	108.00	3.50	−1.50
13	8.50	110.50	2.50	−1.31
14	8.00	112.00	1.50	−1.14
15	7.50	112.50	0.50	−1.00
16	7.00	112.00	−0.50	−0.88
17	6.50	110.50	−1.50	−0.76
18	6.00	108.00	−2.50	−0.67
19	5.50	104.50	−3.50	−0.58
20	5.00	100.00	−4.50	−0.50
21	4.50	94.50	−5.50	−0.43
22	4.00	88.00	−6.50	−0.36
23	3.50	80.50	−7.50	−0.30
24	3.00	72.00	−8.50	−0.25
25	2.50	62.50	−9.50	−0.20
26	2.00	52.00	−10.50	−0.15
27	1.50	40.50	−11.50	−0.11
28	1.00	28.00	−12.50	−0.07
29	0.50	14.50	−13.50	−0.03
30	0.00	00.00	−14.50	—

case of a "normal"–i.e. a downward sloping–demand curve, a fall in price will always cause more of commodity X to be sold. Recognition of this simple truth brings us to two important and closely related concepts in demand analysis–*marginal revenue* and *price elasticity*.

You have almost certainly met these two ideas in your first course in economics. But that was sometime ago. Since we shall make use of marginal revenue and price elasticity on many occasions, a quick review is in order.

Marginal revenue

Let us suppose that information on the demand for a commodity Z is provided by columns a and b in table 3.1. Our decision to switch the discussion from commodity X to commodity Z is not capricious. Nor is it a misprint. We make the switch to avoid confusion. We already have a demand curve for commodity X (which is *DD'* in figure 3.1). But we assume a different demand curve in table 3.1—one that has no kinks. To be more precise, a linear demand curve is assumed in table 3.1. It seems wise to assign the new demand curve to a new commodity Z.

In table 3.1 information on price is entered in column b. Information on quantity demanded at each price is entered in column a. In column c, the good genie comes out of his bottle and enters information on total revenue (price multiplied by quantity demanded) for each of 31 possible outputs and prices. For example, from columns a and b it is clear that when price is $12, quantity demanded is 6 units of commodity Z. Hence in column c, the corresponding entry for total revenue is $72.

We need a definition of marginal revenue. As a first approximation, we accept the conventional definition of the basic economics course which makes marginal revenue *the amount added to total revenue by the production and sale of an additional unit of output.*

Suppose that we want to calculate the marginal revenue of 4 units of commodity Z. Calculation is a simple three-step operation with the aid of table 3.1.

Step 1   Write down the total revenue collected by sellers when 4 units of commodity Z are offered on the market. This figure, found in column c, is $52.
Step 2   Write down the total revenue collected by sellers when 3 units of commodity Z are offered on the market. This figure, found in column c, is $40.50.

Step 3 From the total revenue brought in by 4 units, subtract the total revenue brought in by 3 units. The result is $52 minus $40.50, or $11.50.

Hence, the marginal revenue of 4 units of commodity Z is $11.50. Again, the good genie performs all the subtractions necessary to obtain the marginal revenue for every output listed in table 3.1. The results are entered in column d.

One more time. Let us reckon the marginal revenue of 25 units of commodity Z. The total revenue collected by sellers when 25 units are offered on the market is $62.50. The total revenue collected by sellers when 24 units are offered on the market is $72. Therefore, the marginal revenue of 25 units is $9.50.

Whenever a demand curve is the graph of a mathematical function that can be differentiated (as is true of every linear demand curve), a more elegant definition of marginal revenue is possible. By resorting to the calculus we can make the additional unit of output "infinitesimally small." We can then define marginal revenue as simply the first derivative of total revenue with respect to output.

Columns a and b in table 3.1 contain a number of solutions for the equation

$$p = 15 - \tfrac{1}{2}q \qquad (3.1)$$

where p denotes price and q quantity demanded.

Total revenue r is obtained by multiplying both sides of equation 3.1 by q; hence

$$r = pq = 15q - \tfrac{1}{2}q^2. \qquad (3.2)$$

When we take the first derivative of r with respect to q, the result is

$$\frac{dr}{dq} = 15 - q. \qquad (3.3)$$

To repeat: when the demand curve is the graph of a mathematical function that can be differentiated, marginal revenue is dr/dq. In figure 3.2 line DD' is the graph of equation 3.1; line DM is the graph of equation 3.3.

Note that a linear demand curve has a most useful property. The marginal revenue curve implied by a linear demand curve always falls twice as fast as the linear demand curve itself. This relationship largely explains the immense popularity of linear demand curves with teachers of economics. Their use makes it much easier to draw revenue curves with tolerable accuracy on a blackboard.

From table 3.1 and figure 3.2, it is apparent that, when the demand curve is linear, as output increases total revenue will rise for a time, reach a maximum, and then decline. Thus when zero units of commodity Z are offered on the market, total revenue is zero. When 15 units are sold, the maximum possible total revenue ($112.50) is earned. And when output reaches 30 units, total revenue is again zero. Why? Because, of course, price has been driven down to zero. Likewise, it is apparent that, when the demand curve is linear, as output increases, marginal revenue steadily falls and ultimately becomes negative.

Finally, from table 3.1 and figure 3.3, it is clear that as output increases, the corresponding changes in total revenue and marginal revenue depend upon how a fall in price affects quantity demanded. For example, when the amount of commodity Z offered on the market increases from one to two units, total revenue increases from $14.50 to $28 (table 3.1). This is because a 100 percent increase in output is accompanied by a mere 3.5 percent fall in price. (As output of commodity Z goes from one to two units, price falls very little—from $14.50 to $14.)

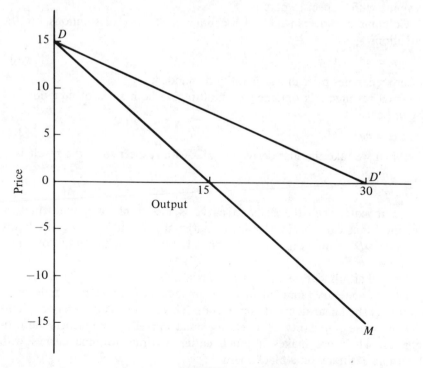

FIGURE 3.2

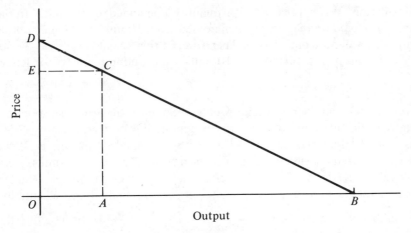

FIGURE 3.3

But note what happens in table 3.1 when the amount of commodity Z offered on the market goes from 29 to 30 units. Total revenue falls from $14.50 to zero. Here a mere 3.5 percent increase in output is accompanied by a 100 percent fall in price.

To sharpen the connection between a change in total revenue and the corresponding changes in price and quantity demanded, we need the help of an old acquaintance from the introductory course in economics—the concept of the price elasticity of demand. Recall that price elasticity of demand is simply the percentage change in quantity demanded divided by the corresponding percentage change in price. The following notation is more or less conventional in microeconomics. We shall use it.

p = price
q = quantity demanded
Δp = a small change in price
Δq = a small change in quantity demanded

Using the above notation, we can write

$$\eta = \frac{\Delta q}{q} \bigg/ \frac{\Delta p}{p} \tag{3.4}$$

or

$$\eta = \frac{\Delta q}{\Delta p} \cdot \frac{p}{q} \tag{3.4a}$$

Suppose that we wish to calculate the price elasticity of demand for commodity Z when price is $10. Table 3.1 provides all of the necessary information. When price is \$10, quantity demanded is 10 units. If the amount offered on the market is increased from 10 units to 11 units, price will fall to \$9.50 from \$10.00. Therefore, in this instance $\Delta p = -\$0.50$, $\Delta q = 1$ unit, $p = \$10$, and $q = 10$ units. Substituting numbers for letters in $\eta = \dfrac{\Delta q}{\Delta p} \cdot \dfrac{p}{q}$ we have $\eta = -2.0$.

Let us take another elasticity problem. Suppose that we wish to calculate the price elasticity of demand for commodity Z when price is \$7.50. As table 3.1 indicates, at this price quantity demanded is 15 units. If the amount offered on the market is increased from 15 units to 16 units, price will fall to \$7 from \$7.50. Therefore, in this instance $\Delta p = -\$0.50$, $\Delta q = 1$ unit, $p = \$7.50$, and $q = 15$ units. Again, making the substitution of numbers for letters in $\eta = \dfrac{\Delta q}{\Delta p} \cdot \dfrac{q}{p}$, we have $\eta = -1.0$. In table 3.1 the coefficient of price elasticity of demand for 29 selected prices on commodity Z is entered in column e.

Computing price elasticities of demand arithmetically can quickly become very tedious. Fortunately, here again we can save ourselves much vexation whenever the demand for a commodity can be expressed as a mathematical function that can be differentiated. As we have noted already, the demand for commodity Z is given by

$$p = 15 - \tfrac{1}{2} q \tag{3.1}$$

Suppose that we want to calculate the value of η when the price of commodity Z is \$8. We can find it in four steps.

Step 1   Find the value of q in equation 3.1 when $p = \$8$. The result is $q = 14$ units.

Step 2   Differentiate q with respect to p in equation 3.1. The result is $dq/dp = -2$ (since $dp/dq = -\tfrac{1}{2}$ and $dq/dp = 1 \div dp/dq$).

Step 3   In equation 3.4 replace $\Delta q/\Delta p$ by dq/dp; so that we have

$$\eta = \dfrac{dq}{dp} \cdot \dfrac{p}{q} \tag{3.5}$$

Step 4   In equation 3.5 replace letters with numbers. The result is $\eta = -2 \cdot 8 \div 14 = -1.143$.

A normal demand curve is downward sloping. Hence, dq/dp always takes a negative sign and the coefficient of price elasticity of demand η also takes a negative sign. Rightly or wrongly, it has become the custom in economics to forget about the negative sign of η. For example, economists usually say that "price elasticity of demand falls as price falls." What we really mean is that η, the *absolute value* of price elasticity of demand, falls as price falls.

In figure 3.3, line DB is the graph of the equation, $p = 15 - \frac{1}{2} q$ for $0 \leqslant q \leqslant 30$. Since $dq/dp = -2$, η decreases as price decreases; hence, η takes a different value for every value assigned to q.

Not all of the demand curves that you will meet in economics have the linear form of DB in figure 3.3. But the vast majority of these demand curves will have the property that η decreases as price decreases. There is an excellent reason for this uniformity. So long as η always decreases as price decreases, we know that if the price of a commodity is raised to some (high) level, that commodity will be priced out of the market; that is, quantity demanded will fall to zero. By the same token, so long as η always decreases as the quantity of a commodity offered on the market increases, we know that its price will finally reach zero.

It is impossible to think of a commodity whose price would not ultimately reach zero if its output were continuously increased. Therefore, in the interest of realism, we use demand curves which have the property that price elasticity of demand falls as price falls.

A final word on price elasticity of demand. Since your calculus may be a bit rusty (if non-existent, for Heaven's sake sign up for calculus next semester) you may find the following bit of geometry helpful. It allows us to obtain a precise estimate of price elasticity of demand for any point on a demand curve.

In figure 3.3, the demand curve is DB. The broken line EC is drawn parallel to OA which lies along the quantity axis. The broken line AC is drawn parallel to OE which lies along the price axis. Suppose that we are given the following problem. Find the price elasticity of demand η at point C on the demand curve DB. (Point C implies a price OE in figure 3.3.) We proceed as follows:

Step 1   Write down the absolute value of dq/dp. Since $dq/dp = 1/(dp/dq)$, the entry is EC/DE. The ratio EC/DE can be rewritten as OA/DE.

Step 2   Write down the value of p/q. The result is OE/OA.

Step 3   Substitute for dq/dp, p, and q in the equation, $\eta = \dfrac{dq}{dp} \cdot \dfrac{p}{q}$

The result is

$$\eta = \frac{OA}{DE} \cdot \frac{OE}{OA} = \frac{OE}{DE} = \frac{AC}{DE}$$

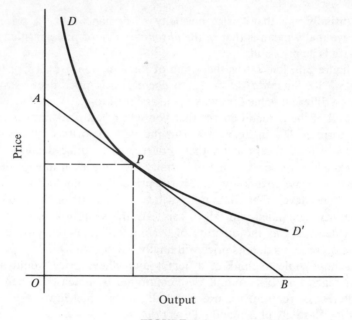

FIGURE 3.4

Step 4 Since triangle *ACB* is similar to triangle *EDC*, we have *AC/DE = CB/DC*. Therefore we can write $\eta = CB/DC$.

The method described above is sometimes called the "bottom over top" technique for estimating price elasticity of demand at a given point on a linear demand curve.

What about non-linear demand curves? Suppose that the problem is: Find price elasticity of demand η at point *P* on demand curve *DD'* in figure 3.4. We simply draw the straight line *AB* tangent to *DD'* at point *P*. Since point *P* now lies on *AB*, we know that elasticity of demand at point *P* is given by *PB/AP*.

Price, marginal revenue, and elasticity

You will have noted that both marginal revenue and price elasticity of demand are affected by changes in price. Let us make explicit the relationships among these three variables.

Step 1 In figure 3.5, draw line *GB* parallel to line *OF* which lies along the quantity axis. Now *EF = BF − BE*; and *GA/GB = BF/FC*. Therefore, since *BE = GA*, *BE = GB (BF/FC)*.

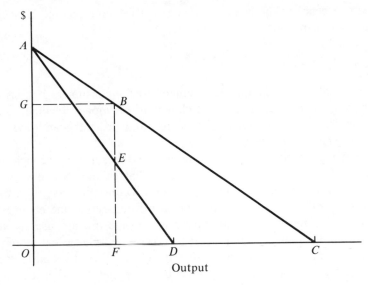

FIGURE 3.5

Step 2 Rewrite $EF = BF - BE$ as $EF = BF - GB \ (BF/FC)$. Thus $EF = BF(1 - GB/FC)$.

Step 3 Note that $GB/FC = AB/BC = \eta$; $m = EF$; and $p = BF$.

Step 4 Therefore, we can express the relationships among price, marginal revenue and, price elasticity of demand as follows:

$$m = p\left(1 - \frac{1}{|\eta|}\right) \tag{3.6}$$

Here a reminder on terminology is in order. When $|\eta| > 1$, economists say that demand for the commodity is *price elastic*. When $|\eta| < 1$, we say that demand is price inelastic. And when $|\eta| = 1$, we say that demand has unitary price elasticity. Thus, when demand is price elastic, marginal revenue is positive. When demand is price inelastic, marginal revenue is negative. And when demand has unitary price elasticity, marginal revenue is zero.

Income elasticity of demand

When economists speak loosely of "elasticity of demand" they almost always mean price elasticity of demand. However, there is also such a thing as income elasticity of demand. Using η_y to denote income elasticity of demand, we can write

$$\eta_y = \frac{\Delta Q}{Q} \bigg/ \frac{\Delta Y}{Y}. \tag{3.7}$$

Here Q is the original quantity demand by the consumer, Y is his original money income, ΔY is a small change in his money income, and ΔQ is the increase in quantity demanded resulting from the addition of ΔY to his original money income Y.

Whereas price elasticity of demand always takes a negative sign, this is not true of income elasticity of demand. That is, $\eta_y \leq 0$ and $\eta_y \geq 0$ are both economic possibilities. This is because a consumer may wish to substitute one commodity for another when his money income changes. For example, to a meat-eater, hamburger and prime cut are usually substitutes. When his money income increases, he may prefer to eat more prime cut and less hamburger. If so, the income elasticity of demand is negative for hamburger and positive for prime cut. We might note that just as price elasticity of demand usually varies with price, so income elasticity of demand usually varies with a consumer's money income. Thus, when the meat eater moves up the income scale from austerity to moderate comfort, the income elasticity of demand for prime cut may well become positive because he is substituting prime cut for hamburger. But when he moves on up from moderate comfort to undoubted affluence, the income elasticity of demand for prime cut may well become negative because he begins to replace it with oysters and pheasant.

Perfect price discrimination

So far we have examined the properties of a market (aggregate) demand curve on the assumption that a commodity is sold in a perfect market. We have defined a perfect market to be one in which arbitrage has completely eliminated all differences in price. Let us now move to the other extreme by assuming:

A3.2 The seller of a commodity is able to practice perfect price discrimination among people who buy it; and he can do so at no cost to himself.

In order to enforce this ultimate degree of price discrimination, the seller must be in a position to do two things. First, he must be able to suppress completely all arbitrage in the sale and re-sale of his commodity. This is equivalent to saying that he must be in a position to prevent the emergence of a second-hand market for his commodity. Since price discrimination involves charging some customers higher prices than other customers, the power to discriminate will obviously be limited by the activities of arbitragers—the people who engage in arbitrage.

Suppose that one buyer in the market is allowed to purchase any amount of the commodity at a price (per unit) of $10. Suppose further that this buyer can promptly, and at no cost to himself, resell the commodity to other people at, say $10.01. Clearly the original supplier of the commodity cannot charge more than $10.01 to any other customer. Otherwise he will be undersold by his favored customer. In this example, the possibility of price discrimination among customers had not been wholly eliminated; the example allows for a negligible amount of price discrimination—a price of $10 per unit for some units versus a price of $10.01 per unit for other units.

To frustrate the arbitrage that perfects the market, the seller must be able to limit the power of his customers to resell the commodity after they buy it from him. The seller can do this directly by exacting a legally binding pledge from each customer that he will refrain from acts of arbitrage. Or the seller can indirectly thwart arbitrage by restricting the amount of the commodity each customer can buy to that customer's "personal needs."

In order for the seller to practice perfect price discrimination, the complete suppression of arbitrage is not enough. The second requirement is that he must be able to deal with each customer on a "take it or leave it" basis. In a perfect market the buyer has the opportunity to buy as much— or as little—of the commodity as he wishes at a given price. If perfect price discrimination is to be achieved, the buyer must somehow be deprived of this option.

We obtained the market demand curve for a commodity by laterally summing up the demand curves of individual consumers. (Figure 3.1) To see how perfect price discrimination is enforced, we reverse this procedure. That is, we begin with a market demand curve and break it down into its individual components. Consider figure 3.6.

Here the market demand curve is *DC*. Thus *DC* is the demand curve which would be relevant to our analysis if the commodity were sold in a perfect market. In figure 3.6 the market is presumed to consist of two customers only. Line *DA* is the demand curve for customer #1 and line *DB* is the demand curve for customer #2.

From figure 3.6 one truth is self-evident. If the seller brings *OC* units of the commodity into a perfect market, then the only price which can

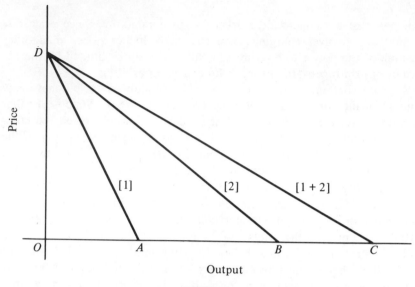

FIGURE 3.6

clear the market is a zero price. That is, if the seller brings *OC* units to such a market, he must give the stuff away. In a perfect market, the total revenue obtainable from selling *OC* units is precisely nothing.

Now suppose that the seller is able to practice perfect price discrimination. He has wholly eliminated arbitrage from the market. And he can say to customer #1: You will either buy a block of *OA* units of my commodity or you will buy no units at all. How much revenue can the seller collect from customer #1?

The economic benefit of *OA* units to the customer #1 is easily found. It is given by the area of the triangle *OAD*. Of course, customer #1 would prefer to obtain a block of *OC* units for less than *OAD;* ideally, he would like to get them free. But he will pay up to (and including) the sum *OAD* in order to obtain *OA* units rather than do without the commodity completely.

Suppose that the seller offers *OB* units to customer #2 on the same take-it-or-leave-it basis. The economic benefit to customer #2 is given by the triangle *OBD*. Therefore, *OBD* is the maximum sum that the seller can collect from customer #2 for a block of *OB* units.

In figure 3.6, *OA* +*OB* = *OC;* and $\triangle OAD + \triangle OBD = \triangle OCD$. Thus we have a rather startling result. When *OC* units are sold in a perfect market, price per unit will be zero; and total revenue will be zero. When *OC*

units are sold under conditions of perfect price discrimination, the sum
OCD—the "area under the market demand curve"—is the maximum total
revenue that can be obtained from buyers.

Note that, under conditions of perfect price discrimination, there is,
strictly speaking, no such thing as "price per unit." There can be no such
price since a block of the commodity is sold to each customer on a take-
it-or-leave-it basis. (Some economists would say that, under conditions
of perfect price discrimination, the *marginal price* at which *OC* units can
be sold in figure 3.6 is zero. But marginal price is not among the standardized terms of microeconomics.)

In short, a demand curve can be viewed in two different ways. It can
be viewed as providing information on the total revenue which can be
collected from the sale of various amounts of a commodity provided that
the sale takes place in a perfect market. Alternatively, the demand curve
can be viewed as providing information on the total revenue which can
be collected from the sale of various amounts of a commodity provided
that the sale is made under conditions of perfect price discrimination.

Imperfect price discrimination

In the markets of the real world price discrimination is absolutely ubiquitous but always far from perfect. Paul Samuelson has written in exas-
peration that the perfectly discriminating monopolist, so often referred to
in textbooks, does not exist on land or sea and never will. "He is just another name for God."[2] Typically, the firm that discriminates has only limited power to divide its customers into separate markets in which different
prices prevail. Consider the case of a monopolist who is able to sell his
commodity in two markets but must charge the same price to all customers located in the same market; that is, he can discriminate only to the
extent of charging two different prices. This situation is depicted in figures
3.7a and 3.7b. Once again in the interest of keeping things simple we assume that the monopolist has no costs of production and so maximizes
his economic rent by maximizing his total revenue.

Suppose that the monopolist sells his output in markets A and B. In
market A (figure 3.7a) his demand curve is given by *AA'* and the corresponding marginal revenue curve by *AM*. The monopolist maximizes
economic rent in market A by equating marginal cost (which is zero) to
marginal revenue. This is done by selling output *OM* and charging OP_A.

2. P. A. Samuelson, "Pitfalls in the Analysis of Public Goods," *Journal of Law and Economics,* 10 (1967), 100.

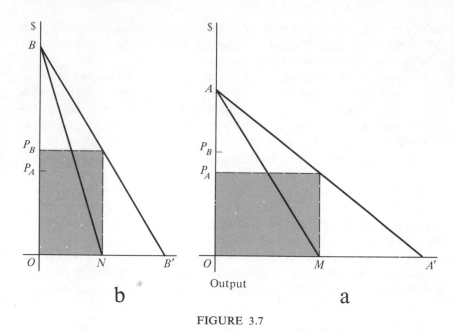

FIGURE 3.7

The maximum economic rent obtainable in market A is given by the shaded area in figure 3.7a.

In market B (figure 3.7b) the monopolist's demand curve is given by BB' and the corresponding marginal revenue curve by BN. Here he maximizes economic rent (again by equating marginal cost to marginal revenue) by selling output ON and charging price OP_B. The maximum economic rent obtainable in market B is given by the shaded area in figure 3.7b.

Since $P_B > P_A$, price discrimination is being practiced by our monopolist with the lower price being set in market A. Why the favoritism to customers located in market A when the cost of selling to them is the same as the cost of selling to customers in market B? A close inspection of curves AA' and BB' provides the answer. At any given price, the price elasticity of demand is greater in market A than in market B. For instance, at price P_B, $\eta = 1$ in market B; but at price P_B, $\eta > 1$ in market A. In fact, we can now generalize about imperfect price discrimination with the following theorem.

  T3.1 Assume that (i) a firm can sell its output in two different markets; (ii) the cost of selling a given output is the same in each market; and (iii) at every price, the price elasticity of demand is greater in one market than in the other. Then the firm will practice price discrimination, charging the lower price in the market which, at any given price, has the greater price elasticity of demand.

Hidden price discrimination

We have seen that a demand curve can be viewed in two different ways: (i) as providing information on the total revenue which can be obtained by selling different amounts of a commodity in a perfect market and (ii) as providing information on the total revenue obtainable when perfect price discrimination is practiced. Economists have usually emphasized the information provided by the first view of the demand curve. This is probably because of our abiding interest in perfectly competitive markets which are perforce perfect markets. As noted earlier, the converse does not hold: a perfect market is not *necessarily* a perfectly competitive market. Unless the seller has the monopoly power that allows him to affect price by varying his output, he cannot practice price discrimination among his customers. However, it is conceivable (though not probable) that he can have such power and still lack the additional power needed to suppress arbitrage in his commodity after he has made a sale to a customer. In the language of the Thomist philosophers, monopoly power is a necessary condition but not a sufficient cause for the practice of price discrimination by a seller.

The preoccupation of economists with perfect markets is rather unfortunate since, in the real world, price discrimination is nearly universal. Adults pay more to see movies than do children. Students usually pay more for books than do professors. Officers pay more for sex than do privates. And so on. Economic activity without price discrimination is virtually inconceivable. Indeed, unless we have a clear grasp of the concept of price discrimination and how price discrimination is enforced, a large part of the economic activity of the real world is simply baffling.

Consider one example of subtle, indeed nearly invisible, price discrimination—the tie-in sale. Federal courts have long viewed with deep suspicion any contract by which a seller of two commodities, say A and B, requires a customer who wishes to buy commodity A to buy some amount of commodity B as well (or vice versa). What the courts fear is "leverage"—that should the seller already monopolize the production of commodity A he can use the tie-in sale as a lever to gain a monopoly on the production of commodity B. Cases of leverage are not unknown in the business world. Nevertheless, most tie-in sales are best viewed as disguised price discrimination. Indeed, price discrimination may be the *only* economically valid explanation of a tie-in sale. One such case has been analyzed by Professor Ward Bowman, Jr., of the Yale Law School.[3]

A machine was invented for stapling buttons to high-button shoes, an operation formerly done by hand at higher cost. The patentee had a number of prospective customers for his machine, some of whom made a great many shoes, others only a few. The invention saved each user a fixed amount on each button attached. Thus the machine was worth more to the more intensive users. If the patentee attempted to sell it as different prices to the different users, however, he would have encountered two problems. To determine in advance how intensively each buyer would use the machine would have been difficult; to prevent those who paid a low price from reselling to those who paid a high price might have proved impossible. A tie-in would resolve these difficulties. The machine might be sold at cost, on condition that the unpatented staples used in the machine be bought from the patentee. Through staple sales, the patentee could obtain a device for measuring the intensity with which his customers used the machines. Hence by charging a higher than competitive price for the staples, the patentee could receive the equivalent of a royalty from his patented machines.

Although a tying sale may thus be used as a "counting device" for setting discriminatory prices on the tying product, the patentee creates no new and additional monopoly over the tied product. He could have achieved exactly the same return by attaching a meter to the button-stapling machine to measure the intensity of use, leasing the machine and charging a meter rate. . . . [T]ying is used simply as a means of insuring the full monopoly return on the tying product, where a monopoly already existed. No leverage can be found because the output of tied product, staples, is exactly the same when machine payment is charged directly and staples are sold competitively as when the staples are tied to the machine. The two outputs under the two equivalent methods of discrimination are identical.

Perhaps a numerical example of price discrimination through a tie-in sale will help. A tie-in long favored by movie producers in the distribution of films is so-called block booking.[4] The producer does not offer individual films to his theater or television station customers but instead offers them a block of films.

Suppose that a producer is promoting two films—the Art Film and the

3. Bowman, W. S., "Tying Arrangements and the Leverage Problem," *Yale Law Journal,* 67 (1957-58), 19-36. The case discussed by Bowman is Heaton-Peninsular Button-Fastener Co. *v.* Eureka Specialty Co., 77 Fed. 288 (6th Cir. 1896).
4. Block booking of films as a form of imperfect price discrimination is examined in G. J. Stigler, *The Organization of Industry* (Homewood, Ill., 1968), pp. 165-70.

TABLE 3.2
Maximum Rentals

	Art Film	Family Film	Art Film & Family Film
Bijou	$14,000	$2,000	$16,000
Rialto	$ 8,000	$3,500	$11,500

Family Film. He wishes to exhibit these films in two theaters, say the Bijou and the Rialto. Table 3.2 shows the maximum sum that each theater will pay in order to show each film. If the movie producer could practice perfect price discrimination between the theaters, he could collect the maximum sum from each theater for each film. That is, with perfect price discrimination he could collect a total of $27,500.

Suppose that he practices no discrimination at all and quotes the same rental on each film to each theater. Obviously he will charge a rental of $8000 on his Art Film; if he tried to charge more, the Rialto would not buy it. Likewise he will charge a rental of $2000 on his Family Film; if he tried to charge more, the Bijou would not buy it. Thus when no discrimination is practiced, the producer can collect a total sum of only $20,000.

Observe what block booking can do for the producer. The Bijou will play a maximum of $16,000 to obtain both Art Film and Family Film; while the Rialto will pay a maximum of $11,500 to obtain them both. Thus by setting a rental of $11,500 on the block that contains the two films, he will sell to each theater and so obtain a total sum of $23,000. This sum, of course, is greater than that to be gained by pricing the films individually though less than that to be gained if perfect price discrimination were possible.[5]

Does price discrimination, on balance, increase or decrease economic welfare? This is a tough question. We shall sidestep it until Chapter 13

5. An even less obvious form of price discrimination is associated with vertical integration. Manufacturers often "integrate forward" by buying their own warehouses, delivery trucks, and retail outlets even though economists and other businessmen do not see how average total cost is reduced by such integration. One explanation is that the manufacturer who sells his commodity through a chain that contains a large number of wholesalers, jobbers, and retailers has scant power to practice price discrimination; these "middlemen" are in a position to act as arbitragers. Consumers who buy at retail for their own use, however, have not the time, inclination, or storage facilities to engage in arbitrage. Hence, if the manufacturer wishes to increase total revenue by discriminating he often must deal directly with consumers, and this involves "eliminating the middleman."

when we have learned some more microeconomics. In case you are impatient, our conclusion will be that there is a presumption that most real-world forms of price discrimination increase economic welfare.

Summary

In this chapter and the previous chapter we have made the acquaintance of the "theory of demand." We found how the demand curves of individual consumers can be laterally summed up to obtain a market (aggregate) demand curve for a commodity. We saw that, when the commodity is sold in a market made perfect by arbitrage, the market demand curve shows the amount of the commodity that can be sold at each price (per unit). In such a market, when the market demand curve has been derived, we can go on to compute the following magnitudes for any price-output combination: total revenue, marginal revenue, and price elasticity of demand.

When the commodity is not sold in a perfect market, the market demand curve provides another sort of information. We examined the limit case where the seller is able to practice perfect price discrimination; that is, at no cost to himself, he can both suppress arbitrage among customers and deal with each customer on a take-it-or-leave-it basis. In this case, the market demand curve provides information on the *maximum* amount of revenue that the seller can collect when he discriminates. The seller can always increase his *total revenue* by practicing price discrimination. However, he may not be able to increase his *total profit* by discriminating. Like everything else in this world, price discrimination does not come free; it can only be implemented with the use of scarce resources. To say the obvious, the real world is a world of imperfect price discrimination.

REFERENCES

Hicks, J. R., *A Revision of Demand Theory* (London, 1956), chapters 2 and 3.
Ferguson, C. E., *Microeconomic Theory* (Homewood, Ill., 3rd ed., 1972), chapter 4.
Friedman, Milton, "The Marshallian Demand Curve," *Journal of Political Economy,* 57 (1949), 463-95.
Lancaster, Kelvin, *Consumer Demand: A New Approach* (New York, 1971).
Mansfield, Edwin, *Microeconomics: Theory and Applications* (New York, 1970), chapter 4.
Pigou, A. C., *The Economics of Welfare* (London, 4th ed., 1932), chapter 27.
Robinson, Joan, *The Economics of Imperfect Competition* (London, 2d ed., 1969), chapters 2, 3, 15 and 16.
Wu, Shih-Yen, and Jack Pontney, *An Introduction to Modern Demand Theory* (New York, 1967), chapter 9.

4
Production

Production and specialization

In the preceding two chapters we employed a technique for describing how a consumer would choose to spend his income when allowed to buy different commodities at specified prices. Whatever its merits or defects, this theory of consumer behavior is at least one of the more standardized parts of economic theory. (You can easily verify this statement by looking up the chapter labeled consumption, consumer behavior, indifference curves, or some such title, in any other economic theory textbook published in the last twenty years.) But the commodities which are offered to the consumer do not appear mysteriously from Merlin's magic cave or outer space. They are "produced." And for openers, it is reasonable to assume that the set of commodities available to consumers depends both on the resource endowment of the economy and on the technology available for making use of this endowment.

Unhappily, the theory of production is among the least standardized (and most difficult) parts of economics. (You can also verify this statement by checking the treatment of production in a few recently published textbooks.) Provided that no one asks us to define our terms very carefully we can all agree on one self-evident truth. Every commodity desired by consumers is produced by combining the services of a very large number of "productive agents." The trouble is that in order to make any sense out of the incredibly complicated process of production, we must first arbitrarily group these productive agents into a manageable number of categories. That is, we have to specify the *factors of production.*

But where in the world do we begin? In a plant that manufactures shoes, a pair of men's size 10 work shoes is produced by making use of leather, rubber, water, fuel oil, electricity, unskilled labor, skilled labor, and maybe ten different kinds of machines. Moreover, each machine can be resolved into its component parts—nuts, bolts, wheels, motors, *etc*. Nobody in his right mind will argue that every last type of nut or bolt should be treated as a separate "factor of production."

In the theory of production one feature of the enormous diversity of things used to produce shoes is significant above all others. Some of these things are much more specialized to the production of shoes than others. Unskilled labor (janitors, file clerks, receptionists) and raw materials (leather, rubber) can easily be shifted to a great number of other uses. But an elderly skilled workman cannot move to another industry without a big loss in income. His income will drop, of course, because he has no special skill that other industries want. Again, if a machine expressly designed to stitch shoe tops to shoe soles is not used for this task, it might as well be melted down and sold for scrap.

Our first need then is for a classification scheme that explicitly recognizes that some productive agents are more specialized to particular uses than are other productive agents. Our second need is for a classification scheme that reduces the productive agents to be discussed to a manageable number. To this end we proceed as follows.

We shall specify a model in which there are two wholly unspecialized factors of production—capital and labor. The "labor supply" can be thought of as a given number of man-hours of equal efficiency. Capital can be thought of as a kind of all-purpose putty. This approach will allow us to treat the inputs of labor and capital in the production process as physical quantities. This in turn will allow us to go behind the "veil of money" and so make clear the technological character of production. Our model will contain productive agents that are specialized to particular uses—the making of shoes, fork lift trucks, transistor radios, *etc*. We shall also specify for our model a state of technology which can be defined as the knowledge needed to build productive agents that are specialized to particular uses—the making of shoes, fork lift trucks, transistor radios, *etc*. These specialized productive agents we shall call, with good reason, machines. You may find it helpful to think of a machine as coming into existence when a certain number of man-hours are devoted to shaping and transforming a certain quantity of putty into hard-baked clay.

In addition, we make the following explicit assumptions.

A4.1 At least two production techniques are available to produce every commodity desired by consumers.

A4.2 Each production technique requires the use of the following: a machine, a direct capital input ("raw materials"), and a direct labor input ("production workers").

A4.3 The construction of a machine requires the use of a capital input and a labor input.

By the above assumptions, the amount of a commodity that can be produced is a function of three variables: (1) the amount of capital used, (2) the amount of labor used, and (3) the way in which some part of the capital and labor is specialized—that is, upon the production technique chosen.

It would not be wrong to say that, in our model, the amount of a commodity that can be produced depends ultimately on the amount of capital and labor used to produce it. We note, however, that our two factors of production figure in the production process in two ways. First, some part of the capital and labor inputs—namely, that part which is regularly employed with a machine—is employed *directly* to produce a commodity. Second, the remaining part of the capital and labor inputs—that which is used to build the machine—is employed *indirectly* to produce the commodity.

If we bear in mind that capital and labor can be used either directly or indirectly in production, we will avoid a very common error in economic theory. Industries that use a great deal of expensive machinery and few workers are often described as "capital intensive." This description can be misleading since machines are also produced with labor—often with a very high ratio of labor to capital. One cannot really say whether an industry is "capital intensive" without having information on both its *direct* capital and labor inputs and on its *indirect* capital and labor inputs.

Failure to recognize this truth is the source of a very old error in economic theory. It is often asserted that if the level of wages rises in the economy, firms will substitute machines for men in the production process.[1] The rise in the level of wages may produce this result; but it need not do so. For the wage increase will also raise the cost of building machines and may (not necessarily will) cause firms to shift to an alternative production technique. This alternative may (not necessarily will) involve the use of less expensive machines and a greater direct labor input.

The inputs of capital and labor that are used directly with a machine to produce a commodity we call variable inputs. Such inputs are variable in

1. The English economist David Ricardo (1772-1823) had argued early in the nineteenth century that "machinery and labor are in constant competition, and the former can frequently not be employed until labor rises." *On the Principles of Political Economy and Taxation* (3rd ed., London, 1821), p. 479.

the sense that they are not specialized to one particular use and so can easily be shifted to the production of other commodities. The inputs of capital or labor that are used to build the machine used to produce a commodity we call fixed inputs. Such inputs are locked into the machine during its useful life. A certain quantity of capital putty has, so to speak, been baked into the hard clay of the machine. And the man-hours used to engineer this transformation have been swallowed up by history. Hence, the capital and labor used to build the machine—the "investment" of capital and labor in the machine, if you prefer—can have an economic payoff only as it is used to produce one particular commodity. From now on, for ready reference, let us again call this unique end product commodity X.

Choosing a production technique

Suppose that we decide that we want to produce commodity X. Never mind how we reached this decision or what we plan to do with commodity X when we have produced it. Suppose further that the present state of technology allows us to choose between two production techniques for

TABLE 4.1A
Alpha Technique

commodity X (units)	fixed capital (units)	fixed labor (units)	variable capital (units)	variable labor (units)
0	6	5	0	0
1	6	5	2	2
2	6	5	3	3
3	6	5	4	4
4	6	5	5	6
5	6	5	6	8
6	6	5	7	10
7	6	5	8	12
8	6	5	10	14
9	6	5	13	16
10	6	5	17	19
11	6	5	23	23
12	6	5	29	26
13	6	5	36	30
14	6	5	44	34
15	6	5	53	38

TABLE 4.1b
Beta Technique

commodity X (units)	fixed capital (units)	fixed labor (units)	variable capital (units)	variable labor (units)
0	12	6	0	0
1	12	6	2	2
2	12	6	3	3
3	12	6	4	4
4	12	6	5	5
5	12	6	6	6
6	12	6	7	7
7	12	6	8	9
8	12	6	10	11
9	12	6	12	13
10	12	6	14	16
11	12	6	17	19
12	12	6	20	22
13	12	6	23	25
14	12	6	27	29
15	12	6	31	33

producing commodity X. Again, for ready reference, let us call them the alpha technique and the beta technique. To use the alpha technique we must build an alpha machine; and to use the beta technique we must build a beta machine.

According to assumption A4.2, neither the alpha machine or the beta machine by itself will produce any amount of commodity X. Production requires that the machine, once built, be used directly with a certain quantity of capital and labor input.

Information on the alpha technique is given in table 4.1a. Information on the beta technique is given in table 4.1b. At first glance, these tables are rather puzzling. But only a little concentration is needed to get their meaning. Note especially the following points.

1. To build an alpha machine, we need 6 units of capital and 5 units of labor. Since the alpha machine is completely specialized to the production of commodity X, we can say that the alpha technique requires a fixed capital input of 6 units and a fixed labor input of 5 units.

2. To build a beta machine, we need 12 units of capital and 6 units of labor. The beta machine is also completely specialized to the production of commodity X. Hence the beta technique requires a fixed capital input of 12 units and a fixed labor input of 6 units.
3. It takes more capital and labor to build a beta machine than to build an alpha machine. However, once the beta is operational, it uses less variable capital and less variable labor at most rates of output. For example, when 10 units of output are produced with the alpha technique, the variable capital input is 17 units while the variable labor input is 19 units. When 10 units of output are produced with the beta technique, the variable capital input is only 14 units and the variable labor input is only 16 units.

If we want to produce commodity X, should we use the alpha or the beta technique? Which is more efficient? That is, which technique gives the greatest amount of product for each dollar spent? On the basis of the information provided in tables 4.1a and 4.1b, we cannot answer this question.

Consider table 4.2 which summarizes in more convenient form some of the facts in these first two tables. Note that table 4.2 gives only the total capital input and total labor input for selected outputs of commodity X. For example, table 4.1a shows that if one unit of commodity X is produced using the alpha technique, we need 6 units of fixed capital, 2 units of variable capital, 5 units of fixed labor, and 2 units of variable labor. Table 4.2 shows that if one unit of commodity X is produced using the alpha technique, we need a total of 8 units of capital and a total of 7 units of labor.

From table 4.2, it is clear that if we want only one unit of commodity X, we should always use the alpha technique. It needs less labor (7 units versus 8 for the beta) and less capital (8 versus 14 for the beta). Suppose that we wish to produce 15 units of commodity X. Now table 4.2 indicates that we should always use the beta technique. When output is 15 units, the beta technique needs less labor (39 versus 43 for the alpha) and less capital (43 units versus 59 units for the alpha).

But suppose that we want 7 units of commodity X. Now we simply cannot tell from table 4.2 alone which of our two techniques is best. The alpha technique uses less capital (14 units versus 20 for the beta) but more labor (17 units versus 15 for the beta). We cannot make a sensible choice between the alpha and beta techniques until we have information on the price of a capital input and the price of a labor input.

Assume that the price per unit of capital is $10 and the price per unit of

TABLE 4.2

commodity X (units)	production technique	total capital input (units)	total labor input (units)
1	alpha	8	7
	beta	14	8
7	alpha	14	17
	beta	20	15
15	alpha	59	43
	beta	43	39

Source: tables 4.1a and 4.1b

TABLE 4.3A
Capital Input = $10
Labor Input = $1

alpha technique*			
commodity X (units)	total capital (units)	total labor (units)	total cost
7	14	17	$157
beta technique			
commodity X (units)	total capital (units)	total labor (units)	total cost
7	20	15	$215

* preferred technique

TABLE 4.3B
Capital Input = $1
Labor Input = $10

alpha technique			
commodity X (units)	total capital (units)	total labor (units)	total cost
7	14	17	$184
beta technique*			
commodity X (units)	total capital (units)	total labor (units)	total cost
7	20	15	$170

* preferred technique

labor is $1. We can now construct table 4.3a. It shows that when 7 units of commodity X are produced with the alpha technique, the total cost is $157. When 7 units of commodity X are produced with the beta technique, the total cost is $215. Clearly, we have an answer. At the prices of capital and labor inputs that we have specified, we would choose alpha over beta if we want to produce 7 units of commodity X.

But let us interchange our factor prices. The price per unit of capital becomes $1 and the price per unit of labor becomes $10. We construct table 4.3b to show the changed situation. Now the beta technique is best for producing 7 units of commodity X. When beta is used, the total cost of these 7 units is $170. Should alpha be used, the total cost of these 7 units would be $184.

At this point you can breathe easier and relax a little. We are back in territory already familiar from your previous work in economics. Once we know the production technique to be used and the prices of the factor inputs that it requires, we can compute the total cost of producing any given quantity of output.

Given information on the production technique to be used and factor input prices, we can also reckon: (a) total fixed cost; (b) average fixed cost; (c) total variable cost; (d) average variable cost; (e) average total cost; and (f) marginal cost—the most troublesome and important cost of all.

No doubt you recall from your first course in economics how these costs were defined. But since the definitions are of crucial importance in economic analysis, we quickly review them.

Total fixed cost is that part of total cost that does not change as the rate of output changes.

Average fixed cost is total fixed cost divided by the rate of output.

Total variable cost is that part of total cost that does change as the rate of output changes.

Average variable cost is total variable cost divided by the rate of output.

Average total cost is total cost divided by the rate of output. Therefore average total cost can also be defined as the sum of average fixed cost and average variable cost.

Marginal cost is the amount added to total cost by the production of one additional unit of output. Therefore, since only variable cost changes as the rate of output changes, marginal cost can also be defined as the amount added to total variable cost by the production of one additional unit of output.

In your first course in economics all of these costs were defined with reference to the firm. It was assumed that the firm had already decided on the best, i.e. most economical, production technique for carrying on its business. In this chapter, we have defined these costs with reference to a given production technique since our concern is with how the firm chooses from a set of alternative production techniques.

Once we have information on the capabilities of the alpha and beta techniques, and the prices of capital and labor inputs, we can compare the relative efficiency of alpha and beta over a range of outputs. Let us try two comparisons.

From tables 4.1a and 4.1b we know the capital and labor inputs needed to produce different amounts of commodity X. These amounts range from 0 through 15 units. Table 4.1a provides information on the alpha technique and table 4.1b provides information on the beta technique.

We shall first calculate the *average total cost* of producing each of the 16 different outputs with both the alpha and beta techniques on the assumption that the price per capital input is $10 and the price per labor input is $1. Once more a helpful genie has made all the necessary calculations for you and summarized the results in figure 4.1a.

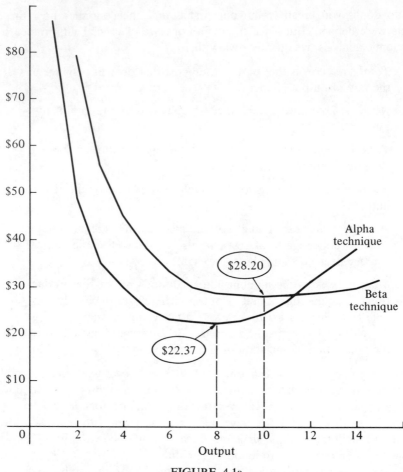

FIGURE 4.1a

Two features of figure 4.1a should be noted very carefully. (i) The curve of average total cost implied by each of our two production techniques has a minimum point. (ii) One minimum point represents a lower average total cost than does the other.

To be specific. If the alpha technique is used, average total cost is lowest when 8 units of commodity X are produced. At this output, average total cost is $22.37. If the beta technique is used, average total cost is lowest when 10 units of commodity X are produced. At this output, average total cost is $28.20.

Which technique is "better?" Remember that, by our assumptions, the price per capital input is $10 and the price per labor input is $1. Here we have to be very careful indeed.

Our first instinct is to say that our choice of technique depends upon how much of commodity X we intend to produce. If 10 units or less of the product are desired, we can produce it most cheaply by using the alpha technique. If 12 or more units are desired, we can produce it most cheaply by using the beta technique. This answer may seem reasonable. You are warned that it deserves no more than half credit on a final exam.

This answer is correct provided that 10 units or less of commodity X are wanted. For over this range of output, average total cost is always less for alpha than for beta. The answer is also correct if we wish to produce somewhat more than 10 units of commodity X—say 12 units.

But suppose that we set out to produce 15 units of commodity X. *Then the correct decision is to use the alpha technique twice.* That is, the average total cost of producing 15 units will be minimized if 7 units are produced on one alpha machine and 8 units are produced on another alpha machine. The production of these units also requires, of course, the variable inputs of capital and labor specified in table 4.1a. Therefore, at our given input prices ($10 per capital input and $1 per labor input), the alpha technique is more efficient than the beta technique *at almost all rates of output.* In short, at given input prices, there is almost always one production technique which is clearly better than others irrespective of level of production desired.

Only one step remains before we can pass on to less abstract and, let us hope, more interesting matters. The cost of producing commodity X is a function both of the particular production technique used and the prices of capital and labor inputs. Hence a change in these input prices may encourage the firm to substitute one technique for another. To make sure that we have a firm grip on this truth, let us try interchanging the prices of our two factor inputs once again. The price per capital input becomes $1. The price per labor input becomes $10.

With the aid of tables 4.1a and 4.1b, our good genie goes to work again, makes the necessary calculations, and comes up with figure 4.1b. Now when the alpha technique is used, average total cost is lowest when 9 units of commodity X are produced. At this output, average total cost is $25.44. If the beta technique is used, average total cost is also lowest when 9 units of commodity X are produced. At this output, however, average total cost using beta is $23.77. Given our new set of factor prices, figure 4.1b shows that the beta technique is clearly best for all rates of output.

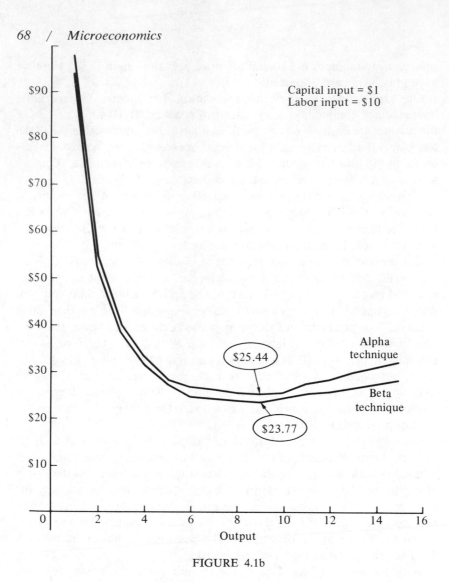

Capital input = $1
Labor input = $10

$25.44

Alpha technique

Beta technique

$23.77

Output

FIGURE 4.1b

For the rest of this book we will hardly ever have any reason to refer to *production techniques*. Instead, we shall usually talk about *cost functions* or *cost curves* whenever production is mentioned. But never forget that production techniques lurk behind cost functions and cost curves. If the object of a firm is to produce, say, 80 units of some commodity, there will ordinarily be a very large number of production techniques available to produce it. Henceforth we shall assume that the firm has already solved the problem of choosing the production technique that is most efficient given the prices which must be paid to hire the needed factors. We have to make this assumption about the behavior of the firm before we can move on to other topics in microeconomics. Otherwise, we could get bogged down for the entire course in a study of how a firm evaluates production techniques. The importance of such a study is not to be doubted. But it is more appropriate to an engineering course than to an economics course.

Specialization and the U-shaped ATC curve

One final word on production techniques. We have said that every such technique requires the use of a machine specialized to the production of a particular commodity; and that this machine, in effect, constitutes a fixed input of capital and a fixed input of labor. It is the specialized nature of the machine that gives the average total cost curves in figures 4.1a and 4.1b their distinctive shapes. As output increases from zero, average total cost declines, reaches a minimum, and then rises. This is true irrespective of the production technique chosen or the prices that must be paid to hire factors. The curve of average total cost (ATC) is sometimes described as being *U-shaped*. (This description is accurate enough provided that one does not insist on a neatly drawn letter U.)

Economic analysis would be vastly simpler if we could forget about U-shaped curves of average total cost and assume instead that average total cost is always independent of the rate of output. If we could make this substitution, average total cost would always be equal to marginal cost. But to deny the existence of a U-shaped curve of average total cost in the plant would be to deny a most important truth: that efficient production in a technologically advanced economy requires that capital and labor be specialized to particular uses for considerable periods of time.

Most of the time in economics our concern is with efficient production in a technologically advanced economy. Hence, we can hardly ever get along without the U-shaped ATC curve cost in the plant. Since a firm can operate more than one plant, it does not follow that the firm must have a U-shaped ATC curve merely because each of its plants must have a U-shaped ATC curve. We consider the properties of the firm's cost functions in the next chapter.

Summary

A theory of production is indispensable in economics because, in the real world, a very great number of production techniques is usually available to produce any given commodity. Some factor inputs used in commodity production are totally unspecialized and so can be used with a great many production techniques. However, each production technique requires that some factor inputs be specialized to a particular use. A firm presumably wishes to select the production technique that will maximize its income. In order to choose wisely from among alternatives, it needs information on (i) the physical properties of each production technique, i.e. on how much output will result from various combinations of factor inputs (specialized and unspecialized); (ii) the prices that must be paid to secure factor inputs; and (iii) the amount of output that it wishes to produce.

Corresponding to every production technique and set of factor input prices, there is a set of cost curves for the "plant." In economic analysis we usually choose to make life easier for ourselves by assuming that the firm has somehow already discovered the set of cost curves—and hence the production technique—that allows it to produce most efficiently. That is, we treat choice of the correct techniques as an engineering problem rather than a problem in economic analysis. The justification for this treatment of the theory of production is that we wish to use our limited time to discuss other matters.

REFERENCES

Becker, G. S., *Economic Theory* (New York, 1971), chapter 7.
Chenery, H. B. "Engineering Production Functions," *Quarterly Journal of Economics,* 62 (1948-49), 507-31.
Ferguson, C. E., *Microeconomic Theory* (Homewood, Ill., 3rd ed., 1972), chapters 5 and 6.
Mantell, L. H. and Sing, F. P., *Economics for Business Decision* (New York, 1972), chapter 8.
Robinson, Joan, *The Accumulation of Capital* (London, 2d ed., 1966), chapter 10.
Stigler, G. J., *The Theory of Price* (New York, 3d ed., 1966), chapters 6, 7, and 8.
Stigler, G. J., *Production and Distribution Theories* (New York, 1946).
Vickrey, W. S., *Microstatics* (New York, 1964), chapter 4.

5
Costs of Production

Cost in the plant

In Chapter 4 we saw how we could construct the curve of average total cost (ATC) of producing commodity X in a "plant" when information is provided on (i) the production techniques available to produce commodity X and (ii) the prices of the necessary factor inputs. In fact, we worked through an example in which such information was provided in order to construct the ATC curves for two different types of plant (alpha and beta). When the prices of factor inputs are given, we noted that ordinarily one type of plant is superior to all others; so that ordinarily there is only one ATC curve in the plant that need concern us.

In Chapter 4 we also briefly reviewed the definitions of total fixed cost, average fixed cost, total variable cost, average variable cost, average total cost, and marginal cost. We did not spend much time on these costs. Given their importance in microeconomic analysis, a little more review is in order before proceeding.

In the case where a producer of commodity X has only one plant, the ATC curve of the plant is necessarily the ATC curve of the firm. There is an output (or a range of outputs) at which average total cost in the plant is minimized. Therefore, in the one-plant firm, as in the single plant, the ATC curve is U-shaped.

Consider table 5.1. It should look familiar since a similar representation of costs is found in every modern textbook on economic principles. Table 5.1 shows, for various outputs, the following costs of producing commodity X *in a single plant:* total fixed cost, total variable cost, total cost, average fixed cost, average variable cost, and marginal cost.

TABLE 5.1
Cost in the Plant

(1) output (units)	(2) total fixed cost ($)	(3) total variable cost ($)	(4) total cost ($)	(5) average fixed cost ($)	(6) average variable cost ($)	(7) average total cost ($)	(8) marginal cost ($)
0	80.00	0.00	80.00	—	0.00	—	—
1	80.00	7.50	87.50	80.00	7.50	87.50	7.50
2	80.00	13.20	93.20	40.00	6.60	46.60	5.70
3	80.00	17.70	97.70	26.67	5.90	32.57	4.50
4	80.00	21.60	101.60	20.00	5.40	25.40	3.90
5	80.00	25.50	105.50	16.00	5.10	21.10	3.90
6	80.00	30.00	110.00	13.34	5.00	18.33	4.50
7	80.00	35.70	115.70	11.43	5.10	16.53	5.70
8	80.00	43.20	123.20	10.00	5.40	15.40	7.50
9	80.00	53.10	133.10	8.89	5.90	14.79	9.90
10	80.00	66.00	146.00	8.00	6.60	14.60	12.90
11	80.00	82.50	162.50	7.27	7.50	14.77	16.50
12	80.00	103.20	183.20	6.67	8.60	15.27	20.70
13	80.00	128.70	208.70	6.17	9.90	16.06	25.50
14	80.00	159.60	239.60	5.71	11.40	17.11	30.90
15	80.00	196.50	276.50	5.33	13.10	18.43	36.90
16	80.00	239.60	319.60	5.00	14.98	19.98	43.10
17	80.00	290.30	370.30	4.71	17.06	21.77	50.70
18	80.00	349.20	429.20	4.40	19.40	23.84	58.90
19	80.00	416.10	496.10	4.21	21.90	26.11	66.90
20	80.00	492.00	572.00	4.00	24.60	28.60	75.90

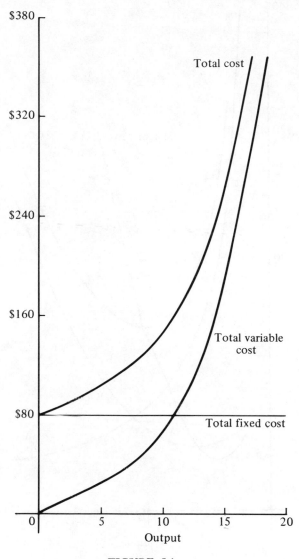

FIGURE 5.1

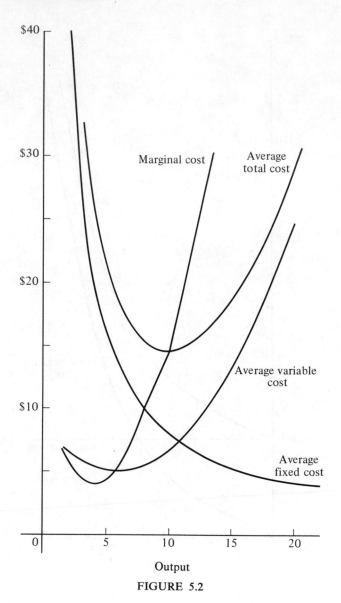

Output

FIGURE 5.2

Figures 5.1 and 5.2 should also be familiar to you from your first course in economics. Figure 5.1 shows total fixed cost, total variable cost, and total cost as a function of output. Figure 5.2 shows average fixed cost, average variable cost, average total cost, and marginal cost as a function of output.[1]

Plant cost versus firm cost

Let us emphasize again that the cost data in table 5.1, figure 5.1, and figure 5.2 are assumed to relate *to a single plant*. In many discussions of cost, no distinction is drawn between the cost of production in the plant and cost of production in the firm on the concealed premise that the firm has only one plant. There are two decisive objections to treating cost of production in this simple-minded way.

First, the premise of "only one plant to a firm" is wildly unrealistic.[2] In the real world, the large firm typically distributes its output among a large number of relatively small plants. (The Ralston Purina Company, not even among the fifty largest American manufacturing firms, operates over ninety mills that process animal and poultry feed.) Second, economic reasoning based upon the assumption that the firm has only one plant easily leads to a very misleading conclusion. As we shall presently see, this conclusion is that there is a unique "optimum size" of firm for every industry.

We have found that whenever some resources are specialized to a particular use, the ATC curve in the plant must be U-shaped. Since produc-

1. The wide-awake reader will have noted a discrepancy between table 5.1 and figure 5.2. Both provide the same information on average fixed cost, average variable cost, and average total cost. But they do not provide quite the same information on marginal cost. For example, table 5.1 indicates that when 10 units of commodity X are produced in the plant, marginal cost is $12.90. Figure 5.2 indicates that when 10 units of commodity X are produced, marginal cost is $14.60—the same amount as average total cost.
The information in figure 5.2 is based on the equation
$$T = 80 + 8.6Q - 1.2Q^2 + 0.1Q^3 \qquad (5.1)$$
where T denotes total cost and Q denotes the output of commodity X. When a total cost function is given, we can treat marginal cost as the first derivative of total cost with respect to quantity, that is, as dT/dQ. Differentiating equation 5.1 we have
$$dT/dQ = 8.6 - 2.4Q + 0.3Q^2 \qquad (5.2)$$
The marginal cost curve in figure 5.2 is the graph of this equation.
However, in table 5.1 the marginal cost of n units of output is treated as the difference between the total cost of n units and the total cost of $(n-1)$ units when n is an integer. Provided that $1/n$ is "small," these two ways of reckoning marginal cost yield results that differ very little.
2. In this chapter we speak of the multiplant firm for the sake of brevity. But the discussion could just as well be conducted in terms of the *multishop* firm or the *multidepartment* firm.

tion without specialized resources is non-existent in the real world, we can state categorically that, in the real world, every plant has an ATC curve that is U-shaped. Hence, in every real-world industry there is, at any moment in time, both an optimum size of plant and an optimum output per plant. (Of course, if the prices of factor inputs are constantly changing, these two optima also may be constantly changing.) When a firm can have only one plant, an obvious conclusion follows: in a real-world industry composed of such firms there is also an optimum size of firm and an optimum output per firm. When a firm can have only one plant, the existence of an optimum size for the plant constitutes a natural impediment to "monopoly" in most industries. That is, unless demand is very small relative to the optimum size of plant (and firm), the industry will ordinarily consist of more than one plant (and firm).

Once we allow for the possibility that a firm can have more than one plant, the ATC curve of the firm *need not* be U-shaped. Hence, there need be no optimum size of firm in each industry and no natural impediment to "monopoly." We place *monopoly* in quotation marks for a very good reason. As we shall presently see, the word is commonly applied to a number of market situations which have very little in common.

Cost in the multiplant firm

Let us examine cost of production in a firm that owns three identical plants on the following assumptions.

 A5.1 The prices that the firm must pay for its factor inputs are given; these prices neither rise nor fall as the firm changes its output.

 A5.2 There are neither economies nor diseconomies of scale to be had by bringing plants under common ownership and control.

Incidentally, assumption A5.2 is not as unrealistic as it may seem at first glance. In many industries of the real world, economies and diseconomies of scale "external to the plant" but "internal to the firm" are so small that they may reasonably be ignored. Some common examples of scale economies external to the plant but internal to the firm are the savings which multiplant firms realize in legal fees, management training, inventory control, and raw material purchasing. In other cases, while particular economies and diseconomies of scale external to the plant are not insignificant, they largely cancel out over a wide range of output and so can be disregarded.

Let table 5.1 give the information on cost of production in each of the three plants owned by a 3-plant firm. (To repeat, its plants are identical.)

Now suppose that the 3-plant firm wishes to produce, say, 18 units of commodity X in the cheapest possible way. We can immediately note two features of the production problem as viewed by this producer.

1. He may produce all of commodity X in one plant and shut down the other two. Or he may divide the production of commodity X between two plants and shut down the third. Or he may use all three plants to produce commodity X.
2. In the short run—that is, before any existing plant wears out or a new plant can be built—the producer's decision as to how many plants should operate is not affected by fixed cost. By definition, fixed cost remains the same for every plant whether it operates or shuts down.

When the 3-plant firm operates only one of its three plants, there can be no output allocation problem. If the object is to produce 18 units, they must all be produced in the one plant that operates.

Should the 3-plant firm decide to operate two of its three plants, there is an output allocation problem. As an income maximizer the firm solves the problem by adhering to the rule: divide output between the two plants in a way that equalizes marginal cost in the two plants. For clearly, if marginal cost is lower in plant A than in plant B, the firm's total cost can be reduced by transferring a unit of output from plant B to plant A. Should the firm choose to operate all three of its plants, the output allocation rule becomes: divide output among the three plants in a way that equalizes marginal cost among them.

A given condition of our problem is that the three plants of the 3-plant firm are identical. Thus, when two plants are operated average variable cost of 18 units is usually minimized by dividing output equally between them. And when three plants are operated the average variable cost of 18 units is usually minimized by dividing output equally among all three.[3]

---

3. The problem of constructing the AVC curve for the multiplant firm (with all plants identical) is somewhat more complicated than the above discussion may suggest. It is complicated because the marginal cost (MC) curve in each plant is U-shaped. Consequently, it is possible that an unequal division between two plants will make marginal cost equal in them. That is, marginal cost while equal in the two plants, may be rising in one and falling in the other. And this unequal division may yield a lower average variable cost for the output than would an equal division.

Fortunately, when the AVC curve is U-shaped in each plant, the division of output which allows each plant in the multiplant firm to operate at the minimum point on the AVC curve must be an equal division. (Recall that all plants are presumed to be identical.) Thus the technique that we use to construct the AVC curve of the multiplant firm allows us to locate precisely the minimum points on this curve (and also the points on the AVC curve close to these minima). However, our technique

TABLE 5.2
The 3-Plant Firm

	total fixed cost ($) 18 units	total variable cost ($) 18 units	total cost ($) 18 units
1 plant operates	240.00	349.20	589.20
2 plants operate	240.00	106.20	346.20
3 plants operate	240.00	90.00	330.00

Once we know how many plants the 3-plant firm chooses to operate, we know how it will allocate output among them. But how does it decide on the number of plants to operate in the first place? The information needed to answer this question when the goal of the 3-plant firm is to produce 18 units in the cheapest way is implicit in table 5.1. We make this information explicit in table 5.2.

Fixed cost in a single plant is $80. Since the firm has three plants, its total fixed cost is $240. In the short run, the firm must incur this $240 expense whether it operates three, two, one, or zero plants. Should the 3-plant firm produce all 18 units in one plant (keeping the other two plants idle) its total variable cost is $349.20 and its total cost is $589.20.

Should it choose to operate two plants, each will produce 9 units. With two plants operating, total variable cost is $106.20 and total cost is $346.20. Should the firm choose to operate all three plants, each will produce 6 units. With all three plants operating, total variable cost is $90 and total cost is $330. In the short run, the 3-plant firm will minimize the total cost of producing 18 units by (i) operating all three plants and (ii) producing 6 units in each plant.

Why do we keep inserting the qualification "in the short run" into our discussion? Simply because the firm is momentarily stuck with one plant too many given that its goal is to produce 18 units of commodity X in the cheapest way. If the firm had only two plants, total fixed cost would be only $160. And if 9 units were produced in each plant, total variable cost

—divide output equally among the plants that operate—may give only approximations to other points on the AVC curve of the multiplant firms.

The problem of constructing cost curves for the multiplant firm is considered in Don Patinkin, "Multiple-Plant Firms, Cartels, and Imperfect Competition," *Quarterly Journal of Economics,* 61 (1947), 173-205.

of 18 units would be only $106.20. And the total cost of these 18 units would be only $266.20. Therefore, if the firm wants to produce 18 units (say, per month) of commodity X over the long haul, it *will not* replace one of its three existing plants when it wears out.

Average variable cost

In the short run, we can forget about fixed cost. Therefore let us derive the cost curves for the 3-plant firm beginning with the curve of average variable cost (AVC). We continue to assume that each of its three plants has the costs described in table 5.1, figure 5.1, and figure 5.2.

Consider figure 5.3. If the 3-plant firm decides to operate one—and only one—of its three plants, its AVC curve is given by AA'. Thus AA' in figure 5.2 corresponds to the AVC curve of the plant in figure 5.1. If the firm elects to operate two of its three plants, it will allocate output in a way that keeps marginal cost equal in the two plants. Since these two plants are identical, it will usually divide output equally between them. When two plants are operated, the AVC curve for the 3-plant firm is given by BB' in figure 5.3. Finally, should our firm want to operate all three of its plants, it will usually divide output into three equal parts. In this case, its AVC curve is given by CC' in figure 5.3.

One truth is now obvious with the aid of figure 5.3. For most rates of output, average variable cost in the 3-plant firm depends upon the number of plants operated; and, for most rates of output, one way of organizing production is cheaper than the two alternative ways of organizing production. For example, if only two units of commodity X are to be produced, the firm will prefer to operate one plant. If 12 units are to be produced, it will prefer to operate two plants; and if 18 units, then all three plants. Clearly, the 3-plant firm will want to organize production in a way that places it on the lowest of its three possible AVC curves in figure 5.3.

The "true" AVC curve for the 3-plant firm is given by AC' in figure 5.4. It consists of the lowest segments of the AVC curves in figure 5.3. It shows that, for rates of output of less than 8 units, one plant will operate. For rates of output greater than 8 units but less than 14 units, two plants will operate. And for rates of output exceeding 14 units, all three plants will operate.

At an output of exactly 8 units, the firm is indifferent between operating one or two plants. At an output of exactly 14 units, it is indifferent between operating two or three plants.

We now have a technique for constructing the curve of average variable

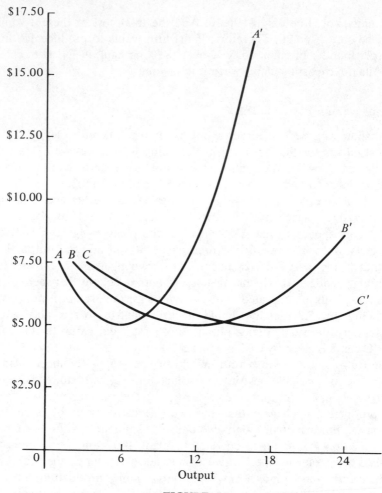

FIGURE 5.3

cost for a firm with three identical plants. Recall that it assumes that there are neither economies nor diseconomies of scale to be had by placing plants under common ownership and control. This technique can easily be generalized to cover the cases of firms with more than three plants and with plants of unequal efficiency. For, to repeat, the multiplant firm will always, *in the short run,* operate that number of its plants which will allow it to minimize the total variable cost of a given output. This behavior means that *in those plants the firm operates,* marginal cost will everywhere be equal.

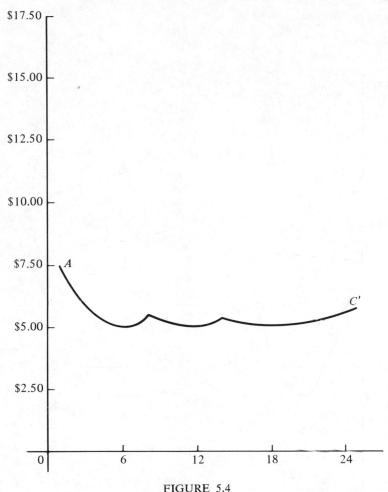

FIGURE 5.4

Marginal cost

Once we have derived the AVC curve for our 3-plant firm, it is an easy matter to derive the corresponding curves of average total cost (ATC) and marginal cost (MC). Marginal cost depends only upon variable cost. Since the AVC curve is kinked in figure 5.4 (a kink occurs whenever it pays to bring an additional plant into production as output increases) the MC curve is discontinuous. In figure 5.5, the relevant segments of the MC curve for the 3-plant firm (these segments are *aa'*, *bb'*, *cc'*) have been imposed on the AVC curve (labeled *AC'*) taken from figure 5.4.

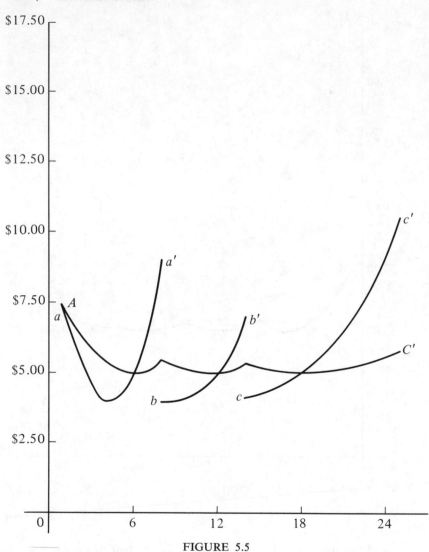

FIGURE 5.5

Average fixed cost

Drawing the curve of average fixed cost (AFC) in the 3-plant firm is no problem at all. Since fixed cost in each plant is $80 (table 5.1), total fixed cost in the 3-plant firm is $240. The AFC curve is the rectangular hyperbola *FF'* in figure 5.6.

Average total cost

The curve of average total cost we obtain by summing up the AVC curve and the AFC curve. This is done in figure 5.7. The ATC curve in the

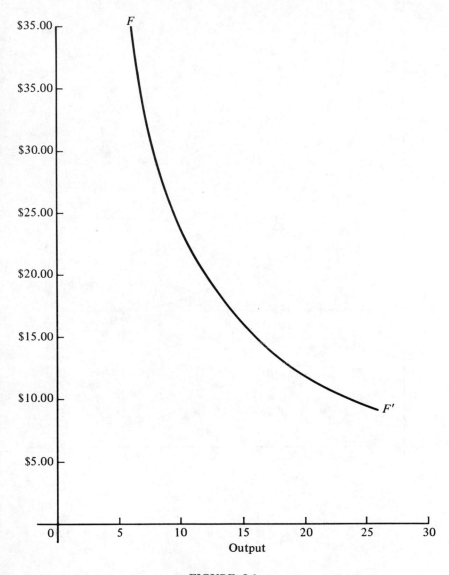

FIGURE 5.6

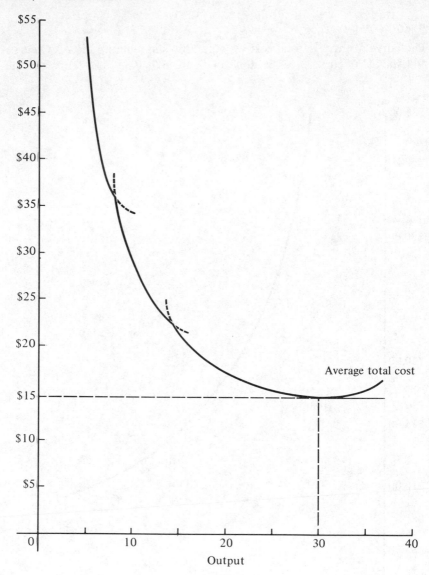

FIGURE 5.7

3-plant firm must, of course, be kinked since one of its two components, the AVC curve, is kinked. Note that the ATC curve in figure 5.7 is U-shaped in the limited sense that average total cost is minimized when 30 units are produced (10 units in each plant).

Cost in the multiplant firm: the long run

According to assumption A5.2, there are neither economies nor diseconomies to be had by bringing plants under common ownership and control. If so, it follows that a firm with one plant can be as efficient as a firm with a hundred plants. But while this inference is correct, its economic significance is not self-evident. Some elaboration is in order. Let us compare the ATC curves of the 1-plant firm, the 2-plant firm, and the 3-plant firm.

In figure 5.8, UU' designates the ATC curve for the 1-plant firm, VV' the ATC curve for the 2-plant firm, and WW' the ATC for the 3-plant firm. Thus UU' in figure 5.8 corresponds to the ATC curve of the plant in figure 5.1; and WW' in figure 5.8 corresponds to the ATC curve of the 3-plant firm in figure 5.7.

For each size of firm, *minimum* average total cost is $14.60. This minimum is realized at an output of 10 units in the 1-plant firm; at an output of 20 units in the 2-plant firm; and at an output of 30 units in the 3-plant firm. In the n-plant firm, this minimum would, of course, be realized at an output of $10n$ units.

In short, in the long run—in the time that it takes to build a new plant or phase out an existing plant—the multiplant firm subject to assumptions A5.1 and A5.2 operates under conditions of approximately constant average total cost. It can always produce at an average total cost of $14.60 provided that it produces some multiple of 10 units—the optimum output of the single plant.

In figure 5.8 a broken line connects the minimum points of UU', VV', and WW'. Should this broken line be viewed as a "curve of long-run average total cost"? The answer is an emphatic NO.

The efficient production of a commodity presupposes specialization of resources. Specialization ensures a U-shaped ATC curve *in the plant*. Every cost curve in the plant, and hence in the firm, is a short-run cost curve. *There is, strictly speaking, no such thing as a long-run cost curve. The firm has only the possibility of substituting one short-run cost curve for another at some time in the future.*

At this point, we might do well to recall the reason why we bothered to construct cost curves for the multiplant firm. In the plant, there is always

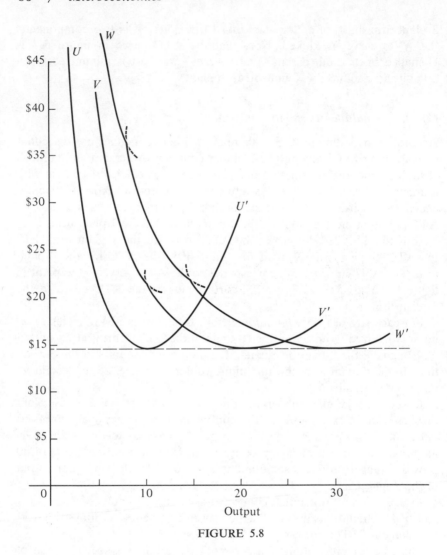

FIGURE 5.8

an optimum output, this output being that which minimizes average total cost. Hence, when a firm can have only one plant, there is an optimum output in the firm as well. Unless demand for aggregate output is very small—so small, in fact, that aggregate demand will support only a single plant—control of production will never pass into the hands of a single firm so long as the rule is "one plant to a firm."

These last two conclusions do not hold when multiple ownership of plants by the firm is possible. When multiplant firms are allowed, there is *not necessarily* an optimum output for the firm that constitutes a natural barrier to industrial concentration.

In the short run, the multiplant firm has a U-shaped ATC curve of sorts. (Remember that the ATC curve of the multiplant firm is always kinked.) And, in the short run, the output that minimizes average total cost depends upon the number of plants owned. The greater the number of plants owned, the greater the output needed to reach this minimum. However, there is no reason dictated by Nature why minimum average total cost should rise as the number of plants in the multiplant firm increases. When there are neither economies nor diseconomies of plant ownership, this minimum expense is independent of the number of plants owned. (Figure 5.8)

In economic analysis it is often useful to assume that there are neither economies nor diseconomies to be had by bringing plants under common ownership and control. (Assumption A5.2) But this assumption is obviously inapplicable to certain real-world industries. Virtually all heads are barbered in individually owned barber shops. Let us accept that other assumptions about scale economies in the firm are possible and consider the economic implications of these alternative assumptions.

We begin again by noting the obvious. When economies or diseconomies can be had by bringing plants under common ownership and control, three possibilities are present. (i) Average total cost will fall as the number of plants in the firm increases. (ii) Average total cost will rise as the number of plants in the firm increases. (iii) "Up to a point" average total cost will fall as the number of plants in the firm increases; after this point, average total cost will rise. These three possibilities are illustrated for up to three plants by figures 5.9a, 5.9b, and 5.9c.

Figure 5.9a gives the case where there are *economies of scale* which are "external to the plant but internal to the firm." Again, UU' is the ATC curve for a firm that owns only one plant; VV' is the ATC curve for the firm that owns two plants; and WW' is the ATC curve for the plant that owns three plants.

As figure 5.9a shows, the minimum point on the ATC curve of the 3-plant firm lies below the minimum points on the ATC curves of the 1-plant firm and the 2-plant firm.

The economic meaning of figure 5.9a? It is simply this: In those industries whose cost behavior it depicts there will ultimately be only a single firm. If aggregate demand is very small, the surviving firm will have only one plant; otherwise it will be a multiplant firm. In this case of economies "external to the plant but internal to the firm," the 1-plant firm cannot survive in competition with the multiplant firm. It is inefficiently small.

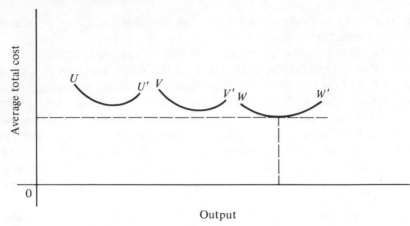

FIGURE 5.9a

Figure 5.9b gives the case where there are *diseconomies of scale* "external to the plant but internal to the firm." Here the 1-plant firm has a lower minimum average total cost than either the 2-plant firm or the 3-plant firm. Once more, *UU'* is the ATC curve for the 1-plant firm, *VV'* the ATC curve for the 2-plant firm, and *WW'* the ATC curve for the 3-plant firm.

The economic meaning of figure 5.9b? Clearly, it is that the industry will consist, in the long run, of 1-plant firms only.

Finally, figure 5.9c describes the case where a 2-plant firm is more effi-

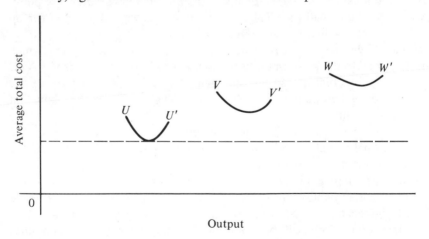

FIGURE 5.9b

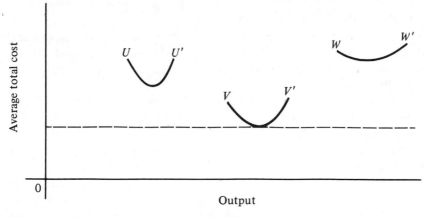

FIGURE 5.9c

cient than either a 1-plant firm or a 3-plant firm. For here the minimum point on VV' below the minimum points on UU' and WW'. In this case, the industry in the long run must consist only of 2-plant firms.

We shall presently find that assumptions concerning the nature of scale economies "external to the plant but internal to the firm" have a crucial role to play in that part of microeconomic theory known as the "theory of the firm." To anticipate our future results, we will say now and prove later that in the long run:

(1) When there is an optimum size of firm, an industry will consist usually of two or more firms.

(2) When there is no optimum size of the firm, the industry will consist of one firm only; this single firm will usually be a multi-plant firm.

(3) The organization of production through two or more firms *is not* to be equated with "competition."

(4) The organization of production through a single multiplant firm *is not* to be equated with "monopoly."

Industry cost

So far we have discussed cost functions in the firm on the assumption that the prices of factor inputs are given. Hence any firm, acting alone, cannot affect the prices of the factor inputs that it uses. (Assumption A5.1) However, in economics we must eternally guard against falling victim to the fallacy of composition. What is true of one firm acting alone is not necessarily true of all firms acting together.

In the analysis that follows we revert to assumption A5.2 which says (in effect) that there are no economies or diseconomies of scale external to the plant but internal to the firm. Hence, if average total cost changes as an industry increases or decreases its output, this change must have some other cause.

We have seen that when (i) minimum average total cost is not affected by the number of plants that a firm owns and (ii) the prices of factor inputs are given to all firms, then we have a "constant cost" industry. Let average total cost be minimized in the plant at $5 when it produces 10 units of output. In the constant cost case, average total cost must be minimized in the 2-plant firm at the same $5 when 20 units are produced (10 in each plant). The industry may consist of firms which own only one plant. Or it may consist of firms which own two or more plants. The pattern of plant ownership is economically uninteresting. In the constant cost case, it cannot affect minimum average total cost.

Economic analysis is greatly simplified whenever we assume that the firm has no control over the prices of the factor inputs that it hires. Nor is the assumption especially unrealistic. In a mature, "mixed" economy (e.g. the United States, Britain, Italy) the largest private firm usually employs less than 1 percent of the economy's labor force. Should even General Motors decide to increase its work force by 20 percent, this expansion is not likely to have any appreciable effect upon the level of wages in the United States, though it might have some noticeable impact (at least in the short run) in the Detroit area.

For many purposes it is useful to assume that an industry, like a single firm, is so small relative to the whole economy that it cannot, acting alone, affect the prices at which it hires factor inputs. In the case of an industry, however, this assumption of constant cost is "unrealistic." This conclusion follows directly from the fundamental assumption of all economic theory that factors of production are (a) "scarce" and (b) have alternative uses. Should industry A wish to expand its output, it can do so only by bidding factors away from industries B, C, D, etc. But as factors are attracted out of these other industries, the outputs of the commodities that they produce must go down; and the prices of these commodities must go up. Thus the "productivity" of the factors that are still employed in industries, B, C, and D must also go up; and it becomes more difficult for industry A to bid them away. In fact, the greater the amount of any factor that industry A needs to attract from other industries, the higher the price that it must pay for the factor.

Figure 5.10 offers a perspective on the connection between cost in the

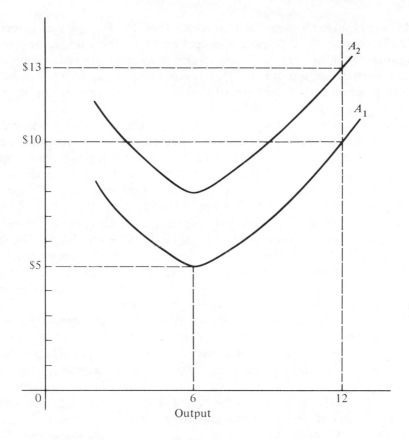

FIGURE 5.10

industry and cost in the firm. Suppose that $A1$ is the ATC curve for one of fifty identical firms that comprise an industry. Figure 5.10 indicates that if this single firm, acting alone, expands output from 6 to 12 units, its average total cost will rise from $5 to $10. (That is, we assume that cost will change in this way because the other 49 firms continue to produce 6 units each.)

Why does average total cost rise in this case? Simply because the firm is adding variable inputs to a fixed plant. However, a single firm uses such a small fraction of the economy's resources that we can reasonably assume that factor input prices do not change merely because one firm goes from an output of 6 units to an output of 12 units.

Now suppose that all fifty firms simultaneously go from an output of

6 units per firm to an output of 12 units per firm. The factor inputs needed to make possible this expansion of output have to be bid away from other industries. A movement of factors of this magnitude can only occur as factor input prices are bid up. This rise in factor input prices is represented in figure 5.10 as an upward shift in the ATC curve of the single firm.

Thus, in figure 5.10 curve $A1$ is the ATC curve for the single firm drawn on the assumption that each of the other 49 firms produces 6 units of commodity X. Curve $A2$ is the ATC curve for the single drawn on the assumption that each of the other 49 firms produces 12 units of commodity X. When all firms simultaneously expand output from 6 to 12 units, average total cost in each firm goes from $5 to $13.

In the real world, increasing cost industries really do exist. In the real world, constant cost industries do not really exist. Still, it is often useful to reason "as if" they did. For example, when we are studying the pattern of competition among firms in an industry, changes in the factor prices paid by the industry can be ignored so long as they affect all firms in the same way. What can we say about "decreasing cost" industries?

Whenever an industry consists of a single firm, there are obviously some scale economies. They are described by the declining segment of the firm's ATC curve. Again, whenever average total cost can be reduced by creating a multiplant firm, there is an additional scale economy. (Figure 5.9a)

The difficult question is: Can the firms that comprise an industry push down the prices of the factors that they use by increasing output? The answer that most economists would give goes about as follows. In the real world, it may—or may not—be possible for an industry to obtain a lower average total cost as output expands because this expansion allows it to obtain lower factor prices.

Suppose the output of industry E constitutes the factor input of industry F. Suppose further that industry E (the factor input supplier) can cut its own average total cost by increasing output because it has not yet realized all of the economies of scale in the plant and/or firm.

We now have the possibility of a chain reaction should the demand for the output of industry F increase. Industry F, needing more factor inputs, will increase its demand for the output of industry E. As industry E expands output, its average total cost decreases. This cost reduction *may*—not necessarily will—cause it to quote lower prices to industry E. We can be more specific. Industry E will lower its price to industry F provided that marginal cost also falls as output expands.

Two types of decreasing cost industries

"Decreasing cost" industries thus are of two sorts. First, there are those industries which consist of a single firm because all the economies of the single plant or of multiplant ownership in the firm have not yet been realized. These industries are sometimes described as "natural" monopolies. The term is a bad one because such industries have little in common with "true" monopoly, i.e. the case of a single producer who does not have to fear that the economic rent (sometimes called profit) which he earns may attract rivals into his industry and so reduce this rent. So-called natural monopoly exists for one reason only: because it is not worthwhile for a second firm to enter.

Second, there are decreasing cost industries that deserve the name because they can lower the prices of their factor inputs by expanding output. There is no reason why such industries should consist of a single firm. A change in factor input prices *need not* change the optimum size of firm. And if a change in factor input prices does change the optimum size of firm, it can lower this size as well as raise it.

Utility of the constant factor prices assumption

When an industry increases its output, the prices of the factor inputs that it uses may rise, fall, or remain unchanged. However, most of the time nothing is gained in microeconomics by genuflecting before this truth. Economists find it much easier to proceed on the assumption that factor input prices are "given" to the firm and, indeed, to all firms that comprise the industry. This assumption allows us to analyze the behavior of cost functions with the aid of a straightforward English and basic mathematics. Without it, we are compelled to treat average total cost in the firm not as a function of its own output alone but also as a function of the output of every other firm in the industry. In most of our remaining work in microeconomics we shall not unreasonably assume that the prices of factor inputs are given both to the firm and to the industry.

Summary

For the last two chapters we have discussed cost of production in the plant, firm, and industry. We derived for the plant the basic costs, i.e. total fixed cost, average fixed cost, total variable cost, average variable cost, average total cost, and marginal cost. We then described a technique by which, in the case of the multiplant firm, the cost curves of its plant can be summed up to yield the cost curve of the firm.

We saw that the ATC curve of the single plant must always be (approximately) U-shaped. This is so because production requires the specialization of some factors that creates a fixed cost. We saw that in the short-run—the time period during which the number of plants cannot be changed—the ATC curve of the firm is also (approximately) U-shaped. But we also noted that, in the case of the multiplant firm, the output at which average total cost is minimized can, in the long run, be altered by altering the number of plants. Therefore, when multiplant firms are possible, there is not necessarily an optimum size of firm which stops a single firm from "taking over" an entire industry. In this chapter it was affirmed but not demonstrated—this demonstration is left until Chapter 7—that the apparent domination of an industry by a single multiplant firm that can result when there is no unique optimum size of firm should not be equated with "monopoly."

Finally, we found that, in order to construct the cost curve for a single firm in an industry, some assumption must be made about the behavior of other firms. In the real world, an industry will ordinarily bid up the prices of its factor inputs when all of its member firms increase output at the same time. Likewise, the prices of factor inputs used by an industry will ordinarily fall when all of its member firms decrease output at the same time. But it was argued in this chapter that, for many purposes, economists can usefully assume that to all firms in the industry the prices of factor inputs are given. For example, when we study competition between big firms and small firms, we can legitimately ignore those changes in factor input prices that affect all firms equally. For no firm will gain or lose a competitive advantage as a result of such price changes (assuming, of course, that all firms use factor inputs in the same proportions).

REFERENCES

Cohen, K. J., and Cyert, R. M., *Theory of the Firm: Resource Allocation in a Market Economy* (Englewood Cliffs, N.J., 1965), chapter 6.
Dewey, Donald, *The Theory of Imperfect Competition: A Radical Reconstruction* (New York, 1969), chapter 3.
Ferguson, C. E., *Microeconomic Theory* (Homewood, Ill., 3rd ed., 1972), chapter 7.
Joseph, M. F. W., "A Discontinuous Cost Curve and the Tendency to Increasing Returns," *Economic Journal,* 43 (1933), 390-98.
Liebhafsky, H. H., *The Nature of Price Theory* (Homewood, Ill, rev. ed., 1968) chapter 7.

Mansfield, Edwin, *Microeconomics: Theory and Applications* (New York, 1970), chapters 5 and 6.
Patinkin, Don, "Multiple-Plant Firms, Cartels, and Imperfect Competition," *Quarterly Journal of Economics,* 61 (1947), 173-205.

APPENDIX TO CHAPTER 5
LONG-RUN COST AND THE ENVELOPE CURVE

Many discussions of cost of production describe a bit of geometry that is usually called the firm's curve of *long-run average total cost.* This geometry is based upon two eminently realistic assumptions.

A5.3 The type of plant that the firm will choose to build in order to minimize cost depends upon the expected rate of output.

A5.4 Every plant that is built will wear out eventually.

Suppose, for example, that the present state of technology allows the firm to build three different types of plant whose cost properties are described by figure 5.11. If the firm expects to produce 2 units of commodity X, it will choose to build a plant of type P1. When 2 units are produced in a plant of type P1, average total cost is $6.50. If two units are produced in a plant of type P2 or P3, average total cost will exceed $6.50.

Should the firm intend to produce 8 units of commodity X, it will build

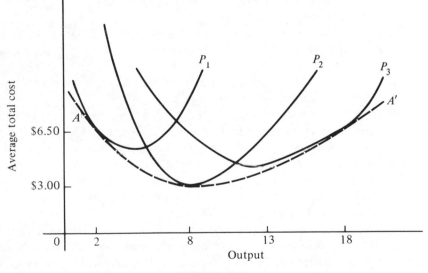

FIGURE 5.11

a plant of type P2 and so obtain an average total cost of $3. For reasons that we shall note in a minute, it is unlikely that the firm will ever want to build plants of types P1 and P2. However, as figure 5.11 indicates, 18 units can be more cheaply produced in a type P3 plant than in any other type.

When any existing plant wears out, it must be replaced by a plant of the same type or a plant of a different type (if production is to continue). This possibility of shifting from one type of plant to another as obsolescence occurs has led some writers to argue that the broken line AA' in figure 5.11 should be viewed as the curve of long-run average total cost. (For a self-evident reason, AA' is often called the "envelope" curve.) Unfortunately, this view of cost is distinctly misleading.

There are two good reasons why AA' in figure 5.11 is not a "true" curve of long-run average total cost.

(1) In a competitive industry no firm that built a plant of any type other than type P2 could survive. It would be driven from the industry by firms that built plants of type P2, produced 8 units in each plant, and gained an average total cost of $3. For at any rate of output, average total cost will be greater than $3 in a plant of type P1 or P3.

(2) If the industry was in the hands of a monopolist, he would choose to build a P1 plant in order to produce 2 units, a P2 plant in order to produce 8 units, and a P3 plant in order to produce 13 units. However, he *would not* build a type P3 plant should he wish to produce 18 units. Clearly, he would be better off by building two plants of type P2 and producing 9 units in each plant.

Whenever a firm can expand output by building additional plants it would be more reasonable to view the curve of long-run average total cost as given by the broken line BB' in figure 5.12. Yet even this view of the matter is not too satisfactory because most of the cost-output pairs that lie on BB' cannot be realized—only approximated.

BB' incorrectly indicates that, in the long run, any rate of output of 8 units or more can be achieved at an average total cost of $3. In fact, the firm must always produce some multiple of 8 units in order to get this minimum. For example, even in the longest run there is no way of producing 9 units at an average total cost of $3. Efficient production of 9 units would require one plant of type P2. But in a P2 plant the $3 minimum is obtained only at an output of 8 units.

In economic analysis, the curve of long-run average total cost is sometimes useful for describing how certain government policies can lead to firms of sub-optimal size. In New York state, for instance, liquor is sold through a large number of very small stores that sell only liquor. This is

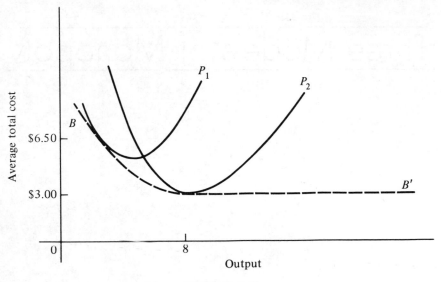

FIGURE 5.12

an extremely inefficient form of marketing; but the method is mandated by a state law which allows liquor to be sold only in specialized stores and forbids any owner to have more than one store. Still, the curve of long-run average total cost is a largely obsolete tool of economic analysis. Virtually anything that can be done with it can be done better with the short-run cost curves of a multiplant firm.

6
Three Models of Monopoly

Monopoly versus pseudo-monopoly

Monopoly is an ancient and still very much alive form of market organization. Since monopoly is also the simplest form of market organization, it is the proper place to begin our study of the major forms of market organization. For our purposes, the following definition will suffice. Monopoly is the control of the sale of a commodity by a single seller who does not fear the entry of other firms into his market.

By this definition monopoly requires the presence of two conditions—(i) control of output by a single seller and (ii) blocked entry. There are, of course, many instances in the real world where a commodity is sold by only one firm in a particular locality—for example, .the only cement firm in a small city. But these examples of apparent monopoly *must not* be confused with the real thing. The cement firm is left alone precisely because its city is small and "everybody knows" that the local market will not support two cement producers. Moreover, there are dozens of firms in the country that manufacture cement. If our local seller sets his price too much above the price charged by his nearest rival, his customers will pay the shipping charges and buy their cement out of town.

Again, in the real world there are many cases in which the market is occupied by two or more firms but no new firms are able to enter. Most major American cities are served by two or more airlines but new competitors cannot offer air service without obtaining permission from the federal government. And this permission is, for all practical purposes, impossible to obtain. Competition among the airlines, especially in the form of advertising, the sexual desirability of stewardesses, and haste to introduce new equipment, is far from perfect. Nevertheless, it is vigorous enough to ensure that, in most years, most airlines earn a very modest rate of return on their capital investments. For honest-to-God monopolies one must ordinarily look to economic creations of the State—the United States Postal Service, the privately owned but state-protected gas company, or the inventor who has been given seventeen years of patent protection.

In short, if we observe that the industry which produces commodity X consists of a single seller, there are three possibilities.

    (i) Demand for the product is so small relative to its cost of production that the market can support only one efficient producer, e.g. the typical American railroad.

   (ii) The sole seller enjoys no protection against the entry of newcomers but is pursuing a policy of charging a low price in order to discourage them from coming in.

  (iii) Law or Nature has given the sole seller protection against the entry of newcomers.

The first type of sole producer does not interest us. His splendid isolation is a technological accident. Any substantial increase in demand for commodity X, or any substantial fall in its cost of production, will increase the profitability of the industry and so induce the entry of new firms. This entry will, in turn, eliminate all (or almost all) profit in excess of the normal rate of return on capital. (Recall that a normal return on capital is that return which is necessary to keep production in an industry at its present level but not great enough to cause production to increase.)

The second case of the sole seller describes a form of competitive behavior—stayout pricing—that we shall consider in Chapter 9. The case of the third sort of sole producer—that where the entry of new firms is blocked—alone constitutes what economists call pure monopoly.

We can easily determine price and output under conditions of monopoly with the tools that we have already acquired. We have learned how to construct demand curves and marginal revenue curves for commodity X. We have learned how to construct a variety of cost curves for the single plant firm or multiplant firm that produces commodity X. The analysis of monopoly is simplicity itself: it merely involves superimposing the demand and marginal revenue curves for the commodity upon the cost curves of the firm. When this is done, the effects of monopoly on price and output are easily calculated.

Monopoly without price discrimination

In the first instance, let us assume that arbitrage in the market for commodity X is perfect. That is:

A6.1 The monopolist has no power whatsoever to practice price discrimination and so must charge the same price to all customers.

Figures 6.1 and 6.2 illustrate two instances where a monopolized industry can support one plant but not two. Consider figure 6.1 first. Demand is given by *DD'* and marginal revenue by *DM*. Here ATC designates the curve of average total cost and MC the curve of marginal cost. When the monopolist produces *OA* units, he exactly breaks even. At any other output he incurs a loss. Obviously nobody in his right mind—neither the monopolist nor anyone outside the industry—would want to build a second plant in order to produce more units of commodity X in the situation depicted by figure 6.1. Here any protection given by the State or Nature to the monopolist would be an example of overkill of potential competition.

Now consider figure 6.2. The ATC curve and MC curve are the same as in figure 6.1. But this time we assume that demand has increased

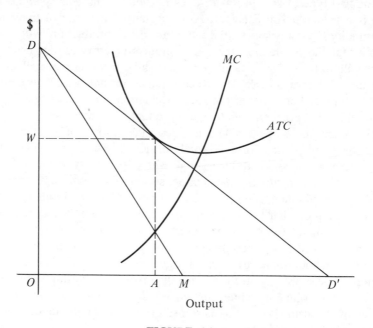

FIGURE 6.1

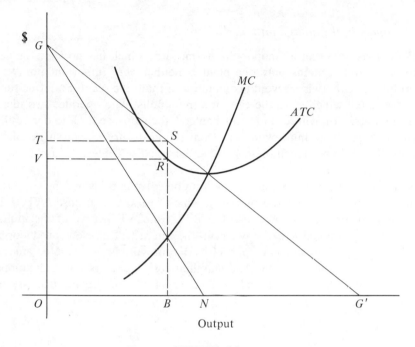

FIGURE 6.2

slightly and that, in figure 6.2, demand is given by *GG'* and marginal revenue by *GN*. At the income maximizing output *OB*, price is *OT*. Hence price is above average total cost and the monopolist earns the small economic rent *VRST*. (Some books call VRST a monopoly profit or supranormal profit.)

Will the improvement in the monopolist's fortune due to higher demand cause him to build another plant? Obviously not. In figure 6.2 he still produces an output (*OB* units) at which average total cost is falling. Would anyone wish to enter the industry if the monopolist's protection were taken away? Again, obviously not. Should this happen and a new firm enter, the industry becomes saddled with excess capacity. And what is a modest economic rent for one firm in figure 6.2 would be replaced by an economic loss for two firms.

We will examine the problem of entry in greater detail later on (Chapters 7 and 9). For the present it will suffice to note that if we increase demand by moving *GG'* toward the upper right corner in figure 6.2, we will clearly cross a threshold where a second firm would wish to enter.

Monopoly in the multiplant firm

We can assume that a "monopolized" industry which has no legal barrier to entry and contains only one plant is neither very important nor very profitable. Otherwise it would contain more than one plant. So let us turn to figure 6.3 which gives the case of a monopolist who operates two identical plants. You will recall from Chapter 5 the steps we took to derive the cost curves of the multiplant firm from the cost curves of a single plant firm. If you do not recall these steps, enlightened self-interest should move you to look them up.

In Chapter 5 we saw that, as the number of plants owned by the firm increases, so also does the output at which average total cost (ATC) is minimized for the firm. We also found that the ATC curve of the multiplant firm is kinked because when, in the interest of efficient production, one plant is shut down, some part of its output will be redistributed among the plants that remain open. And marginal cost in each of these remaining plants will fall. The marginal cost curve of the multiplant firm is, of course, discontinuous.

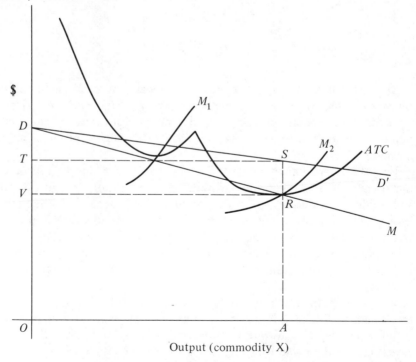

Output (commodity X)

FIGURE 6.3

In figure 6.3 demand is given by *DD'* and marginal revenue by *DM*. Since the ATC curve of a 2-plant firm contains one kink, the marginal cost curve is discontinuous. In figure 6.3, *M1* denotes marginal cost when one plant operates and the other is shut down; *M2* denotes marginal cost when both plants operate.

If a monopolist in a multiplant industry is to maximize income, he must solve two problems simultaneously. (i) He must decide how many plants to build and (ii) he must decide how many units of output to produce in each plant. In figure 6.3 we make the problem easy for him.

The monopolist will build two plants. He will produce a total of *OA* units which he will divide equally between his two plants. When he behaves in this way, he achieves the lowest of all possible average total costs —which is *OV* in figure 6.3. He equates marginal cost *M2* to marginal revenue *DM*. And he earns the economic rent *VRST*. Any output other than *OA* will earn the monopolist less than *VRST* no matter how efficiently it is produced.

In the interest of an uncluttered diagram, we make the marginal revenue curve *M2* in figure 6.3 pass through the minimum point of the ATC curve. But, of course, a monopoly equilibrium is possible even though the marginal revenue curve intersects the ATC curve either to the right or left of minimum average total cost. You can easily verify, however, that as the number of plants increases in the multiplant firm, the ATC curve flattens out. Therefore, the amount by which marginal revenue (and hence marginal cost) can differ from average total cost in equilibrium becomes progressively smaller as the number of plants increases.

By way of generalizing, we can say that the multiplant monoplist maximizes his income by observing two rules.

Rule 1 He selects the number of plants that would maximize the difference between total revenue and total cost if each plant were to operate where average total cost is lowest.

Rule 2 Having found the "correct" number of plants, he equates marginal cost to marginal revenue.

By observing these two rules, the monopolist ensures that he produces an output which places him either (a) at the minimum point of the ATC curve in each plant or (b) "in the neighborhood of" this minimum point. Rule 1 can be thought of as the "investment rule," and Rule 2 as the "operating rule."

Whenever monopoly is discussed, two closely related questions are invariably raised. (i) Does monopoly compel consumers to pay higher prices? (ii) Does monopoly lead to wasteful production? The first question can be easily disposed of. It presents an issue of "fact" only. The second question requires more attention since we must make clear our definition of "wasteful."

Let us turn back to figure 6.1. Here the 1-plant monopolist produces *OA* units at an average total cost of *OW*. He also sells *OA* units at price *OW*. If he expands output somewhat beyond *OA,* average total cost will fall below *OW*. But in the absence of a government subsidy, the 1-plant monopolist will never produce more than *OA* units; he would incur a loss by going above the output at which marginal cost equals marginal revenue. Since there is no cheaper way that the 1-plant monopolist can produce *OA* units, we can say that he is *technically* efficient.

Some economists argue that, while output *OA* is efficiently produced in figure 6.1, it is not the output that maximizes consumer welfare. By this view, consumer welfare cannot be maximized unless an economy's resources are distributed in a way that makes price equal to marginal cost in all firms; so that in figure 6.1 output *OA* is too small on welfare grounds. For the moment this conception of optimum output is noted but not endorsed. We leave the complicated subject of welfare economics until Chapters 13 and 14.

Does the 1-plant monopoly of figure 6.1 raise price to consumer? Obviously not. When demand is *DD',* the monopolist earns no excess profit or, more accurately, no economic rent. That is, he earns nothing above the "normal" return on capital embedded in average total cost. Even if demand were *GG',* as in figure 6.2, it would not pay a second firm to enter. If it did, the industry would promptly become unprofitable for both. Thus in figures 6.1 and 6.2, there is no efficient alternative to the concentration of production in a single plant.

Turn now to figure 6.3. Here the 2-plant monopolist produces *OA* units at an average total cost of *OV,* and he sells them at price *OT*. There is no cheaper way of producing *OA* units; nor can average total cost be brought below *OV* by changing the rate of output. Undoubtedly the 2-plant monopoly of figure 6.3 is technically efficient. But here, as in the case of 1-plant monopoly, we acknowledge that equilibrium output may be too small on welfare grounds (since marginal cost is not equal to price).

There is, however, an important difference between the 1-plant monopolist and the 2-plant monopolist whose price-output policies we have considered. Either the former earns no economic rent (figure 6.1) or he earns an economic rent so small that it would not tempt a second firm to enter his industry (figure 6.2). Thus the 1-plant monopolist does not need any other barrier to entry to preserve his position. The barrier provided by "weak" demand is enough.

The 2-plant monopolist, since he earns the substantial economic rent *VRST* in figure 6.3, is onto a good thing. But he can enjoy it only so long as the State or Nature protects him against the entry of newcomers. Should he lose this protection, only two options are open to him. (i) He can supinely await the entry of one or more new firms and see price and profit fall as they add their outputs to his own. (ii) He can deliberately increase output and reduce price in order to block their entry. This is the policy of stayout pricing which we will examine in detail in Chapters 7 and 9. Either way one result is inevitable should the 2-plant monopolist lose his power to exclude rivals: price will fall and output increase.

We can now set down a truism which is intellectually trivial but immensely important in its policy implications. *Any barrier that excludes producers from an industry that, in the absence of the barrier, they could profitably enter, will almost always raise price to consumers.*[1] The implacable resolution with which lawmakers and government regulators deny that the entry restrictions which they enforce (often at the instigation of producers) will raise prices to consumers is one reason why teachers of economics sometimes succumb to black pessimism.

Note that the above truism is merely a statement of fact—though a pretty damning one. It does not follow that monopoly is always a bad thing because it raises price to consumers. In some industries, notably in the distribution of liquor through state-owned liquor stores, monopoly is regarded by some people as a good thing precisely because it raises price to consumers and so curtails their drinking and presumably the consequences that are commonly thought to follow from drinking—wife beating, drunken driving, excessive generosity to casual barroom acquaintances, premature death, etc. Of course, it is painfully obvious why monopolists—be they private firms or government agencies—like monopoly. The problem is to explain why they are so often successful in persuading consumers to cooperate in being their victims. This is mainly a job for psychologists, not economists.

Monopoly and sloth

Before ending our discussion of the efficiency of monopoly we should take note of a widely held view that monopolists "go soft" because they lack

1. One of the rare cases (ocean fisheries) where a restriction on entry might actually benefit consumers is considered in Chapter 13.

the stimulus of competition. That is, they do not carefully audit the expense accounts of their salesman, check out new ideas in technology, etc. Or so the argument goes. (There is also the contrary view that only a firm with monopoly power has an incentive to innovate since, without such power, a successful innovation that it developed would promptly be adopted by rival firms at no cost.) Our model, however, assumes a monopolist who has complete information on costs and demand; this criticism cannot be applied to him.

In the real world, monopolists obviously do not have complete information and they may indeed go soft. The inefficiency associated with real-world monopoly is an empirical question that lies outside the scope of this book. We can only enter the following judgment. To the extent that a real-world monopoly approximates the conditions of a static model of monopoly, it is a technically efficient form of market organization.

Discriminating monopoly

The remarks upon price and output in the last section were based squarely upon assumption A6.1, which denied the monopolist any power whatsoever to practice price discrimination. It is possible to imagine a case of non-discriminating monopoly. In the real world, though, such a case is almost never found. Why not? For the very good reason that perfect arbitrage is a necessary precondition for the emergence of a perfect market. And arbitrage can never be perfect in a market dominated by a single seller who does not have to worry about the entry of other sellers. A monopolized market totally free of price discrimination—i.e. a "perfect" market—could exist only as an artificial creation of the State. Probably the closest approximinations to non-discriminating monopoly are to be found in the private concessions operated in public parks—hot dog stands, amusement rides, hotels, etc. Here the terms of the concession often explicitly or implicitly rule out the crasser forms of price discrimination.

Now let us go to the other extreme and posit that:

> A6.2 The monopolist is able to practice perfect price discrimination against every customer.

As we noted earlier, perfect price discrimination requires that the monopolist must possess two powers: (i) the power to keep his customers separate from one another and hence to suppress arbitrage in the commodity market; and (ii) the power to deal with each customer on a take-it-or-leave-it basis. When the monopolist can deal with the customers in these ways he can transfer the whole of each consumer's surplus to him-

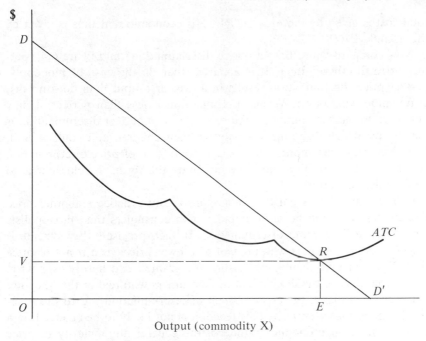

FIGURE 6.4

self. But, of course, to state the conditions necessary for perfect price discrimination is practically to indicate why it can never be achieved by a monopolist in the real world—only approximated.

When price discrimination is practiced, there is no single "price" per unit of commodity X. Indeed, given perfect price discrimination, the customer is not even permitted to buy single units of commodity X—only a block of units. However, the discriminating monopolist can always choose between offering n units and $n+1$ units to his customers. And, borrowing a term from older economists, we may describe the amount added to his total revenue by the sale of the $n+1$ unit—the marginal unit of output—as marginal price.

Figure 6.4 shows how a monopolist who can practice perfect price discrimination will maximize income. He builds three plants; and he produces that rate of output at which marginal cost is equal to marginal price. (Note that in figure 6.4, *DD'* gives the marginal price which clears the market for each quantity of output produced; for example, at output *OE* marginal price is *OV*.) Thus, the discriminating monopolist produces output *OE*. His total revenue is given by the area *OERD* in figure 6.4. His total cost is given by the area *OERV*. His economic rent thus is given by the triangle *VRD*.

Now compare figure 6.3 (no price discrimination) and figure 6.4 (perfect price discrimination). It is apparent that, in the case of monopoly, perfect price discrimination results in a greater output than does no discrimination whatsoever. When discrimination is less than perfect, it may not serve to increase output.[2] (An example of imperfect discrimination is the theater which discriminates only between children and adults.) Still, there is a clear presumption that an elaborate form of price discrimination results in greater output; the more elaborate the form, the closer it is to perfect discrimination.

Offhand, it might seem that monopolists who practice elaborate price discrimination would be more popular with consumers than monopolists who practice little or no discrimination. In fact, precisely the opposite is usually true. Consumers who are charged lower prices as a result of price discrimination take their good fortune for granted and hardly ever write thank-you notes to the discriminator. Consumers who realize that they are being charged higher prices as a result of discrimination regard the practice as monstrously unfair. (This reaction is not likely to be changed by a college course in economics.) Indeed, the general unpopularity of price discrimination explains why discriminators often go to such great lengths to disguise what they are doing. Recall that we met one highly disguised type of price discrimination in Chapter 3—the contract that ties the sale of one commodity to the sale of another.

Summary

Monopoly—the simplest form of market organization—is not to be confused with the case of a market occupied or "dominated" by a single seller. Monopoly is the case where the market is occupied by a single seller who need not fear the entry of other sellers no matter how great his income.

2. Since price discrimination can be perfect in only one way but imperfect in any number of ways, it is difficult to generalize about the effect of imperfect price discrimination on output. As noted above, a monopoly that practices perfect price discrimination will always produce a greater output than one which, with identical cost and revenue conditions, practices no price discrimination.

However, when it is possible to practice an imperfect price discrimination that merely divides consumers into two separate groups (with all consumers in the same group being charged the same price) discrimination may increase, decrease, or leave output unchanged. The effect of price discrimination in this case will depend upon the properties of the demand curves that the seller faces in the two markets. For details see Joan Robinson, *The Economics of Imperfect Competition* (London, 2nd ed., 1969), 190-92.

When the monopolist (a) cannot practice any price discrimination and (b) can have only one plant, he maximizes income by equating marginal cost to marginal revenue. When the monopolist (a) cannot practice any price discrimination but (b) can have two or more plants, he must first determine the number of plants which would maximize the difference between total revenue and total cost if each plant produced the output that minimized its average total cost. This number of plants having been determined, the multiplant monopolist then maximizes income by equating marginal cost to marginal revenue *using all plants*. (Recall that the marginal cost curve of the multiplant firm is always discontinuous.)

When the monopolist can practice perfect price discrimination, he equates marginal cost to *marginal price*. The multiplant monopolist who discriminates must, of course, first determine the number of plants that will maximize the difference between total revenue and total cost if (i) perfect price discrimination is practiced and (ii) each plant produces the output which minimizes average total cost.

Equilibrium output will always be greater in perfectly discriminating monopoly than in non-discriminating monopoly. In the real world, of course, there are no perfectly discriminating monopolies and very few non-discriminating monopolies. Virtually all real-world monopolists practice some amount of price discrimination, but this amount is limited by Law and Nature.

Many economists condemn monopoly because it "restricts output" and so look with less disfavor on discriminating monopoly than on the simple kind. However, price discrimination can also affect the distribution of real income; hence no judgment about the goodness or badness of the discrimination practiced by a monopolist should be made in a particular case until one has been provided with more information. Thus, many—if not most—readers would not approve a discriminatory price policy that systematically raises price to very poor people and lowers it to the very rich.

REFERENCES

Bain, J. S., *Industrial Organization* (New York, 2d ed., 1968), chapters 8 and 9.
Buchanan, J. M. and Tullock, Gordon, "The 'Dead' Hand of Monopoly," *Antitrust Law & Economic Review*, I (1968), 85-96.
Fellner, William, *Competition Among the Few* (New York, 1949), chapters 4 and 5.
Ferguson, C. E., *Microeconomic Theory* (Homewood, Ill., 3rd ed., 1972), chapter 9.
Leftwich, R. H., *The Price System and Resource Allocation* (Hinsdale, Ill., 5th ed., 1973), chapter 11.

Machlup, Fritz, *The Political Economy of Monopoly: Business, Labor and Government Policies* (Baltimore, 1952), especially chapters 1, 2, and 3.
Machlup, Fritz, *The Economics of Sellers' Competition: Model Analysis of Sellers' Conduct* (Baltimore, 1952), chapter 17.
Robinson, Joan, *The Economics of Imperfect Competition* (London, 2nd ed., 1969), chapters 3, 15, and 16.

APPENDIX TO CHAPTER 6
TWO-STAGE (BILATERAL) MONOPOLY

Monopolist versus monopolist

In economic analysis it is convenient to assume that the firm uses factor inputs to produce a commodity that then is sold directly to consumers. In the real world, of course, the production process is not so simple. In most industries production is organized in stages. The commodities produced by firms at the primary (raw materials) stage are not sold directly to consumers but rather to other firms which treat them as their own factor inputs. For example, in the aluminum industry bauxite may be transformed into aluminum ingot by one firm; the ingot aluminum may be transformed into aluminum sheet by another firm; and aluminum sheet into aluminum pots and pans by yet a third firm. To say the obvious: we live in a world of middlemen.

An interesting pricing problem arises when in an industry with several production stages, each stage is monopolized by a different firm. Let us consider the simple case of two-stage monopoly (which some economists call bilateral monopoly and others call monopoly-monopsony).

To keep things uncomplicated, let us again make use of that venerable heuristic device—the homogeneous commodity that has both zero production costs and zero distribution costs. (If this assumption bothers you, think of the production and distribution costs as being so small that they can usefully be ignored.) But let us also assume that Nature's intention to give mankind a free good has been frustrated by a wicked king (or maybe a wicked Federal Communications Commission). Specifically, the wicked king has given a monopoly on the production of the commodity to one court favorite and a monopoly on the distribution (direct sale to consumers) of the commodity to a second court favorite.[1] That is, the wicked

1. In the bad old days (mainly before 1700 in Europe) the grant of an exclusive monopoly franchise was often used by sovereigns to reward court favorites, including mistresses and sychophants, and pay debts to moneylenders. In our enlightened

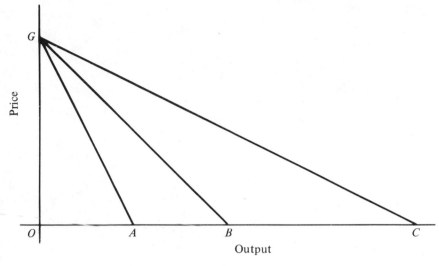

FIGURE 6.5

king has interposed a middleman between the producer-monopolist and the ultimate consumers of the commodity.

In figure 6.5, line *GC* is the demand curve for the commodity derived from consumer preferences; that is, *GC* gives the quantities that consumers will buy at various prices. In figure 6.5, line *GB* is the marginal revenue curve of the distributor-monopolist who sells directly to consumers. But he is only a conduit (and tribute collector) for the delivery of the commodity. He must get his supplies from the producer-monopolist. Therefore line *GB* is also the distributor-monopolist's demand curve for the commodity. And line *GA* is the marginal revenue curve of the producer-monopolist.

What will be industry output in this case? As you no doubt suspect, the answer depends upon how much price discrimination is possible. And upon how much collusion is possible.

---

age governments are not usually so crass. Monopoly franchises to bilk consumers are still liberally given by government to its own agents and favored private parties, but not until exhaustive administrative and court hearings have ostensibly demonstrated that it is in "the public interest" that consumers should be so bilked.

In the United States, in the last thirty years, the Federal Communications Commission, at the direction of Congress, has passed out monopoly franchises to television stations that are now worth millions (possibly billions) of dollars. The fact that the public is being held to ransom has gone largely unprotested. Controversy has rather centered on whether the rights to bilk the public with local TV monopolies were allocated fairly and without corruption.

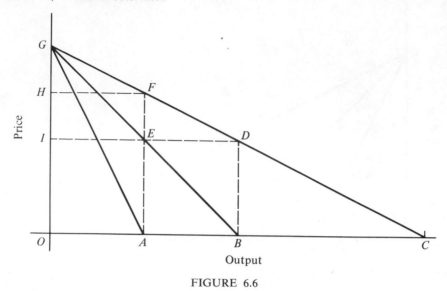

FIGURE 6.6

Neither collusion nor discrimination

First, consider the case where neither price discrimination nor collusion is possible. Now the answer can be read off from figure 6.6. The first-stage producer (the producer-monopolist) equates marginal cost (which is zero) to marginal revenue and so produces output *OA*. This output he sells to the distributor-monopolist at price *OI*. The distributor-monopolist then resells output *OA* to consumers at price *OH*. Thus total consumer expenditures are equal to the area *OAFH* in figure 6.6. Of this amount, *OAEI* goes to the producer-monopolist, and *IEFH* goes to the distributor-monopolist.

Incidentally, figure 6.6 points upon an important moral in the art of monopolization. Monopoly at an early stage of production in an industry is always more valuable than monopoly at a later stage (and usually more to be feared by consumers).

Collusion without discrimination

Next, suppose that while no price discrimination may be practiced against consumers, the two monopolists are free to engage in collusion and profit sharing. Now it is clear from figure 6.6 that joint profit for the two monopolists is greatest when they cooperate to produce and distribute output *OB*. For output *OB* can be sold to consumers at price *OI;* and joint profit will be *OBDI*. (Remember that in this example profit is always equal to total revenue since there are no production or distribution costs.)

It is sometimes said that price and output are "indeterminate" under conditions of two-stage (bilateral) monopoly. This is not really true. Price and output are always determinate in two-stage monopoly when collusion is possible. The only uncertainty surrounds the division of profit between the monopolists. For example, in the last illustration (collusion but no price discrimination) we cannot say with precision how the maximum profit *OBDI* will be divided. We only know that the producer-monopolist must receive at least *OAEI;* and that the distributor-monopolist must receive at least *IEFH*. (Figure 6.6) For these amounts are the respective profits that each monopolist could collect without consenting to collusion.

Collusion plus discrimination

Finally, suppose that both collusion between monopolists and price discrimination against consumers is possible. Now the output that maximizes joint profit is *OC* in figure 6.6. And the sum that can be extracted from consumers by perfect price discrimination is *OCG*. Again, we cannot state with precision how the sum *OCG* will be shared between the two monopolists.

Instability of multistage monopoly

For nearly obvious reasons, it is very unusual in the real world for different stages of production in an industry to be monopolized by different firms. Whenever monopoly is fragmented in this way, it always pays the monopolists to cooperate with one another or for one monopolist to buy out the others. Note also that there is a strong presumption that consumers will benefit from the consolidation of multistage monopoly. Thus, if only one set of railroad tracks connects two cities, it is almost certainly in the consumer interest that the entire right-of-way be managed by a single firm.

7
Natural Monopoly, Cartels, and Labor Unions

So far our analysis of monopoly has assumed that the single seller does not fear the entry of new firms no matter how great the income that he earns. Much confusion could be avoided if the term monopoly were always reserved for the case of the single seller who can relax behind an insurmountable barrier to entry. Alas, this cannot be. The term monopoly has had too many other connotations for too long.

We cannot stop to list and analyze all of the market situations that are popularly equated with monopoly. However, we shall examine three situations that are often so identified—"natural" monopoly, cartel monopoly, and labor monopoly. You are warned that each of these will turn out to involve a much smaller restriction of output than the "pure" monopoly described in Chapter 6.

"Natural" monopoly

So-called natural monopoly occurs whenever one firm in industry always has decreasing average total cost over the "relevant range of output," i.e. the range within which an equilibrium output can occur. To keep things simple, let us assume that initially the industry consists of a single firm; that this firm has only one plant; and that its single plant has fixed costs but no variable costs. In such a firm marginal cost is, of course, zero at all outputs since marginal cost depends only upon variable costs. In short, we assume a firm whose curve of average total cost can be represented by a rectangular hyperbola. In figure 7.1 we give our firm at ATC curve which is a rectangular hyperbola and the demand curve *DD'*. The marginal revenue curve corresponding to *DD'* is *DH*.

Suppose that the owners of the firm described by figure 7.1 have read one too many books about how monopolists behave. Foolishly believing themselves to possess a monopoly, they decide to maximize income by equating marginal revenue to marginal cost. The firm will produce output *OH* (since marginal revenue is zero at output *OH*), incur an average total cost *OW*, and sell the output *OH* at price *OV*. Now the firm expects that economic rent (often called profit) will be equal to the area *WRSV*.

When the firm in figure 7.1 tries to behave as would a monopolist with a protected market, it will soon be made aware of its mistake. The expected rent *WRSV* in figure 7.1 is much greater than total cost *OHRW*. Entry into the industry is open to all comers; hence a second firm will enter if it can profitably do so.

We can easily show that if the poor, deluded "natural monopolist" pro-

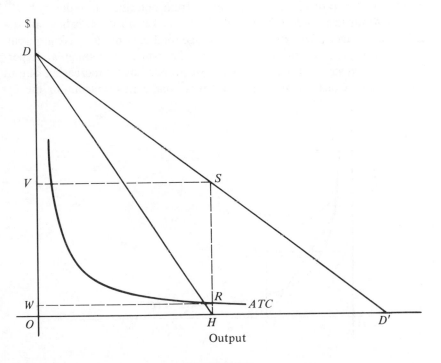

FIGURE 7.1

duces output *OH* in figure 7.1, entry will be profitable for a second firm. Since the second firm has access to the same technology and resources, it will have the ATC curve of figure 7.1. It will have the same ATC curve as the natural monopolist. When the natural monopolist produces output *OH*, the second firm will have as its demand curve the "unused" portion of the demand curve *DD'* in figure 7.1. That is, the second firm will have the segment *SD'* of *DD'* in figure 7.1.

In figure 7.2 the segment *SD'* is taken from figure 7.1 and moved laterally to the left until point *S* lies on the vertical axis; that is, in figure 7.2, *SD'* is drawn as a "normal" demand curve. The ATC curve of figure 7.1 is transferred (with no change in its position) to figure 7.2.

From figure 7.2 it is clear that a second firm can enter the industry, produce output *OF*, and gain the profit *klmn*—provided, of course, that the poor, deluded "natural" monopolist continues to produce output *OH* in figure 7.1.

Obviously it does not pay the natural monopolist of figure 7.1 to be too greedy. But how much greed is too much? How much profit must he forgo in order to discourage other firms from entering the industry?

Should our firm undertake to defend its market position, it has one decisive advantage. It can always cut average total cost by increasing output. More precisely, since the ATC curve of the firm is a rectangular hyperbola, it can always cut average total cost 50 percent by increasing output 100 percent. Consequently, the only way that a new entrant to the in-

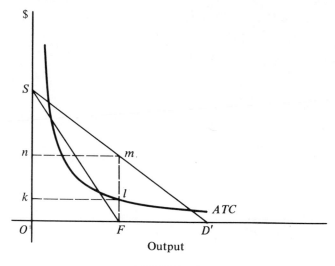

FIGURE 7.2

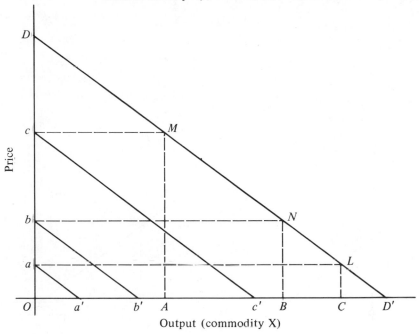

FIGURE 7.3

dustry can get an equally low average total cost is by doubling the output
of the industry.

Once the defending firm has raised output to some (as yet unknown)
level, the new entrant will only make the industry unprofitable both for
himself and the defending firm if he doubles the industry's output in order
to be as efficient as his established rival. The problem that the defending
firm faces is quite clear. It must produce the output that will drive price
and profit low enough to block the entry of other firms. Actually, there
are likely to be many such outputs. For the defending firm, the tough
problem is to find the *minimum* output that will block the entry of new
firms. It is this minimum that will allow the greatest long-run economic
rent.

To enforce a policy of stayout pricing, the natural monopolist will behave as follows. In figure 7.3 the demand for the industry's product—let
this commodity be commodity X again—is DD'. Should the firm produce
output OA it preempts segment DM of DD'. The segment MD' of DD' in
figure 7.3 is available to a newcomer. Now move MD' laterally to the left
until point M lies on the price axis. The curve cc' is drawn parallel to

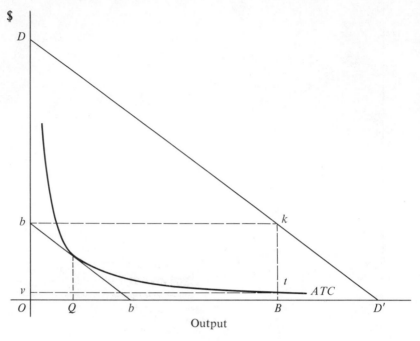

FIGURE 7.4

MD'; hence *cc'* is a conventional demand curve. In fine, in figure 7.3, when the industry demand is *DD'* and the defending firm produces output *OA,* a newcomer has the demand curve *cc'.*

Now suppose that the defending firm produces output *OB* in figure 7.3. It preempts segment *DN* of *DD'.* Now the segment of *DD'* available to a newcomer is *ND'.* Move *ND'* laterally to the left until point *N* lies on the price axis. The curve *bb'* is drawn parallel to *MD';* hence *bb'* is also a conventional demand curve and is available to a newcomer.

Finally, suppose that the defending firm produces output *OC* in figure 7.3. The segment of *DD'* available to a newcomer becomes *LD';* and it implies the conventional demand curve *aa'.*

In short, the output produced by the defending firm determines the demand curve that is available to a newcomer. The greater the output of the defending firm, the lower will be the demand curve of a newcomer. In the limit case where the defending firm produces output *OD'* in figure 7.3 (that is, when commodity X is given away) there is no demand at all for the output of a potential entrant.

Which of the many possible demand curves will the defending firm choose to impose on a potential entrant? The answer is readily apparent in figure 7.4. Here the industry demand curve *DD'* is taken from figures 7.1 and 7.3. The demand curve for a potential entrant *bb'* is taken from figure 7.3. The ATC curve for the potential entrant is taken from figure 7.1. (Recall that this ATC curve is a rectangular hyperbola, there being only fixed cost in the plant.)

The economic meaning of figure 7.4 is simply this. If the defending firm—the natural monopolist—produces output *OB,* then a second firm can enter the industry and, by producing output *OQ,* exactly break even. Therefore, if the defending firm produces any output greater than *OB,* a second firm will not enter. For now the second firm will incur a loss no matter how much or how little it produces. By producing in excess of *OB* units the defending firm blocks the entry of newcomers. It will, of course, prefer an output as close to *OB* as possible. Thus in figure 7.4 the economic rent enjoyed by the natural monopolist can approach the limit given by the area vtkb.

We can say then that the "natural" monopolist of figure 7.1—remember that he is a natural monopolist because he can always cut average total cost by increasing output—maximizes income by resorting to a policy of stayout pricing. (Some writers prefer to describe this income maximizing behavior as limit pricing or entry-blocking pricing.) You should study the behavior of the natural monopolist very carefully. For, as we shall see in Chapter 9, the policy of stayout pricing that he employs will, in many marketing situations, be followed by firms with perfectly normal cost function, i.e. cost functions which yield a U-shaped ATC curve in each plant.

Cartels

Another variety of market organization that economists have often classified as a kind of monopoly is the cartel. For our purposes, a cartel can be defined as an association of firms in the same industry—the association may be either formal or informal, strong or weak—that tries to restrict output in the interest of higher prices and higher profits for all. With the monumental exception of certain labor unions, cartels have been illegal in the American economy since 1899 unless expressly authorized by statute. Cartels may be *illegal* in most industries in the United States, but they are not for this reason either unnatural or unknown. (Many European and Japanese businessmen regard the American antitrust efforts to stamp out cartels with the same incredulity as they view the efforts of some American cities to suppress gambling and prostitution.) Illegal

cartels of the weak, furtive sorts (e.g. agreement among building contractors to rig the bids on government contracts), are regularly discovered
and attacked by federal and state prosecutors. And in all countries where
they are legal, cartels are a conspicuous and accepted feature of the business world. Cartels may or may not be desirable. They are a fact of business life.

All firms that seek to organize cartels meet two major difficulties.
(i) They face the same entry problem as does the natural monopolist
whose dilemma we have just considered. If the cartel successfully restricts
output and earns persistently high profits, new firms will enter the industry. (ii) Cartels face the problem of ensuring that their members do not
cheat; for in any cartel, it will pay one firm to chisel by increasing output
provided that all other members continue to play by the rules.

The entry problem of the cartel can be disposed of summarily. There
are few cases where a cartel acting without government support has been
able to stop newcomers from moving into an industry that the cartel's restriction of output has made profitable. And cases of successful cartelization without government support have usually rested on the control of
some scarce natural resource. Thus the owners of diamond mines in the
Union of South Africa have for many years operated a cartel that has
been able to keep up the world price of diamonds by regulating their export; success has been possible because the cartel in 1972 controlled over
three-fourths of world diamond sales, used a single firm (De Beers) as
its sole export agent, and nobody has yet found a close substitute for diamonds. The reason for the inability of most profitable cartels to protect
themselves against the entry of new firms is quite simple. A cartelized
industry which wishes to exclude newcomers who have a legal right to
enter must be able to respond quickly and ruthlessly to any challenge;
whereas a cartel, being a coalition of firms with imperfectly synchronized
goals and interests, is an awkward, slow-moving fighting machine.

Nevertheless, in the real world it often happens that external forces
confer some protection against entry—usually of short duration—on the
cartel. For example, when the cartel merely helps its members reduce the
losses that they would otherwise suffer, new competition need not be
feared. Again, in time of general business recession, newcomers may find
it impossible to raise the capital needed to enter an industry made modestly
profitable by cartel restrictions.

Cartels that are protected against new competition by government are
quite common in the United States and elsewhere (including socialist
countries). Government-protected cartels, however, are of very little in-

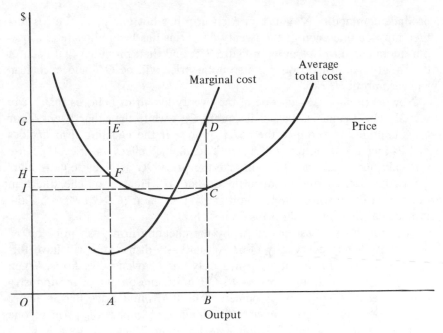

FIGURE 7.5

terest to us. Either they learn to behave in the same way as would the One Big Firm that is protected against competition, or, if they cannot master the techniques needed to rationalize an industry, they will be bought out by a far-sighted promoter. The only notable exceptions to this generalization are agricultural industries that enjoy government protection. Here the number of producers is so great that the cost of organizing them to make maximum use of their protection is prohibitive. Even if the government made it a capital crime for a newcomer to begin the production of wheat for the first time, wheat farmers are already so numerous (there are thousands of them) that they could not make use of this protection by agreeing to restrict output in order to get maximum profits.

In the real world, the entry of new firms takes time—often quite a long time. Hence, it often pays rival firms to enter into a cartel agreement on the assumption that there exists some obstacle which will at least temporarily block the entry of new firms. But the cartel of limited life and modest ambitions must still solve the chiseling problem. It is illustrated by figure 7.5.

Suppose that the industry consists of twenty-five identical firms that produce commodity X; and that each firm has but one plant. Let us further suppose that each of the twenty-five firms has been allocated an output quota equal to *OA* units in figure 7.5; and that, provided that each of the twenty-five firms produces its quota, price will be *OG* and each firm will earn profit *HFEG*.

Now let us suppose that one of the twenty-five firms believes that it can secretly cheat—that is, exceed its quota *OA*—while the other twenty-four firms continue to produce their *OA* quotas. If the cheating firm decides that its increase in output will have a "negligible" effect on price (because it is only one of 25 firms) it will take the price *OG* as given, equate marginal cost to price, and produce the output *OB*. Hence, the cheating firm can earn a profit whose upper limit is given by area *ICDG* in figure 7.5— provided always that other firms do not cheat.

Will not this increase in output by the cheating firm push price below *OG* for itself and everybody else? Actually, its dishonesty will have this effect. However, the cheating firm is only one of twenty-five firms. When it raises its own output from *OA* to *OB* units, the output of the industry is increased by only about 4 percent. The horizontal price line in figure 7.5 merely conveys that we view the downward impact on price of one firm's cheating as so negligible that it can be ignored.

We could alter figure 7.5 to indicate that cheating by a single firm lowers price. But this revision would require the introduction of more lines and letters on the diagram and make it even more difficult to interpret. We forgo this loss of intelligibility in the interest of realism since we wish to make only a simple, virtually self-evident point. In a cartel it always pays the single firm to cheat provided that all other members continue to play by the rules.

Some economists argue that there is really no way that a cartel can stop its members from producing more than the quotas assigned to them. By this skeptical view, there is always a weak link in the chain; and, so the argument goes, the cartel must always be of short duration since it will collapse when the treachery of the weak link is discovered. By this view, the American antitrust effort is largely a waste of time to the extent that it invests resources in the harassment of cartels that will shortly break down anyway.

This skepticism greatly underestimates the self-discipline and ingenuity of businessmen (including the managers of government-owned airlines who operate the cartel that sets fares on international air routes). Strictly speaking, it is not necessary that a cartel be able to secure the complete cooperation of its members in order to raise profits above a non-cartel level. In fact, a cartel may well decide to limit its membership to large, efficient producers and let small, high-cost producers do as they please. The activities of the latter may not be important enough to frustrate the output restrictions of the large firms. Even cheating by large firms will not cause the cartel to break down provided that the cheating is sporadic and quickly detected. To say the obvious: cartelization "pays" to the extent that, to its members, the economic benefits exceed economic costs.

Moreover, the difficulty of preventing cheating in the cartel should not be exaggerated. In an electronic age it is vastly easier for the cartel to expose rule violations by a member than it is for him to conceal them. And the cartels of the real world have devised a hundred and one ways to keep cheating within economically tolerable bounds. One very simple and effective device is the "fidelity fund." During the year, each member pays a royalty into the fund on every unit of product marketed. At the end of the year, the royalties paid in are refunded to each contributor on condition that he has observed the rules. In the case of a rule violation, the chiseler forfeits all or part of his contribution to the fidelity fund.

Labor unions as cartels

While many labor unions are properly classified as cartels, they differ in several important respects from the cartels of private businessmen or government agencies. For the record, we might note most labor unions are so weak that they do not deserve to be classified as cartels. They are better viewed as firms that sell a contract-negotiating skill (with a little help from federal and state labor laws) to workers. A union's tax specialist, for example, presumably knows how to divide a wage increase between take-home pay and fringe benefits in a way that will minimize the income tax burden on its members. The following remarks apply only to the minority of unions that are in a position to force wages "perceptibly"—say more than 10 percent—above the non-union level.[1]

Most unions are so weak that they are unable to control directly the quantity of labor available to their respective industries. The American Medical Association and some unions in the building trades are an exception to this generalization. They have some control over the supply of

---

1. One authority has estimated that during the 1950's when union members constituted about 25 percent of the labor force in the United States, the average wage of union workers was 7 to 11 percent higher relative to the average wage of all workers, union and non-union, than it would have been in the absence of unionism. H. G. Lewis, *Unionism and Relative Wages in the United States* (Chicago, 1963), p. 86.

skilled labor because they are able to limit the number of apprentices. Most so-called strong unions, however, can only have an indirect effect upon labor supply. They can enforce a wage above what it would be in their absence and so reduce the amount of labor hired. For example, the Teamsters' Union—most people's idea of a strong union in the United States—has virtually no control over the number of workers in the labor force who are competent to drive trucks (there being milions of such workers). We might note that the position of a union that succeeds in raising wages above the non-union level without being able to restrict the supply of available labor is basically precarious. This circumstance explains why violence more often occurs in labor disputes involving unskilled workers than in those involving skilled workers; unions of unskilled workers have far more to fear from strikebreakers.

Since union wages are a matter of public record and are legally binding upon the employer during the life of a labor contract, cheating by union members is rare. It hardly ever happens that a worker who is a union member will secretly agree to work for less than the wage rate called for in the union contract. (However, it is not uncommon for union workers to moonlight on second jobs with non-union firms at less than the union wage.) The problem is that, to the extent that the union has monopoly power, union jobs become so attractive to workers that, at the union wage, the quantity of labor available to employers will exceed the quantity demanded. Some rationing of jobs becomes necessary.

In the case of those few unions controlled by professional criminals, racketeer officials will, in effect, sell jobs to the highest bidders in return for kickbacks and other favors. (For details, see the fine old Marlon Brando film, *On the Waterfront*.) In a union that is run as a family corporation, jobs will go to sons and nephews. (By and large, women are not yet found in jobs where union nepotism is rife—daughters and nieces are out of luck.) In some, more democratic unions, jobs go to workers who are prepared to pay high initiation fees and accept long apprenticeship periods at low wages in order to make life comfortable for older workers. Large industrial unions, however, make little effort to ration job vacancies. The employer must pay the negotiated wage but he is given a free hand to fill job vacancies. The result is that, in such unions, any success in raising wages is usually followed by what appears to be an "upgrading" of the work force. The higher wage that the employer must pay to satisfy the union contract usually gives him access to a wider range of worker skills and abilities. He reduces the impact of the union contract upon himself by hiring "better" workers as job vacancies occur.

Union success in raising the wage also has another unintended effect. It reduces the costs that the employer must incur in order to practice forms of discrimination against certain workers that are unrelated to income maximization. The higher wage allows him to hire from a larger pool of qualified (and overqualified) applicants and so increases the probability that he will find a competent applicant whose personal or ethnic qualifications are to his liking. It comes as no surprise to economists when the federal government discovers blatant examples of discrimination by race, sex, and religion, in profitable public utility monopolies that are organized by strong labor unions. A garment manufacturer, operating, as he does, in an intensely competitive industry that contains many non-union firms, would risk going bankrupt if he discriminated against competent black or female workers. The local electric power company operates under no such goad.

We will not attempt here to pass judgment on the proper way of rationing jobs in an industry where "labor monopoly" has come into existence, though presumably nobody (except criminals) will favor a job auction, the proceeds of which go to criminals. Indeed, it is difficult to believe that there is a "best" way to ration desirable jobs. For our purposes, it is enough to note that, given the existence of a labor monopoly, jobs must be rationed somehow. The principal question is how the power to ration is to be divided among union officials, employers, and government officials (who, for example, enter the picture when black workers or women are systematically excluded from high-wage union industries).

In this connection we can also note that labor unions with monopoly power but acting alone have met with the same limited success in solving the entry problem as have other cartels. In the long run, unions have little power to stop employers from switching to cheaper non-union labor unless government in some way backstops the union effort to restrict the supply of lower wage, non-union labor that the employer can tap. Government bolsters labor monopoly in a great many ways—by compelling government contractors to pay union rates whether or not they use union labor, by requiring aid supplied to foreign governments to be carried on American ships, by granting tariff protection to industries suffering the competition of foreign products made with "cheap" labor, etc. However, government's commitment to labor monopoly is far from unconditional; and in an economy where over two-thirds of all workers are not members of labor unions, government attempts to strengthen union monopoly are habitually undermined and frustrated.

Summary

We have considered certain monopolistic features of decreasing cost industries, cartels, and labor unions. We have seen that these forms of market organization have little in common with the protected monopolies considered in Chapter 4 because they do not have a comparable power to exclude rivals.

Cartels invariably arise, provided that they are legal, whenever firms are relatively few and short-run obstacles impede the easy entry of new firms. Since such obstacles characterize most industries most of the time, weak cartels are a thoroughly "natural" form of market organization. To be successful, a cartel must see that its members cooperate to restrict output. This it can do in many ways. The cartel, however, is usually too unwieldy to maneuver effectively to block the entry of new firms over the long run; hence it hardly ever earns a really startling economic rent or profit in the real world—unless, of course, government protects it against competitors.

Most labor unions can reasonably be viewed as firms which sell a contract-negotiating service to their members and are without power significantly to raise the level of wages. The few unions which do have this power are often called "labor monopolies." When unions succeed in forcing a wage above its non-union level, the quantity of labor demanded will be lower at the higher wage; and jobs must be rationed among applicants. No single principle governs the rationing of such jobs. But, so-called labor monopolies, like cartels, face the problem of keeping out people attracted by their success. In both cases long-run exclusion of competitors is usually impossible unless the aid of government can be enlisted.

REFERENCES

Becker, G. S., *Economic Theory* (New York, 1971), chapter 6.
Carter, A. M., and F. R. Marshall, *Labor Economics: Wages, Employment and Trade Unionism* (Homewood, Ill., 1967).
Dewey, Donald, *Monopoly in Economics and Law* (Chicago, 1959), chapter 2.
Patinkin, Don, "Multiple-Plant Firms, Cartels, and Imperfect Competition," *Quarterly Journal of Economics,* 61 (1947), 173-205.
Reder, M. W., "Wage Determination in Theory and Practice" in *A Decade of Industrial Relations Research, 1946-1956,* N. W. Chamberlain, ed. (New York, 1958), pp. 64-97.
Stigler, G. J., *The Theory of Price* (New York, 3d ed., 1966), chapter 13.
Stocking, G. W., and M. W. Watkins, *Cartels in Action: Case Studies in International Business Diplomacy* (New York, 1946).

8

Competitive Equilibrium: The Classical View

Competitive equilibrium: no economic rent

In this chapter we shall meet what economists call the partial equilibrium theory of perfect competition. The adjective "partial" is applied because the theory to be examined is concerned with the determination of price and output in a single industry only. We postpone until a later time (Chapter 17) our study of the relationships among industries that constitute the general equilibrium theory of perfect competition. Rightly employed, the partial equilibrium theory of perfect competition is a powerful tool of analysis with a wide range of applications. It has been applied to such diverse economic phenomena as the location of industry, racial discrimination in labor markets, the pushing of heroin, the slave trade of the ante-bellum South, the work habits of married women, and the production of ball-point pens. Indeed, as we shall see, there is a strong presumption that partial equilibrium analysis can be applied with rewarding results to any economic activity that takes place in a market which provides buyers and sellers with a wide range of choice. Nor, for the reasons noted in Chapter 1, is it necessary that such a real-world market be perfectly competitive before it can profitably be analyzed with the aid of the partial equilibrium theory of perfect competition. There are many imperfections of real world competition that are too trivial to merit attention.

Once more we assume:

A8.1 All firms in the industry produce a homogeneous product.

A8.2 The prices of all factor inputs are "given," i.e. they are fixed and unchanging.

A8.3 All firms have equal access to the same technology and to the same factor inputs, i.e. all firms have identical cost functions.

In addition, we now assume for the first time:

A8.4 The industry is capable of supporting a very large number of plants.

A8.5 The cost of bringing two or more plants under a common management is prohibitive; this cost is so great that it is un-economic to create multiplant firms or organize cartels.

Assumption A8.5 provides that the number of firms will always be equal to the number of plants in the industry. Assumption A8.4 states that the industry is capable of supporting a very large number of plants. Since these two assumptions together ensure that the industry will consist of a very large number of firms, each firm contributes only a very small fraction of the industry's total output. Hence, a change in the output of a single firm will have only a very small effect upon market price—provided, of course, that the outputs of all other firms in the industry remain unchanged.[1]

To simplify our analysis, let us assume that, when the number of firms is "very large" the power of a single firm to affect price is so negligible that it can be ignored. That is, we assume

A8.6 Each firm behaves as if it can sell any quantity of output at the present market price.

By assumption A8.6, the firm believes that the demand for its own output is perfectly elastic. As an income maximizer the firm will carry output to the level at which marginal cost is equal to marginal revenue. Given the assumptions set down above the firm believes that marginal revenue is always equal to price; hence, in perfect competition, it will carry output to the level at which marginal cost is equal to price.

Let us first consider the case where our perfectly competitive industry

---

1. Strictly speaking, assumption A8.5 is stronger than necessary in that it rules out as economically inefficient any firm with two or more plants. Firms with two or more plants are compatible with perfect competition in the commodity market provided that two conditions are satisfied: (i) There is an upper bound to the number of plants that the firm can economically operate, i.e. that there is an optimum size of firm; (ii) this optimum size is "very small" relative to aggregate demand for the commodity.

When these conditions are satisfied, each multiplant firm will believe that it faces a perfectly elastic demand curve. However, economic analysis is simplified whenever we can represent marginal cost and average total cost as continuous functions of output. This can only be done by ruling out the multiplant firm. For, as we have seen, in the multiplant firm the ATC curve is kinked and the MC curve is discontinuous. (Chapter 5)

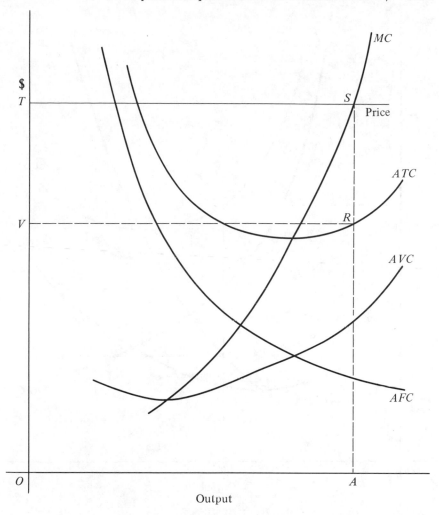

Output

FIGURE 8.1

has not yet reached equilibrium. We define industry equilibrium to be the state where total output will not change over time unless the industry is buffeted by some new and unforeseen shocks that affect its supply and demand conditions. Specifically, industry equilibrium requires that three conditions be satisfied:

    (i) No firm already in the industry has any incentive to change its output.

    (ii) No firm in the industry has any incentive to leave.

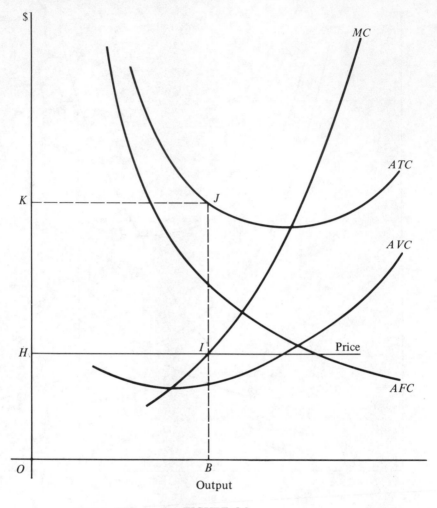

FIGURE 8.2

(iii) No entrepreneur has an incentive to organize a new firm and enter the industry.

Assumption 8.4 requires that all firms have identical cost curves and, hence, that a proposition which is true for one firm is perforce true for all firms. It follows that industry equilibrium will occur only when every firm neither earns a profit nor suffers a loss after it has equated marginal cost to price.

The geometry of disequilibrium is given by figures 8.1 and 8.2. Figure

8.1 depicts the happier and analytically easier case of profitable disequilibrium. Here the perfect competitor equates marginal cost to price by producing an output of *OA* units so gains a profit equal to the area *VRST*.

Let us take care to note why the industry's output is unstable when figure 8.1 depicts the situation of every firm in the industry. The firm has equated marginal cost to price and so has maximized income *with its existing plant*. The firm will not build a second plant because, by assumption A8.5, multiplant ownership is not profitable. However, a new firm does have the incentive to build a plant and enter the industry. For it can expect to earn the profit *VRST in addition to the normal rate of return on its capital*. (Recall that this normal rate of return is a component of average total cost.) In other industries, which a new firm might enter, there is only the prospect of the normal rate of return. The industry is in disequilibrium in figure 8.1 only because new firms have an incentive to enter.

Figure 8.2 depicts the unhappy case of unprofitable disequilibrium. Here the perfect competitor equates marginal cost to price by producing output *OB*. He suffers a loss equal to the area *HIJK*.

Why should the perfect competitor ever operate at a loss? You should remember the answer to this question from your first course in economics. To produce any output at all, the firm must incur certain expenses that are independent of the rate of output. Buildings must be leased, lawyers retained, specialized machinery purchased, etc. These expenses add up to the so-called fixed cost of production. And, virtually by definition, fixed cost must be borne by the firm whether it operates or closes down. Therefore, the firm that "maximizes income" will elect to operate at a loss provided that average variable cost is not greater than price. And in figure 8.2 this condition is satisfied. Indeed, when output *OB* is produced, price is greater than average variable cost. Thus in figure 8.2 the firm incurs a loss on each of the *OB* units of output that it produces. But since at output *OB,* price is greater than average variable cost, the firm has a surplus of revenue over total variable cost that it can apply against its fixed cost.

The strategy of minimizing loss under conditions of perfect competition is further illustrated in figure 8.3. (The AFC curve is omitted from figure 8.3; we have made the point that some costs cannot be avoided by shutting down the firm.) In figure 8.3 the firm must sell its output at a price *OM*. If the firm produces output *OC,* price will equal average variable cost (and also marginal cost since at output *OC* average variable cost is minimized). With price at *OM,* the firm will lose a sum equal to its fixed cost if it produces output *OC*. It will lose precisely the same sum by clos-

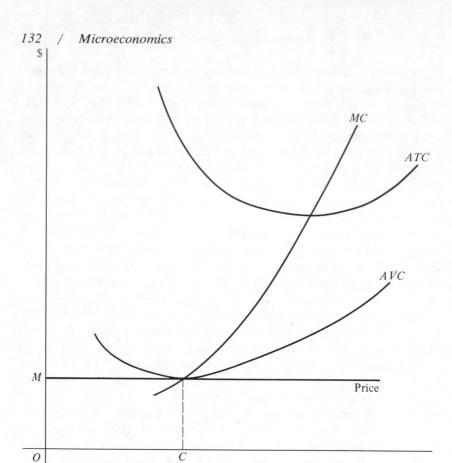

$

MC

ATC

AVC

M

Price

O   C

Output

FIGURE 8.3

ing down. Presumably, the decision to continue to operate or to close is made by tossing a coin or in some similar random manner.

In figure 8.3, should price fall below *OM,* the firm will obviously choose to close down and lose its fixed cost. When price is less than *OM,* loss to the firm is minimized by closing down even though the decision involves turning the plant over to scavengers and vandals.

Reaching equilibrium

So much for disequilibrium under conditions of perfect competition. How does the industry get to equilibrium? When disequilibrium exists because each firm in the industry earns a profit, the answer is easily given. Profit is the magnet which draws capital and labor away from other industries which pay only the prevailing (normal) return on capital and the prevailing (normal) wage. Hence, when there is a profit to be made, new firms will organize and enter the industry. As their production is added to the production of existing firms, price will fall. When price has fallen until it equals average total cost, profit has disappeared. And there is no longer an incentive for new firms to enter the industry.

When disequilibrium exists because each firm in the industry earns a loss (no greater than its total fixed cost) the story is slightly—but only slightly—more complicated. A look at the real world provides us with two good reasons for assuming that unprofitable disequilibrium will eventually give way to an equilibrium in which no firm incurs a loss.

(i) Fixed cost exists because production requires the use of specialized men and machines. But these specialized instruments must ultimately be replaced. Specialized machines wear out and specialized men retire or die. This truth is sometimes expressed by saying that "in the long run all costs are variable."

(ii) In most plants, the ratio of variable cost to fixed cost increases with use (and hence with age). With a reasonable amount of luck the repair bills on a new truck will be low. With the passing of time they will rise. And, as we know, a truck is usually sent to the junkyard not because it cannot be repaired still one more time but because, given the cost of repairs and the price of a new truck, it does not pay to continue the patching process.

For either or both of these reasons, as time passes, the average variable cost associated with the operation of a plant will rise. In a firm where, as of this moment, average variable cost is still below price, it will someday rise above price. When average variable cost exceeds price, the firm must either scrap the old plant and replace it with a new one; or the firm must leave the industry. If there is no prospect that price will ever become equal to, or greater than, average total cost, the firm will leave the industry. Aggregate output will contract in the industry and price will rise.

The exit of some firms will eventually produce a state where, for the firms that remain in the industry, price is equal to average total cost. When this equality finally prevails, each firm will replace its plant with another in the fullness of time. Thus the population of plants is constant over time, with the number of births just equaling the number of deaths.

We are now in a position to state the fundamental equilibrium theorem of perfect competition.

T8.1 Let all firms in the industry have identical cost functions.

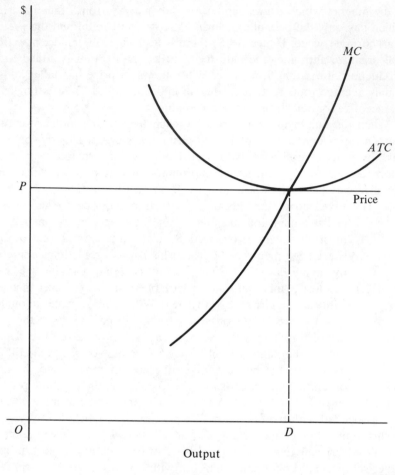

FIGURE 8.4

Then, when the conditions necessary for perfect competition are present, an equilibrium will be reached in which each firm produces an output at which price is equal to both marginal cost and average total cost.

We know that, in the firm, marginal cost can only be equal to average total cost where average total cost is lowest. This is a mathematical truism. Therefore, we are also able to state a most important corollary to the above theorem, namely:

C8.1 Let all firms in the industry have identical cost functions. Then

when an equilibrium under conditions of perfect competition
has been reached, there is no cheaper way to produce the industry's equilibrium output—that is, such an equilibrium is
economically efficient.

Reverting to geometry, we can show the firm's equilibrium under conditions of perfect competition with figure 8.4. No doubt you have already
met something very much like it in your education. In figure 8.4, equilibrium output is *OD* and equilibrium price *OP*. The firm, of course, earns
neither a profit nor a loss since when output *OD* is produced, price is
equal to average total cost.

Competitive equilibrium with economic rent

In the analysis just completed, we have employed assumptions that dictate an arresting conclusion: under conditions of perfect competition, an
equilibrium will be reached in which no firm earns either a profit or a
loss. In order to avoid confusion and error in the future, we must now
examine this conclusion rather carefully.

Our previous analysis assumed that the prices of all factor inputs are
given (assumption A8.2); and that all firms have equal access to technology and factor inputs (assumption A8.3). Strictly speaking, neither
of these two assumptions is necessary for perfect competition to exist in
the commodity market.

Assumptions A8.2 and A8.3 were introduced to allow us to concentrate on essential matters. Assumption A8.3 ensures that all firms have
identical cost functions. Assumption A8.2, by ruling out the possibility
that the prices of factor inputs can change, saves us from the necessity
of considering what happens to the earnings of firms as these prices
change. As we presently shall see, a change in factor input price can (and
probably will) have an impact on the earnings of a firm which "owns"
the factors that it uses, and another, different, impact on the earnings of
a firm that "hires" its factors. Taken together, assumptions A8.2 and
A8.3 ensure that a proposition which is true for one firm in an industry
is necessarily true for all firms in the industry. This is an immense
convenience.

Actually, in order to have perfect competition in the commodity market, it is only necessary that the conditions of assumptions A8.1, A8.4,
and A8.5 be satisfied. That is, in the industry there must be a very large
number of plants; there must be some obstacle to the creation of multiplant firms; and all firms must produce a homogeneous commodity. How-

ever, should the firms in the industry have different cost functions, then an equilibrium will be reached in which some firms produce an output at which total revenue is greater than total cost. As we noted in Chapter 6, in our discussion of monopoly, economists distinguish between economic rent and profit. The term profit is commonly reserved for the disequilibrium case in which total revenue is temporarily above total cost. The term economic rent is applied to the case in which, because new firms cannot or will not enter the industry, total revenue is permanently above total cost for some established firms. Therefore, when perfect competitors have different production functions or own different fractions of the factors that they use, a different sort of equilibrium will be reached. In this equilibrium economic rents will be collected by somebody.

In case you are wondering about our sudden lapse into the passive voice ("economic rents will be collected by somebody"), it was deliberate. When the entry of additional firms fails to eliminate a difference between total revenue and total cost in established firms, production generates economic rent. But unless we are given additional information, it is not possible to say who gets the economic rent.

In order for economic rent to be collected in equilibrium, one or both of the following conditions must be satisfied.

A8.6 The price of at least one factor input rises as the industry's output is increased. (This is the negation of assumption A8.2.)

A8.7 Firms do not have equal access to technology or to factor inputs, i.e. all firms do not have identical cost functions. (This is the negation of assumption A8.3.)

If condition A8.6 is satisfied while condition A8.7 is not, then economic rent is collected only by the factor inputs whose prices rise as industry output expands. To take an ancient but perfectly serviceable example: an increase in the demand for wheat will, for nearly obvious reasons, lead to an increase in the demand for land suitable for growing wheat. Therefore, the rental per acre of land suitable for growing wheat will rise. In the long run—when all leases on wheat land have expired and been renegotiated—the only beneficiaries of the increase in the demand for wheat will be the owners of wheat land. There will be no long-run benefit for hired labor nor for tenant farmers who can grow wheat only by renting other people's land. All this was pointed out by the English economist David Ricardo (1772-1823) many years ago.

Now suppose that condition A8.7 is satisfied while condition A8.6 is not. Let there be a perfectly elastic supply of wheat land but only a limited number of tenant farmers who know how to organize wheat produc-

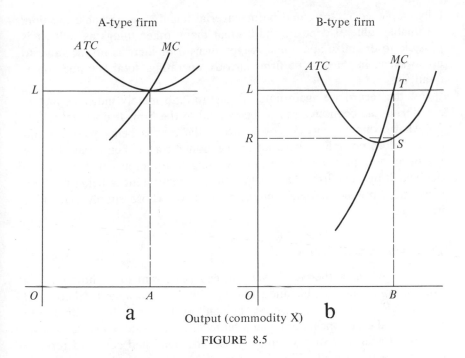

FIGURE 8.5

tion. Then, in the long run, an increase in the demand for wheat will create economic rent only for these tenant farmers.

In the more realistic case where neither the supply of wheat land nor the supply of tenant farmers skilled in wheat production is perfectly elastic, an increase in the demand for wheat will create economic rent for *both* landlords and tenants. We cannot say how the resulting economic rent will be divided between these two groups without more information.

But let us leave wheat and return to our more general commodity X. Suppose that commodity X is produced under conditions of perfect competition in two kinds of firms, say A-type firms and B-type firms. Equilibrium for A-type is given by figure 8.5a and equilibrium for B-type is given by figure 8.5b. Firms of both types sell their outputs at price *OL*. A-type firms earn no economic rent. Each B-type firm earns the economic rent *RSTL* in figure 8.5b.

We might stop to note that A-type firms and B-type firms are in equilibrium for essentially different reasons. No more B-type firms can be organized; the scarce factor (or factors) whose employment allows the B-type firm to collect an economic rent is already fully employed. The fully employed factor could be managerial talent, a geographic location, a valuable mineral deposit, and a great many other things as well. It is possible to organize additional A-type firms. But there is no incentive to do so since, in the A-type firms already operating, total revenue equals total cost.

For the record we again note that figure 8.5b merely indicates that in equilibrium an economic rent is being paid to the firm. It does not tell us for what economic service (or services) the rent is being paid. Specifically, it does not tell us whether the economic rent is being paid for the use of an entrepreneurial skill in combining factor inputs that cannot be duplicated by new firms. Or whether the economic rent is being paid because the firm owns some amount of a factor whose supply cannot be increased.

The capitalization process

Nor are we out of the woods yet. An economic rent may show up in a firm's accounts as a visible and enduring difference between total cost and total revenue. But it may also be "hidden" in the firm's ATC curve even though total cost appears to equal total revenue. (No stock market analyst or federal examiner of tax returns trusts the published cost and revenue data of the real world. Why should you?) In Chapter 11 we shall meet the ubiquitous "capitalization process." Capitalization is a tricky (also a profoundly important) economic phenomenon and deserves careful, detailed treatment. For present purposes, a brief comment must suffice to indicate why we must reckon with capitalization in any discussion of economic rent.

Suppose that an economic rent is earned by a B-type firm in figure 8.5b because it owns a variety of land especially well suited to producing commodity X. Suppose further that the owners of a B-type firm (who are also the owners of the land well adapted to producing commodity X) wish to sell out. They will put a price tag on the economic rent *RSTL* in figure 8.5b. And the investment which the buyer will have to make in order to buy the privilege of collecting rent *RSTL* will become a fixed cost in his bookkeeping. That is, as the B-type firm changes hands, the economic rent of the original owners is capitalized into the firm's value as a "property" in the market. Indeed, when capitalization has done its work, all economic rents of the original owners will have been transformed into fixed costs for the firm organized by the new owners. And price will appear to equal average total cost in the new firm. Thus in the long run the effect of capitalization is to bury economic rent in the ATC of the firm where it is lost from public view.

Summary

For perfect competition to exist, all firms must be free to enter and leave the industry. Further, the output at which a single firm has minimum average total cost must be very small relative to the output of the industry. When these conditions are satisfied, each firm behaves as if it has no power to affect price by varying output. That is, in perfect competition each firm believes that the demand for its own output is "infinitely" or "perfectly" elastic.

We described two types of equilibrium in perfect competition. We derived the first by assuming that (i) every firm in the industry can hire all of the factor inputs that it requires at fixed prices and (ii) all entrepreneurs are equally efficient. On these assumptions, an equilibrium will be reached in which price is equal to average total cost in every firm. If price is above average total cost, new firms will enter the industry being drawn in by the profit. If price is below average total cost, some established firms will leave, being driven out by the loss. In this first type of competitive equilibrium, there is neither profit nor loss, nor economic rent.

If (i) the price of at least one factor input rises as the industry's output expands and/or (ii) entrepreneurs are not equally efficient or do not have equal access to technology and resources, then the entry and exit of firms will still produce an equilibrium. However, in this second case, somebody—factor owner or entrepreneur—will be collecting an economic rent.

We note again the distinction between a profit (or loss) and an economic rent. A profit (or loss) is a difference between price and average total cost that, assuming no new developments, sooner or later, will be eliminated by the entry (or exit) of firms. An economic rent is a difference between price and average total cost that will not be eliminated by the entry (or exit) of firms. An economic rent will eventually "disappear" into a higher ATC curve through the capitalization process. Capitalization will be discussed at length in Chapter 11.

REFERENCES

Clark, J. M., *Competition as a Dynamic Process* (Washington, D.C., 1961), chapters 1 and 2.

Ferguson, C. E., *Microeconomic Theory* (Homewood, Ill., 3rd ed., 1972), chapter 8.
Knight, F. H., *Risk, Uncertainty and Profit* (London, 1948), especially Part II.
Leftwich, R. H., *The Price System and Resource Allocation* (Hinsdale, 5th ed., 1973), chapter 10.
Mansfield, Edwin, *Microeconomics: Theory and Applications* (New York, 1970), chapter 8.
Robinson, Joan, "What Is Perfect Competition?" *The Quarterly Journal of Economics* 49 (1934), 104-20.
Stigler, G. J., "Perfect Competition Historically Contemplated," *Journal of Political Economy,* 65 (1957), 1-17.

9
Competitive Equilibrium: An Alternative View

We have now surveyed the theory of monopoly and the classical theory of perfect competition. Monopoly and perfect competition are often viewed by people who misuse economic analysis as the opposite ends of a spectrum along which every market situation of the real world can be placed. In their error they assert or imply that a particular industry can be located on this spectrum once its number of firms is given. By their view an industry with three firms is likely to be more competitive than an industry with two firms, an industry with four firms is more likely to be competitive than an industry with three firms, etc.

A little thought will show this approach to competition and monopoly is quite naïve. In Chapter 6 we saw that in order for monopoly to exist two conditions are necessary. (i) There is only one seller and (ii) he is totally protected by Government or Nature against the entry of other sellers into his market. Likewise, we saw that for perfect competition to exist two conditions are necessary. (i) There must be a very large number of firms and (ii) entry into the industry is open to all comers.

Free entry but few firms

What happens if we keep one of these two assumptions necessary for perfect competition but drop the other? What happens to price and output if we retain the assumption that entry into the indusry is free but now assume that, in equilibrium, the industry will consist of a "small" number of firms? Specifically, the number of firms is assumed to be so small (e.g. 2, 3, or 4) that each firm knows perfectly well that any change in its own rate of output will change price for itself and the other firms as well. Each firm clearly realizes that if it increases its output, price will fall; and that if it reduces its output, price will rise. Let us explicitly set down the key assumptions that we shall use in this chapter.

A9.1   All firms are free to enter and leave the industry.

A9.2   All firms are equally efficient.

A9.3   There are neither economies nor diseconomies to be had by bringing plants under common ownership and control.

A9.4   Each firm knows that any change in its rate of output will affect price for itself and all other firms in the industry.

A9.5   All firms have complete information on all matters that are relevant to the price-output decision. (This assumption was also used in our analysis of both monopoly and the traditional treatment of perfect competition.)

A firm that sells its output in a market to which the above assumptions apply, clearly has a problem. On the one hand, it knows that by changing its rate of output it can change the price at which its output sells and hence the profit it will earn. On the other hand, it knows that a policy of equating marginal cost to marginal revenue in order to maximize short-run profit may cause new firms to enter the industry. And the entry of these new firms will reduce and finally eliminate its profit. What should the firm do in this situation?

"Natural" monopoly once more

The clue to the behavior of the rational firm placed in this situation was provided in Chapter 7 in our discussion of so-called "natural" monopoly— the case where average total cost (ATC) always falls as the firm expands its output. There we found that the natural monopolist will always resort to stayout pricing—that is, he will adopt a price policy designed to block the entry of other firms. And we saw why stayout pricing will always work for him.

If the natural monopolist produces, say, 100 units of commodity X, a potential newcomer to the industry cannot produce a unit of commodity X as cheaply as the natural monopolist unless he (the newcomer) also produces 100 units. But if he (the newcomer) adds his 100 units to the 100 units produced by the natural monopolist, the industry may well become unprofitable for both. If the natural monopolist's profit is so great when he produces 100 units of commodity X that it tempts a newcomer to enter the industry, then obviously he should produce more than 100 units. For our purposes, the important truth is this. The natural monopolist is, by definition, the producer who can always cut average total cost (ATC) by increasing output; therefore, there is an output that he can produce which is great enough to ensure that no second firm will enter.

As we noted earlier, it is unfortunate that the label of natural monopoly has been pinned to the case in which average total cost in the firm always decreases as output increases. This case has virtually nothing in common with the case of (pure) monopoly where a firm is so protected by Government or Nature that it can maximize profit without fear of attracting new firms into the industry. Unfortunately, as we also noted earlier, the label of natural monopoly has, for a very long time, been applied to industries where average total cost decreases as output increases. Therefore, we respect tradition by keeping the term in our vocabulary—but with reluctance.

Competitive equilibrium with the multiplant firm

In this chapter the existence of a multiplant firm is made possible by assumption A9.3, which says that there are neither economies nor diseconomies to be had by bringing plants under common management and control. This being so, a firm neither raises nor lowers minimum average total cost by changing the number of plants it owns. Now the firm has a set of cost possibilities of the sort depicted in figure 9.1. This figure gives the cost possibilities up to the limit of three plants.

If the firm has one plant, average total cost is AA'. If it has two plants, average total cost is BB'. And if it has three plants, average total cost is CC'.

We might note again the reason for the kinks in the curve of average total cost for a multiplant firm. (This reason was discussed at length in Chapter 5.) A kink occurs whenever, as output is reduced, it pays the firm to shut down a plant and concentrate production in the remaining plant or plants. The number of kinks in the curve of average total cost of the firm with n plants is always equal to $n - 1$.

When the firm owns only one plant, average total cost is lowest when 10 units of commodity X are produced. (Figure 9.1) When it owns two plants average total cost is lowest when 20 units are produced. And when it owns three plants, average total cost is lowest when 30 units are produced. In each instance, minimum average total cost is $5. As a firm adds

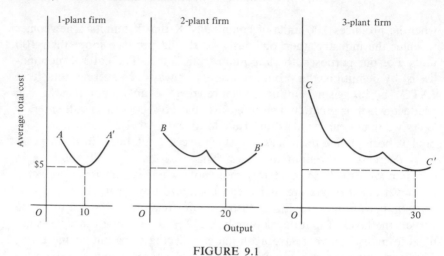

FIGURE 9.1

to its number of plants, this minimum does not change. What does change? Simply the output at which this minimum is reached. We illustrate this truth in figure 9.1, for the firm that can choose to have one, two, or three plants. The analysis can, of course, be extended to cover any number of plants.

Let us suppose that a firm has the chance to produce an entirely new commodity X—one not heretofore offered on the market by anybody. But this opportunity is subject to the following constraint.

The firm may choose to build any number of plants that it wishes and to produce any output that it wishes in the plants built. While the firm is tooling up for production, no other firm will be allowed to build plants. On the day that it produces the first unit of commodity X, its protection against rivals is taken away. All of the five explicit assumptions of this chapter then come into play. In short, we give the firm a head start in the race to make profits by producing commodity X. But this is the only advantage that we give it.

If our firm had the falling ATC curve of a natural monopolist, we know that it would resort to stayout pricing in order to block the entry of other firms and so maximize long-run profit. But our firm does not have such a cost curve. Rather it has an ATC curve that contains a minimum point, though the location of this minimum depends upon the number of plants that it has chosen to build. (Figure 9.1)

Given that the firm cannot reduce minimum average total cost by building more plants and increasing output, can it block the entry of new firms? More precisely, can the firm use its head start to produce an output that yields it a permanent economic rent which, however, is too small to trigger the entry of another firm? We can demonstrate that such a policy of stayout pricing is possible even though the firm is not the conventional natural monopolist defined as the firm whose average total cost decreases as output increases. To demonstrate this possibility we must prove two lemmas.

      L9.1 There is some minimum output which if produced in the multiplant firm will block the entry of additional firms into the industry.

      L9.2 When this minimum output is produced in the multiplant firm, price will be greater than average total cost; hence the multiplant firm will earn an economic rent.

These two lemmas can be proved with the aid of figures 9.2, 9.3, and 9.4. In figure 9.2, let SS' denote the aggregate demand for commodity X. In the beginning, let the industry contain but one firm. Now consider how the prospects for profits in the industry appear to a second firm that is thinking about coming in.

The demand curve that is available to this second firm depends, of course, upon how much of SS' in figure 9.2 has been appropriated by the firm already established in the industry. Suppose that the established firm

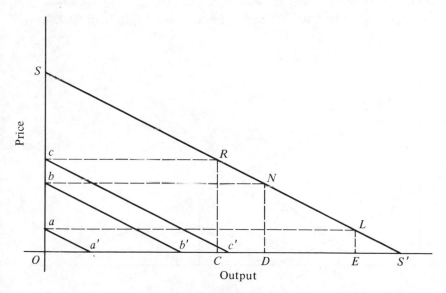

FIGURE 9.2

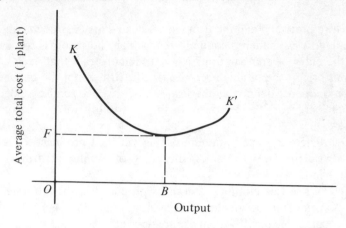

FIGURE 9.3

produces output *OC*. Then the "unused" portion of the industry demand curve *SS'* that can be picked up by a new entrant is the segment *RS'* in figure 9.2. Move *RS'* laterally to the left until point *R* lies on the vertical (price) axis. When so positioned, *RS'* becomes the conventional demand curve *cc'*.

Suppose that the established firm produces not output *OC* but rather output *OD*. Then the unused portion of the industry demand curve that can be picked up by a new entrant is the segment *NS'* in figure 9.2. Move

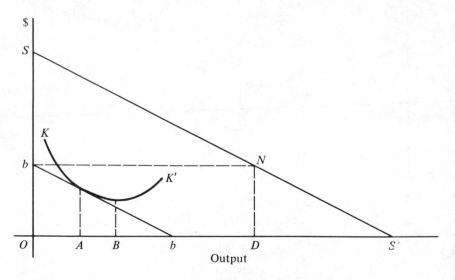

FIGURE 9.4

NS' laterally to the left until point *N* lies on the vertical (price) axis. When so positioned, *NS'* becomes the conventional demand curve *bb'*. Using this same reasoning, we can show that should the established firm produce output *OE,* the demand curve facing the potential entrant would be *aa'*.

In short, the greater the output of the established firm the closer the demand curve facing a potential entrant will lie to the origin in figure 9.2. The limit case occurs when the established firm produces output *OS'*. In this unlikely event, there would be no demand at all for the output of a second firm.

In figure 9.2 the demand curve available to a potential entrant is seen to depend upon the size of the output of the established firm. The costs that a potential entrant must incur in order to produce commodity X, however, are dictated by technology and factor prices—variables that cannot be affected by any action on the part of the established firm. In figure 9.3, the ATC curve for a firm that builds one (and only one) plant is given by *KK'*. It has, of course, the conventional U-shape. Presumably a firm that is thinking of entry will first explore the possibility of beginning production with one plant.

Now let us superimpose figure 9.3 upon figure 9.2. The result is figure 9.4. We do not bother to transfer curves *cc'* and *aa'* from figure 9.2 to figure 9.4 since we have no further use for them.

With the aid of figure 9.4, we see a most important truth. If the established firm produces output *OD,* a second firm has the demand curve *bb'*. It can enter the industry and exactly break even by producing output *OA*. If the established firm produces an output smaller than *OD,* a second firm can enter and make a profit. Hence, if the established firm wishes to block the entry of all other firms, its course is clear. It must produce an output greater than *OD* in figure 9.4. Since the established firm wishes to maximize income, it will aim at the smallest output in excess of *OD* that it is feasible to produce.

We have proved lemma L9.1. There is an output which, if produced by our firm with the head start, will block the entry of other firms. But how will it organize production in order to secure this result? And will such stayout pricing be profitable for the firm that practices it?

Consider figure 9.5. Aggregate demand curve for commodity X is again given by *SS'*. Once more *OD* is the output, which if produced by the established firm, would allow a second firm to enter and exactly break even. In figure 9.5, *OD'* is now the smallest output that is greater than *OD* which the established firm can produce. Thus *OD'* is the entry-blocking output.

How many plants will the established firm want to build in order to produce OD'? (Remember that we are assuming neither economies nor diseconomies of multiplant ownership.) This question is easily answered. We divide the distance OD' in figure 9.5 by the distance OB in figure 9.3. That is, we divide the entry-blocking output by the optimum output per plant. Two results are possible: The division is exact. The division is not exact; it produces an integer n and a fractional remainder r.

When OD' is exactly divisible by OB, the number of plants which the established firm must build in order to block entry is n. Moreover, when division is exact, each plant built will produce output OB and, of course, $OB \times n = OD'$.

In the more likely event that $OD'/OB = n + r$, we have a minor problem. It is not possible for the established firm to organize production so that each plant produces OB—the cost minimizing output. If n plants are built, each plant will have to produce something more than OA units if total output is to equal OD. However, there is another production possibility that must be explored. It may be cheaper for the established firm to build $n + 1$ plants and produce something less than OB in each plant. Still, one thing is certain. The number of plants that the established firm will build is either n or $n + 1$.

Figure 9.6 is constructed to incorporate the information that the cost of producing the entry-blocking output OD' is minimized when three

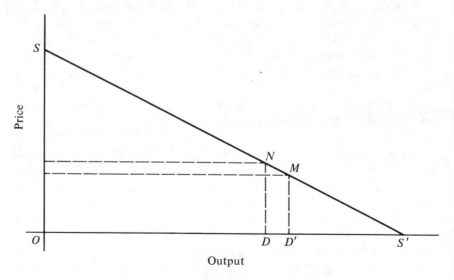

FIGURE 9.5

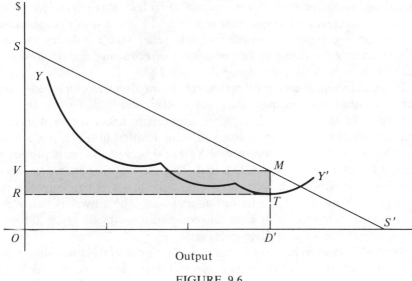

Output

FIGURE 9.6

plants are built. In the interest of neat geometry, we have chosen to make *OD'* in figure 9.5 exactly divisible by *OB* in figure 9.3. That is, our geometry ensures that $3 \times OB = OD'$. And each of the three plants produces *OB* which is the cost-minimizing output. If *OD'* were not exactly divisible by *OB* we could only say that output per plant would be "in the neighborhood" of *OB*.

In any event, the truth that stayout pricing is a profitable option for the multiplant firm is made clear by figure 9.6. Here average total cost in the 3-plant firm is given by *YY'*. (Each of its three plants has the ATC curve given by *KK'* of figure 9.3.) By producing total output *OD'* the 3-plant firm earns the economic rent given by the shaded area RTMV in figure 9.6. Hence lemma L9.2 is proved. A policy of stayout pricing for the multiplant firm is both possible and profitable. We are now in a position to state a most important theorem in economic theory.

 T9.1 If neither economies nor diseconomies of scale result when plants are brought under common ownership and control, then an equilibrium will be reached with only one firm in the industry.

We might emphasize again that an equilibrium with one firm that practices stayout pricing must be carefully distinguished from the case of "pure" monopoly examined in Chapter 6. The true monopolist is protected against the entry of new firms and so blithely maximizes income by equating marginal cost to marginal revenue. The single firm that practices stayout pricing enjoys its position as sole seller in the industry for one reason only: it is willing to accept a level of economic rent so low that the entry of new firms is discouraged.

In the above analysis a most restrictive assumption was employed in order to demonstrate the inevitability of total concentration when no diseconomies of scale result when plants are brought under common ownership and control. We assumed that some one favored firm is given a head start in the production of commodity X; that this favored firm is protected against the entry of others while it is tooling up; and that such protection evaporates at once when production of commodity X is begun by the favored firm. Why use such a far-out assumption? The answer is that it allows our industry to reach long-run equilibrium without going through any intermediate stage of disequilibrium.

We do not have to proceed in this way. We could start with a disequilibrium in which the industry contains several firms, each one of which has excess capacity. That is, we could begin by assuming that each firm has at least one plant which is producing less than optimum output. We could then show how these inefficient firms would be led by the profit motive to join together in order to rationalize production. And we could show how such a rationalization scheme would involve the phasing out of some plants and the adoption of a policy of stayout pricing. Finally, we could demonstrate that the gains from rationalization can only be fully realized when all plants have been placed under the control of One Big Firm or One Big Cartel. We could trace the movement from disequilibrium to equilibrium in this way but it would be a time-consuming exercise and not lead us to any new economic principle. Therefore, we have proceeded directly to the equilibrium case.

Two models of competitive equilibrium compared

We are now able to compare the classical view of competitive equilibrium set forth in Chapter 8 with the view developed above. The comparison is made easy by figure 9.7. Again *SS'* is the aggregate demand curve for commodity X; and curve *KK'* is the curve of average total cost of producing commodity X in a single plant.

According to the classical view, equilibrium output for the firm will be *OB* (since each firm will have only one plant); and *OG* will be the equilibrium output for the industry. By the alternative view, equilibrium out-

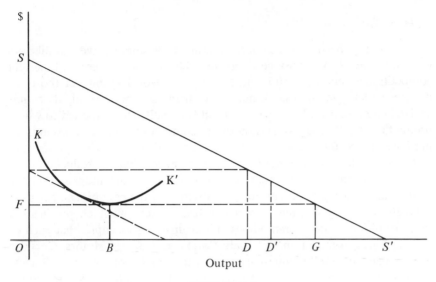

FIGURE 9.7

put for the plant (but not the firm) will also be *OB* (or very close to it); and equilibrium output for both the firm and the industry will be *OD'*. Recall that *OD* is the output which would allow a second firm to enter the industry and exactly break even while *OD'* is the smallest output greater than *OD* which the multiplant firm can produce.

Given a linear demand function (such as *SS'* in figure 9.7) we can identify the main difference between our two types of competitive equilibrium with the following theorem:

> T9.2 Let *industry* output in an equilibrium of perfect competition be designated Z. Let the output at which average total cost in each *plant* is minimized be designated z. Then should the industry be organized by a multiplant firm that practices stayout pricing, equilibrium output will be less than Z but greater than $Z-z$.

One implication of our comparison is clear. So far as equilibrium output is concerned, the difference between an equilibrium of perfect competition and an equilibrium with stayout pricing becomes unimportant as the equilibrium number of plants increases. Note also that both methods of organizing the production of commodity X are economically efficient. In each case, equilibrium output will be distributed among plants in such a way that the total cost of producing it is minimized. In figure 9.7 minimum average total cost is *OF*.

Market strategies in action

Do we really heed the alternate treatment of competitive equilibrium just elaborated? We most certainly do. The classical theory of perfect competition is mainly useful for studying real-world pricing in those industries which contain a large number of firms and produce highly standardized commodities. It gives truly beautiful results when applied to wheat production (a thoroughly standardized commodity, many thousands of producers) and fairly good results when applied to typewriter production (a fairly standardized commodity, a fairly large number of producers).

But to say the obvious, many of the most important industries in the American economy do not remotely approximate the conditions of perfect competition. They contain only a few firms, each of which produces a range of differentiated commodities. To assume, for example, that each of the Big Three in the automobile industry—Ford, General Motors, Chrysler—maximizes income by equating price to marginal cost would be lunacy. Yet it would be equally absurd to treat most of the highly concentrated industries of the American economy as protected monopolists who are engaged in equating marginal cost to marginal revenue in accord with the conventional monopoly theory presented in Chapter 6.

Should the leading firms in these industries make extraordinary profits, there are several quarters from which a challenge could come. They could be challenged by shoestring entrants with little capital and much courage. Battle can be offered by foreign firms with much capital but little experience in the American market. And they face the most dangerous threat of all—the possibility of so-called "lateral entry" by well-financed firms in other, less profitable industries. As a matter of information, in the United States, firms in high concentration industries (those where the top four firms have 50 percent or more of total output) generally appear to earn a higher rate of return on capital than firms in low concentration industries. But, as our theory now leads us to expect, the difference is surprisingly small.[1]

1. For some years now, an inconclusive family debate has been maintained among economists over the connection between industrial concentration and profitability. As you might expect, the strength of the tie can vary from one decade to the next. However, in the manufacturing sector of the American economy, during the period 1935-70, in any five-year interval, after-tax profits expressed as a percentage of stockholders' equity have seldom gone higher than 13 percent per annum even in the most concentrated industries. The corresponding figure for the least concentrated industries has seldom gone below 7.5 percent. Moreover, it is probable that "true" differences in profitability are less than these figures suggest because low-concentration industries contain many small, owner-managed firms in which the owner is

To find really staggering rates of return on capital (say, 25 percent per annum and up) that persist for more than a year or so, one must usually look to industries that are protected against the entry of newcomers by the State. For example, in New York City a $4000 taxicab currently earns a rate of return well in excess of 100 percent per annum! This is possible only because the number of taxicabs has been limited by law since the 1930's. You can buy a taxicab for $4000 or less from Detroit. A permit to operate a taxicab in New York City can only be bought from somebody who already has one. And in 1974 this permit cost more than $15,000.

There is yet another good reason for studying the mechanics of stayout pricing. Many economists have pointed out that large firms in highly concentrated industries will often sacrifice short-run profits in order to preserve or increase their respective market shares. Others have noted that such firms also seem to have a preference for expansion that leads them to make investments that create excess capacity. And the suspect inference is sometimes drawn that they prefer high market shares and rapid corporate growth to maximum profits. The more plausible inference is simply that these firms believe that pricing to protect a market share and accelerated expansion are ways to discourage the entry of competitors. Stayout pricing is simply a policy of giving up short-run profits in order to obtain a long-run economic rent. Thus during the forty years from 1900 to 1940 the Aluminum Company of America (Alcoa)[2] was virtually the sole supplier of virgin aluminum ingot in the United States, and only one other firm made a serious effort to enter the market during these years. Alcoa had, of course, many advantages over a potential entrant by virtue of its head start. But the fact that over this period Alcoa's rate of return on capital averaged only about 10 percent per annum (while competitive industries were averaging about 8 percent) suggests that Alcoa did not believe in tempting fate. Alcoa's "monopoly" of aluminum production was finally destroyed by a government policy of artificial insemination which financed the entry of two new firms during World War II.

Whenever competition is discussed, we are now in a position to keep

able to take his earnings out of the business in the form of a generous expense account, having friendly relatives on the payroll, and charitable contributions. The evidence on profitability and concentration is examined in F. M. Scherer, *Industrial Market Structure and Economic Performance* (Chicago, 1970), pp. 183-86; and Leonard Weiss, "Quantitative Studies of Industrial Organization" in *Frontiers of Quantitative Economics,* M. D. Intriligator, ed. (Amsterdam, 1971), pp. 362-411.
2. The early history of Alcoa is discussed in United States *v.* Aluminum Company of America et al., 148 F. 2d. 416 (1945).

one truth firmly in mind. The first requirement for the operation of a price system that eliminates most economic rent in the production of a commodity is freedom of contract. The number of firms which, at any moment, is actually using this freedom to produce the commodity is a matter of secondary importance.

Summary

The traditional theory of competitive equilibrium assumes that each firm has a U-shaped curve of average total cost which ensures an optimum size for the firm in the industry. And it assumes that, in long-run equilibrium, the industry will consist of "a very large number" of firms. A more modern view of competitive equilibrium assumes that *only the plant* has a U-shaped curve of average total cost. When there are neither economies nor diseconomies to be had by bringing plants under common ownership and control, a multiplant firm is possible, indeed probable. Such a firm, by increasing or decreasing its number of plants, can alter output without altering minimum average total cost.

By resorting to a policy of stayout pricing the multiplant firm can keep for itself an economic rent. But the greater the number of plants that the industry can support in equilibrium, the smaller the difference in the equilibrium outputs of our two competitive models. Both models ensure that, in equilibrium, each plant produces the output at which average total cost is minimized.

Each model of competitive equilibrium has its uses. The classical model gives the best predictive results when applied to the agricultural sector of the economy with its thousands of producers. The modern model gives its best predictive results when applied to highly concentrated manufacturing industries.

REFERENCES

Bain, J. B., "A Note on Pricing in Monopoly and Oligopoly," *American Economic Review,* 39 (1949), 448-64.
Baumol, W. J., *Business Behavior, Value and Growth* (New York, rev. ed., 1967), especially chapters 6, 7, and 8.
Dewey, Donald, *The Theory of Imperfect Competition: A Radical Reconstruction* (New York, 1969), chapters 3 and 4.
Fig, Bjarke, "Stayout Pricing," *Metroeconomica* 9 (1957), 42-51.
Gaskins, D. W., "Dynamic Limit Pricing: Optional Pricing under Threat of Entry," *Journal of Economic Theory,* 3 (1971), 306-22.
Pashigian, B. P., "Limit Price and the Market Share of the Leading Firm," *Journal of Industrial Economics,* 16 (1968), 165-77.
Sylos-Labini, Paola, *Oligopoly and Technical Progress* (Cambridge, 1962), pp. 40-50.

10
A Simple Model
of Oligopoly

Difficult territory

We have now seen how price and output are determined in three models of market organization—monopoly, perfect competition, and stayout pricing. In each of these models, a crucial assumption concerned the cost of bringing plants under common management and control. In the cases of monopoly and stayout pricing, this coordination cost was assumed to be zero; so that, in equilibrium, the industry consists of a single, multiplant firm. In the case of perfect competition, this coordination cost was assumed to be "prohibitive" for all combinations of plants; so that, in equilibrium, the industry consists of firms that have only one plant apiece. We also saw that perfect competition requires a very large number of firms—large enough to convince each firm that, acting alone, it cannot affect price by varying output.

We have not yet considered an obvious possibility. Suppose that we analyze price and output determination on the following assumptions:

A10.1 The cost of bringing any combination of plants under common ownership and control is prohibitive, i.e. only single plant firms are possible.

A10.2 Production costs are so high relative to demand that the industry can support only a small number of plants (and hence only a small number of firms).

A10.3 Firms are free to enter and leave the industry.

A10.4 The total cost curve for each firm is continuous over the relevant range of output, and "normal" in that total cost never decreases as output increases—i.e. marginal cost is always non-negative.

The above assumptions give us the "competition among the few" that has acquired the useful, if inelegant, name of *oligopoly*. Note that assumption A10.1 says nothing about why the cost of bringing plants under common ownership and control is prohibitive. The reason may lie in government policy—for example, in an antitrust rule which makes it a penitentiary offence to form multiplant firms. Or the reason may lie in Nature—perhaps the job of ensuring that all plants operate at peak efficiency is simply too big for a single management team. Later on we will return for another look at the reasons that can bar the creation of multiplant firms.

Unfortunately, oligopoly is one of the most controversial areas in economic theory. Sooner or later we will have to face up to the leading issues in this controversy in the interest of maintaining intellectual self-respect. But let us postpone the confrontation until later (Chapter 16) in the hope that we will then be better equipped to deal with the issues.

The main reason why oligopoly causes so much trouble in economics becomes obvious once we try to answer a deceptively simple question. How should we draw the demand curve for an oligopolist? He is not a monopolist so we cannot use the industry demand curve. He has a U-shaped curve of average total cost so he cannot resort to stayout pricing. He is not a perfect competitor; he would be stupid to act on the assumption that his actions have no effect upon other firms in the industry. What do we do?

The answer is that we cannot do anything with oligopoly until we make some assumption about interaction among oligopolists. That is, we must come up with an interaction rule. A moment's reflection will suggest that we can come up with a number of very plausible rules. For example, we can assume that oligopolists are a collection of distrustful rivals who are always trying to divert business from one another by price cuts. Alternatively, we can assume that oligopolists are men of at least average intelligence who have discovered that frequent price changes touch off price wars which are unprofitable for all.

So great is the uncertainty about the interaction rule that we should specify for oligopolists that a very good argument can be made that oligopoly is not really a part of economic statics. Perhaps it should be treated as a form of competition under conditions of uncertainty. However, the convention is very strong in economics that oligopoly is discussed in connection with monopoly and perfect competition in order to round out "the theory of the firm." It seems advisable to respect this convention to the extent of considering the simplest form of oligopoly in this chapter. Other forms we shall later consider under the heading of "dynamics." There-fore, let us specify an interaction rule for oligopolists with the following assumption:

A10.5 Each firm knows that any change in its own price or output will be matched immediately by all other firms.

Oligopoly with economic rent

The significance of assumption A10.5 is underscored by figure 10.1. Here ED gives the demand curve for the industry's product. (Let it be commod-ity X again.) If the industry consists of two firms, each will believe that its own demand curve is *EC* in figure 10.1. This follows because each firm knows that whatever output it produces or whatever price it charges will be exactly matched by its rival. If the industry consists of three firms, each will believe that its own demand curve is *EB*. And if the industry consists of four firms, each will take demand to be *EA*. Etc. In figure 10.1 the nu-meral designating the number of firms in the industry assumed by each demand curve is superimposed for ready reference.

By assumption A10.3 firms are free to enter the industry. They will continue to do so until it becomes clear that the entry of an additional firm will make the industry unprofitable for all. Entry then ceases and the in-dustry has reached equilibrium.

When the demand for commodity X is given by *ED* in figure 10.1, how many firms will the industry contain in equilibrium? To answer this ques-tion, we impose the curve of average total cost for a single plant on figure

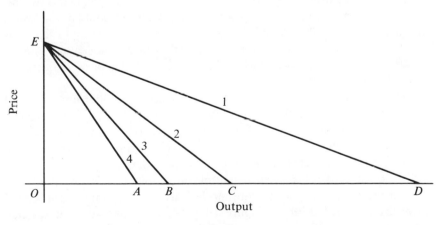

FIGURE 10.1

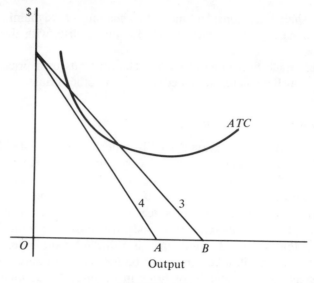

FIGURE 10.2

10.1. This is done in figure 10.2, but since we have no further need for lines *ED* and *EC* in figure 10.1, we do not transfer them to figure 10.2.

From figure 10.2 it is apparent that, in our simple oligopoly model, the equilibrium number of plants (and firms) is three. Should a fourth firm enter, the demand curve that each of the four firms would face would be *EA*. And in figure 10.2, the ATC curve is always above *EA*. That is, should a fourth firm enter and the industry's output be divided into four equal parts, there is no possible way that the four firms could avoid losses. In a static model, all resource owners are presumed to act upon the basis of complete information. Therefore, a fourth firm will not enter. The industry in equilibrium will consist of three firms. Each faces the demand curve *EB* in figure 10.2.

Now consider figure 10.3. It allows us to read off equilibrium price and output for each of the three oligopolists. *EB* is the demand curve taken from figures 10.1 and 10.2. The line *EN* in figure 10.3 is the marginal revenue curve implied by *EB*. The ATC curve is reproduced from figure 10.2; and *MC* designates the marginal cost curve that it implies.

The oligopolist maximizes income when output *OR* is produced and sold at price *OU*. And in equilibrium he earns the economic rent *VSTU* given by the shaded area in figure 10.3. We call this excess of revenue above cost a rent rather than a profit because it will not be competed away

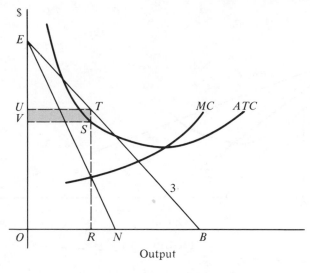

FIGURE 10.3

by the entry of another firm. It is, so to speak, the prize that the oligopolist collects because he is among the first three firms to enter the industry.

Profitability of oligopoly

It is also possible to construct a model of simple oligopoly where, in equilibrium, price equals average total cost in each firm and no economic rent is earned. The case of oligopoly equilibrium with no economic rent is illustrated by figure 10.4. Here the ATC curve of the single plant (and firm) is carefully tailored to ensure that the entry of the third firm into the industry exactly eliminates all economic rent. In figure 10.4, the aggregate demand for commodity X is again given *ED*. And when three firms have entered the industry, the demand curve that each faces is again *EB*. When each firm produces output *OQ*, average total cost is equal to price and no economic rent is earned.

An oligopoly equilibrium where each firm exactly breaks even may be possible. But an oligopoly equilibrium where each firm earns a modest equilibrium rent—one not great enough to cause an additional firm to enter the industry—is much more probable. In short, in an oligopoly market there is no single, unique equilibrium rate of profit; rather there is a set of possible equilibrium profit rates. Can we say anything specific about the characteristics of this set? More particularly, can we show that the upper

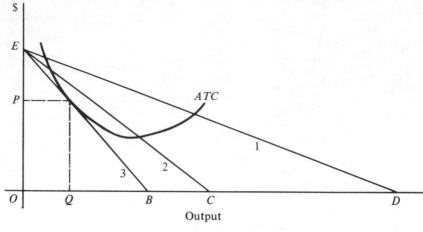

FIGURE 10.4

bound of this set—the maximum rate of profit consistent with equilibrium —is a function of the number of firms that the industry can support in equilibrium? The answer is yes.

Suppose that we write s for the firm's total revenue; t for the firm's total cost; z for the firm's economic rent ("profit"), that is, $z = s - t$; and n for the number of firms in the industry.

In oligopoly our concern is with rate of profit, not total profit, since, in general, big firms earn big profits and small firms earn small profits. Rate of profit can be defined as "profit as a percentage of total revenue." Using r to designate rate of profit we can write $r = z/t$. Thus r corresponds very closely to what businessmen call rate of return on sales.[1]

Equipped with this notation we can prove the following theorem.

> T10.1 In a simple model of oligopoly, in n-firm equilibrium the equilibrium rate of profit must be non-negative and less than $1/(n+1)$

Obviously an equilibrium rate of profit must be non-negative. For if it is negative at least one firm will leave the industry; indeed the exit of firms will continue until the rate of profit becomes non-negative. Our problem

1. In empirical work many economists prefer to define the rate of profit as a rate of return on capital. Some investigators equate profitability with the return on total capital used by the firm (equity capital plus borrowed capital) while others equate it with the return on equity capital. However, we need not be concerned with difficult methodological and statistical problems involved in treating rate of profit as a return on capital. It can be shown that, no matter how rate of profit is defined, the greatest rate of profit consistent with n-firm equilibrium in simple oligopoly with free entry is a function of the equilibrium number of firms.

is to show that the rate of profit r must be less than $1/(n+1)$ in n-firm equilibrium. We proceed as follows.

In a simple model of oligopoly, all oligopolists have equal market shares; hence output per firm is always reduced when an additional firm enters the market (figure 10.1). By assumption A10.4, marginal cost in the firm is always non-negative. (This assumption is realistic as well as useful—nobody has yet discovered a case of negative marginal cost.) Now suppose that $nz \geq t$. Suppose, that is, that the sum of the profits of all n firms is equal to, or greater than, any one firm's total cost of production.

The entry of the $(n+1)$ firm cannot cause t to increase since all firms will contract their outputs. Therefore, should $nz \geq t$, the $(n+1)$ firm will enter the market and claim an equal market share; but its entry will still leave profit non-negative for all $(n+1)$ firms. Clearly a necessary condition of n-firm equilibrium is $nz < t$ and $z < t/n$.

By definition, $z = s - t$ and $r = z/s$; so that we obtain by simple substitution, $r < 1/(n+1)$. Theorem T10.2 is proved. And, of course, the greatest rate of profit consistent with n-firm equilibrium asymptotically approaches zero as n increases. In 1-firm equilibrium the rate of profit r can approximate 0.5; whereas in 5-firm equilibrium r must be less than 0.167.

Let us stop to emphasize one important implication of the above analysis. It leads us to expect that (i) high concentration industries will generally have higher rates of profits than low concentration industries but (ii) there will be many exceptions to this generalization since, in oligopoly, more than one rate of profit is consistent with equilibrium. As we noted in Chapter 9, these expectations have often been confirmed by empirical studies on the connection between industrial concentration and profitability.

Oligopoly not necessarily wasteful

With the aid of our geometry we can now identify a distinctive feature of oligopoly with the following theorem.

> T10.2 Assume that in the industry producing commodity X, entry is free, firms are few, and the cost of organizing the simplest multiplant firm is prohibitive. Then an equilibrium will be reached in which each firm produces an output at which average total cost is falling.

Theorem T10.2 is often called the "excess capacity" theorem but this label is unfortunate. This choice of words implies that oligopoly is, in the nature of things, an economically wasteful form of market organization.

This is not necessarily so. Before we can pass judgment on the economic efficiency of an industry characterized by oligopoly, we must look at the nature of the obstacle to its rationalization via merger or cartel. Recall that for oligopoly to come into existence in the first place there must be some such obstacle; otherwise, mergers and cartels will create the multiplant firm that rationalizes the industry and practices stayout pricing to block the entry of other firms. However, until now we have carefully refrained from specifying the nature of the obstacle to rationalization assumed in the preceding analysis.

If the obstacle that prevents rationalization—the concentration of output in plants that operate at, or very near, the minimum point of their respective ATC curves—is man-made and removable without cost, oligopoly is clearly wasteful. Such an obstacle could be an antitrust rule or the regulation of a government agency that prohibits the formation of multiplant firms or sets a limit on their size.

Suppose that an antitrust rule limiting every firm to one plant has produced the 3-plant (and 3-firm) equilibrium of figure 10.1. Then a repeal of this rule will be followed by rationalization and the eventual closing down of one of the three plants. Its output would be allocated in whole or in part to the two plants that remain in operation. Each remaining plant would produce an output greater than *OR* in figure 10.3 and have an average total cost lower than *OV*.

If the multiplant firm or cartel that is created by rationalization is to block the entry of other firms attracted by the industry profits, rationalization must, of course, be combined with a policy of stayout pricing. We have already been over the details of stayout pricing in Chapter 9 and (it is to be hoped) need not retrace our steps.

If nothing can be done about the obstacle which makes possible the 3-plant (and 3-firm) equilibrium of figure 10.3, rationalization to achieve greater efficiency is clearly impossible. In this case, oligopoly equilibrium may be unfortunate. But since it is "inevitable," we cannot reasonably regard it as inefficient. This would be the situation, for example, if our three oligopolists could only merge to form a multiplant firm by paying "exorbitant" sums to lawyers, business consultants, and property assessors.

At this point it is tempting to say that many oligopolies in the real world —the Big Three in American automobile production, the Big Two in American can making, etc.—owe their existence to the antitrust laws of the United States which place a constraint on the market shares of large firms. After all, the coordination costs in multiplant operations are not all *that* high in most industries. However, the temptation to attribute oligopoly to the antitrust laws should be resisted, for the moment at any rate.

Our analysis of simple oligopoly has assumed that economic decisions are made on the basis of complete information (this assumption being a foundation of all static economic analysis). In the real world, of course, oligopolists, like other people, must act upon the basis of incomplete information. An oligopolist may know, in a general way, that if he cuts his price by 10 percent, his major rivals will respond with price cuts of their own. But he usually does not know how soon the retaliation will come or how severe it will be.

In a static model, it is fair to posit that the payoff from rationalizing the activities of two inefficiently operated plants can be calculated to as many decimal places as one likes. Therefore, depending on the coordination cost that we specify, rationalization either will—or will not—be undertaken. In the real world, the owners of two plants in the same industry may be unable to agree upon what their properties are worth and so a merger is never carried through. *The Wall Street Journal* regularly carries reports of merger discussions that have been begun and later discontinued.

Oligopoly and imperfect competition

In some treatments of microeconomics, a distinction is made between oligopoly and imperfect competition. Oligopoly is equated with the state where firms are so few that each knows full well that any change of price or output on its own part will provoke some reaction among its rivals. Imperfect competition is equated with the state where (i) firms are few enough that each knows full well that it can affect its own price by varying output but (ii) firms are also so numerous that each one ignores the possible reactions of rivals in setting its own output. Imperfect competition, like oligopoly, assumes that firms are free to enter and leave the industry.

Provided that imperfect competition is treated rigorously, it does not differ from oligopoly in any way that need concern us. A rigorous treatment of imperfect competition is one that explicitly relates the demand faced by the imperfect competitor to the demand curve of the industry to which he belongs. In non-rigorous treatments of imperfect competition, the downward sloping demand curve of the imperfect competitor is simply pulled out of the air. This practice is objectionable for the very good reason that the demand curve of the imperfect competitor will shift whenever any rival firm changes its output.

In imperfect competition, as in oligopoly, the entry and exit of firms will produce an equilibrium where each firm earns a modest economic rent or no economic rent and where each produces an output at which average total cost is falling. In imperfect competition, as in oligopoly, the equilibrium that emerges may—or may not—be economically wasteful. Here again the test is whether the obstacle that prevents rationalization through the emergence of a multiplant firm can be traced to man or nature.

Summary

This chapter has described a model of simple oligopoly. Our analysis has assumed that an industry consists of a small number of firms that produce a homogeneous commodity; that firms are free to enter and leave the industry; and, most important, that each firm (correctly) assumes that any change in its own price or output will immediately be matched by all other firms. We saw that, on these assumptions, an equilibrium will be reached where each firm produces an output at which average total cost is falling. In equilibrium, each firm will earn a modest economic rent or no economic rent at all.

We noted that oligopoly is a stable form of market organization if, and only if, "something" prevents the oligopolists from rationalizing production by merging or joining together to form a profit-sharing cartel. If the barrier to rationalization is man-made and removable without cost, oligopoly is economically wasteful. If the barrier to rationalization is provided by Nature, oligopoly is merely unfortunate. In this chapter we considered only the simplest model of oligopoly. More complex models involving behavior of sellers under conditions of uncertainty are considered in Chapter 16.

REFERENCES

Bronfenbrenner, Martin, "Imperfect Competition on a Long-Run Basis," *Journal of Business,* 23 (1950), 81-93.

Dewey, Donald, *The Theory of Imperfect Competition: A Radical Reconstruction* (New York, 1969), chapters 1, 2, and 4.

Fellner, William, *Competition Among the Few* (New York, 1949), chapter 1.

Machlup, Fritz, *The Economics of Sellers' Competition: Model Analysis of Sellers' Conduct* (Baltimore, 1952), chapters 11 and 15.

Mansfield, Edwin, *Microeconomics: Theory and Applications* (New York, 1970), chapter 11.

Robinson, Joan, *The Economics of Imperfect Competition* (London, 2nd ed., 1969).

APPENDIX TO CHAPTER 10
"MONOPOLISTIC" COMPETITION AND
PRODUCT DIFFERENTIATION

Why economists like homogeneous commodities

So far in this book we have always used economic models which assume that all firms produce and market a homogeneous commodity. We might recall the economist's definition of a homogeneous commodity. By his meaning a commodity is homogeneous if, and only if, every consumer thinks that a unit purchased from one seller will provide him with precisely the same services as a unit purchased from any other seller. The consumer may be mistaken. Bombarded by advertising claims every day of the year, he may come to believe that the commodity offered by one seller is "better" even though a research worker from Consumers' Union, after appropriate chemical and engineering tests, finds that it is no different from the wares of other sellers. Conversely, the consumer, lacking complete information, may assume that the competing products of two sellers have identical properties when an expert buyer could detect real differences. To repeat: two or more sellers produce and market a homogeneous commodity if all consumers think that they are doing so.

We know that in the real world a homogeneous commodity is the exception rather than the rule. Menthol cigarettes differ perceptibly from the non-menthol kind. Five-inch ball point pens are not quite the same thing as four-inch ball point pens. A Swiss watch sold without a money-back guarantee is inferior to an otherwise identical watch sold with this guarantee. Indeed, as a matter of everyday experience, we know that a commodity marketed by one seller almost always differs in some respect from what we loosely term the "same" commodity marketed by another seller. To say the obvious, a bottle of Coca-Cola in the office vending machine is not the same product as the same size bottle of Coca-Cola available in the supermarket at the end of the block.

In economic analysis the usual practice is to ignore "small" commodity differences. When the differences between two "things" are substantial, they are treated as different commodities. Conversely, when these differences are not substantial, the things are treated as the "same" commodity. What constitutes a substantial difference must necessarily be decided in the light of what the investigator wants to do. When the United States Department of Commerce collects statistics on the national production of ball point pens, it has no interest in distinguishing between four-inch and five-inch models. A pen is a pen. But the one-inch difference may be critically important to producers of ball point pens. At the limit, the firm that produces the less popular length for too long may go bankrupt.

There is a perfectly good reason why economists usually ignore small commodity differences. This practice allows us to treat both total revenue and total cost as determined entirely by the rate of output of the "commodity" and hence to use simple two-dimensional diagrams. Once we accept that a commodity can be differentiated by packaging, advertising, quality improvement, or a seller's guarantee—and these are only a few of a vast number of possibilities—very little can be done with conventional geometry. Now both cost and revenue become functions of two or more variables. Any elaborate treatment of product differentiation must make use of calculus and linear algebra.

Rightly or wrongly, most economists have felt that the payoff to be had from a mathematically rigorous treatment of product differentiation is not worth the effort. As a result, in economic analysis product differentiation is usually either ignored ("let us assume a homogeneous commodity") or its existence is acknowledged in literary, folksy asides ("advertising designed to make consumers see differences when none exist is pure economic waste").

Chamberlin's "monopolistic competition"

Nevertheless, for nearly fifty years a dissenting minority view in economics has insisted that product differentiation is so important a method of competition in the real world that it should occupy a central place in economic analysis. The most extreme position was adopted by the late Professor Edward Chamberlin of Harvard, who insisted that his theory of "monopolistic competition"—a competition among large numbers of sellers of similar but differentiated products—was the most important contribution to economic thought in the twentieth century.

By Chamberlin's estimate:

> "Monopolistic competition" is a challenge to the traditional viewpoint of economics that competition and monopoly are alternatives and that individual prices are to be explained in terms of either the one or the other. By contrast, it is held that most economic situations are composites of both competition and monopoly, and that, wherever this is the case, a false view is given by neglecting either one of the forces and regarding the situation as made up entirely (even though "imperfect") of the other.[1]

1. E. H. Chamberlin, *The Theory of Monopolistic Competition* (Cambridge, Mass., 8th ed., 1962), pp. 204-5.

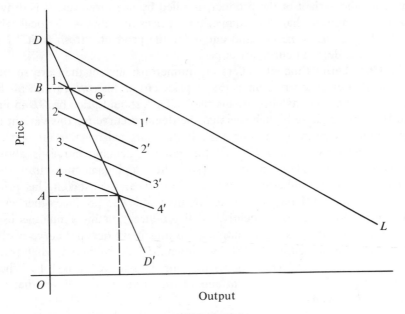

FIGURE 10.5

Unhappily, Chamberlin's rigid and intemperate defense of his ideas provoked a hostile reaction—one so hostile that it regards "monopolistic competition" as a worthless concept.[2]

Most economists (at any rate most economists under age forty) probably believe that the truth lies somewhere between Chamberlin and his critics. However, the controversy over product differentiation has loomed so large in economics in the last fifty years that you should make the acquaintance of the important issues—if only in self-defense.

In Chamberlin's model an industry consists of a large group of firms which produce different varieties of the "product" with each member firm producing a single, unique variant of this product. In figure 10.5 line *DL* gives the quantity demanded for all varieties of the product at different prices. Note that if the product is defined as "fresh fruit," line *DL* necessarily sums up apples, oranges, pears, plums, etc. Line *DD'* is the demand

2. The most intemperate objections to monopolistic competition have come from the "Chicago" school. See, for example, G. J. Stigler, "Monopolistic Competition in Retrospect" in *Five Lectures on Economic Problems* (London, 1949), pp. 12-24; or Milton Friedman, "The Methodology of Positive Economics" in *Essays in Positive Economics* (Chicago, 1953), pp. 38-39.

curve for the variant of the product supplied by one producer. It is drawn on the assumption that "his competitors' prices are always identical with his." Thus if *DL* is the demand curve for the product, "fresh fruit," *DD* could be the demand curve for apples.

In Chamberlin's model, sellers are numerous; in fact they are so numerous that each seller assumes that a price cut on his own variant of the product *will not* be matched by his rivals. Thus should price be *OB* in figure 10.5 the single seller believes that the demand curve for this variant of the product is given by the line 1-1'. If the marginal revenue implied by his demand curve—it is really an "imaginary" demand curve—is above marginal cost, he will expand output (since he is an income maximizer).

However, in Chamberlin's model, the producer is mistaken: his price cuts will, sooner or later, be matched by his rivals who produce other variants of the product. Consequently, as all producers, acting simultaneously or in sequence, increase their outputs, the imaginary demand curve of the single producer in figure 10.5 "slides" down *DD'*. As we noted, when price is *OB,* the single producer believes that his demand curve is 1-1'. When price has fallen to *OA* for all variants of the product, he believes that his demand curve is 4-4'.

One point should be noted here. A postulate that the rival firms produce "differentiated" products is necessary in order to give a negative slope to lines 1-1', 2-2', etc. If the product is homogeneous, then the single producer would behave as if he faced a perfectly elastic demand for his variant of the product. And lines 1-1', 2-2' would be horizontal. Thus in figure 10.5, the angle θ serves as an index of the "degree of product differentiation" in the industry.

The long-run equilibrium of Chamberlin's model is described by figure 10.6—one of the most famous geometrical constructions in the history of economics. When this long-run equilibrium has been reached, three of its features are immediately visible. (1) The imaginary demand curve *dd'* of the single producer is tangent to his curve of average total cost. (2) The single producer has no incentive to change his price *OG* since he thinks that marginal cost is equal to marginal revenue. (3) Since price is equal to average total cost, curve *DD'* is stationary over time; it will not be shifted to the left by the entry of new firms nor to the right by the exit of established firms. We might note that feature #3 depends upon a rather heroic assumption—Chamberlin's premise that all producers have identically shaped curves of average total cost; so that figures 10.5 and 10.6 stand for all producers of differentiated products in the same "industry."

Note that the geometry needed to deal with the case of firms that pro-

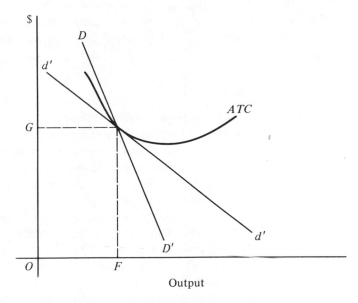

FIGURE 10.6

duce differentiated products, i.e. different variants of the "same" basic product, is much more cumbersome than that needed to handle the case of firms that produce a homogeneous product. For example, in figure 10.5, line *DL* is not fixed in two-dimension space; rather its positioning depends upon the number of differentiated products that are produced by the industry. As additional firms producing additional variants of the same basic product enter into production, *DL* will rotate upward about point *D* (because additional customers are attracted by the additional variety). As this happens, the intercept of *DD′* with the quantity axis moves to the left (since each new producer takes some business away from each established firm).

How does the entry of new firms producing additional variants of the same basic product affect the slopes of the imaginary demand curves 1-1′, 2-2′, etc.? Provided that we adhere strictly to Chamberlin's premise that each producer thinks that a price cut on his part will go unmatched by rivals, the answer is clear. Consumers in general prefer more product variety to less; and the individual consumer prefers a more differentiated product to a less differentiated one. Therefore as product variety increases, it becomes more difficult for the producer of, say, brand X to increase output sold by making a 5 percent price reduction. The slopes of the imaginary demand curves 1-1′, 2-2′, etc., must become steeper as the entry of new firms increases the number of differentiated products available to consumers.

Pitfalls in monopolistic competition

It is clear that, on the assumptions employed by Edward Chamberlin, in equilibrium the firm in monopolistic competition produces where average total cost is falling. But now two questions must be faced. Is Chamberlin's analysis correct? If so, what is the economic significance (if any) of the fact that each monopolistic competitor produces where average total cost is falling? Is such production economically wasteful?

Actually, it is difficult to assign a simple pass or fail grade to Chamberlin's analysis because he never made entirely clear the assumptions on which it rests. In our previous discussion of simple oligopoly with a homogeneous commodity, we have already met the so-called tangency solution. We noted that it could represent stable equilibrium in only one case. This would be where there exists some barrier that prevents the oligopolists from being brought under common central management and their activities rationalized in a way that allows industry output to be produced in the cheapest possible way. If no such barrier exits, then the rationalization of oligopoly is inevitable. It will occur because it will make every oligopolist better off and none worse off.

In our discussion of simple oligopoly, we also learned another truth. When some barrier to rationalization makes oligopoly stable, the goodness or badness of this equilibrium depends upon the nature of the barrier. If the barrier is some silly, man-made rule that prevents mergers, oligopoly is bad. (In New York State, the cost of liquor is higher than need be because state law says that liquor can only be sold in small shops that sell nothing else.) If the barrier is imposed by Nature in the form of unavoidable contract costs, oligopoly is, if not good, at any rate inevitable.

Virtually the same line of reasoning that we applied to oligopoly can be used on Chamberlin's monopolistic competition. In simple oligopoly, all firms were presumed to produce a homogeneous commodity and to have the same production function in the plant; so that the production function itself could not constitute the barrier that prevents rationalization. In Chamberlin's monopolistic competition, differentiated products are produced; and hence the production functions are, by definition, also differentiated.

Does it follow that the fact that each differentiated commodity has a production function peculiar to itself constitutes a barrier to rationalization? The answer is: not necessarily. Consider the case of, say, bubble gum. Peppermint-flavored sticks and cherry-flavored sticks are the same product except for the flavoring imparted to the basic gum at some stage in the production process. Both types are produced with the same fixed investment—machines, skilled workers, warehouses, etc. Expenditures on flavoring fluids to differentiate gum are variable costs. There is no reason to believe that gum will be produced where average total cost is falling simply because the industry produces different flavors. (This proposition would be falsified, of course, if trade secrecy or the patent laws prevented one firm from producing the money-making flavors of its rivals.)

It follows that if the cost of differentiating a commodity from its close substitutes is to constitute a barrier to efficient production, this cost must be a fixed cost. The technology used to manufacture an air-cooled automobile engine is significantly different from that used to manufacture a water-cooled automobile engine. Each type requires its own specialized tools and dies. Hence if the economy produces both types of engine, it is possible that each type will be produced in a plant where average total cost is falling.

Can we say that the existence of two such plants, one producing air-cooled engines and the other producing a water-cooled model, is evidence of "excess capacity"? Obviously not. An economic dictator might feel that the economy would be better off if only one type of engine were offered to consumers. But providing that there is no cheaper way to produce the particular mix of air-cooled and water-cooled engines that is offered on the market, there is no excess capacity. And since consumers, acting through the market, have chosen to have both types when they could have settled for either one engine or the other at a lower price, there is no loss of economic welfare.

Summary

To sum up: Microeconomic analysis most of the time assumes that an industry consists of firms that produce a homogeneous commodity. Analysis is immensely simplified when this assumption is made. Still, there is no insuperable objection to defining an industry as the set of firms that produce similar but differentiated commodities.

At one time, under the influence of the late Edward Chamberlin, it was widely believed that product differentiation was a form of economic waste enforced by the process of monopolistic competition. But now most economists know better. Product differentiation will *not necessarily* cause commodities to be produced where average total cost is falling. Even if product differentiation does impose this result, it does not follow that the industry is economically wasteful. In short, Chamberlin's claim that the concept of monopolistic competition—competition with differentiated products—is a revolutionary idea in economics must be doubted. But there is no reason to deny that, in the study of certain industries, e.g. soap flakes, book publishing, women's fashions, it is a very useful idea.

REFERENCES

Archibald, G. C., "Chamberlin versus Chicago," *Review of Economic Studies*, 29, 1 (1961), 2-28.
Chamberlin, E. H., *The Theory of Monopolistic Competition* (Cambridge, Mass., 8th ed., 1962).
Chamberlin, E. H., "The Chicago School" in *Towards a More General Theory of Value* (New York, 1957), pp. 296-306.
Dewey, Donald, *The Theory of Imperfect Competition: A Radical Reconstruction* (New York, 1969), chapter 5.
Machlup, Fritz, *The Economics of Sellers' Competition: Model Analysis of Sellers' Competition* (Baltimore, 1952), chapters 5 and 6.
Samuelson, P. A., "The Monopolistic Competition Revolution Revisited" in *Monopolistic Competition Theory: Studies in Impact*, R. E. Kuenne, ed. (New York, 1967).

11

Interest, Capital, and Capitalization

Interest and time

The production of anything—consumer good, capital good, work of art, or a child—takes time. But so far our survey of microeconomics has recognized the importance of time in production in only one connection. In our discussion of cost (Chapter 5) we distinguished between the short run and the long run. The short run we equated with the period of time during which the capital stock—the stock of specialized men and machines used in production—is fixed. The long run we equated with the longer period of time during which this stock can be increased by net investment or decreased by not replacing individual items in the capital stock as they wear out. Unhappily, the role of time in production cannot be disposed of merely by making the distinction between short run and long run. Because production takes time, we must always reckon with the rate of interest.

No idea of comparable importance in economics is so cavalierly treated as the rate of interest. This is probably because the study of interest belongs to capital theory which many economists with good reason regard as the most difficult branch of economics. Capital theory is systematically studied only at the graduate level in economics (and not always there).

Some attention, of course, is paid to the rate of interest in courses on money and banking, national income analysis, and monetary theory; but, for our purposes, this attention is often a doubtful blessing. In these macroeconomic courses, one is likely to come away with the impression that the rate of interest is a "tool of monetary policy" to be raised or lowered by the Central Bank in accordance with its game plan for achieving economic stability and/or the right rate of economic growth. No economist doubts that the Central Bank (which in the United States is the Federal Reserve System) can by vigorous action—most notably by suddenly changing the money supply or the re-discount rate—appreciably affect the rate of inter- est in the short run. How much influence the Central Bank can have on the rate of interest in the long run is a matter of much controversy. And not a few economists view its long-run influence as quite small if only because, in the older industrialized countries of the world, interest rates have been remarkably constant over a period of at least 250 years, seldom going be- low 3 percent or above 6 percent on government bonds. In any event, the phenomenon of interest is far older than any surviving Central Bank.

Over the years much ingenuity has been employed in economics in an effort to answer a simple question: why is interest paid? We can easily think of a number of good reasons why interest may be paid. The prob- lem is to find the reason why it is, in fact, paid. Consider two plausible but really unsatisfactory explanations of interest.

Many writers have stressed that a present income is certain whereas an income due next year is necessarily uncertain; the debtor may default, in- flation may destroy some of the purchasing power of the income due to the creditor, or the creditor may die in the interval. Hence they reason that nobody in his right mind will loan $100 to somebody else for a year un- less he is promised more than $100 at the year's end. By this view, inter- est is a risk premium.

Other writers have pointed out that money, virtually by definition, is the most liquid of all economic assets; so that we will not exchange money and its convenience for somebody's IOU payable in the future (stocks, bonds, mortgages, promissory notes are all IOU's) unless we can collect interest. By this view, interest is "payment for parting with liquidity."

It is true that, other things being equal, high-risk investments promise higher rates of return than low-risk investments. And IOU's which can easily be resold, e.g. United States Government bonds as opposed to Lost River County bonds, carry lower rates of return than less liquid IOU's. Nevertheless, in the real world, it is also possible to earn interest without incurring any significant risk or parting with any significant liquidity. You could, for example, buy United States Government bonds which are to be redeemed in the very near future.

Suppose that today you pay a bond trader $1000 for a bond which will be redeemed by the Government one week from today for $1001. You earn the weekly rate of interest of $1/$1000 or 0.001. This is equivalent to an annual rate of interest of 0.001×52 or 0.052. This type of transaction is used mainly by company treasurers who wish to keep part of their firm's assets in highly liquid form without forgoing interest. Individuals can generally get all of the liquidity and security they wish while earning interest by putting income into savings deposits. Some economists even insist that savings deposits should be treated as part of the money supply. (Recall that the money supply is usually defined as cash outside the banks plus demand deposits.)

In short, on every loan contract (IOU), after an allowance is made for a risk premium and payment for parting with liquidity, something remains. What is this "pure" interest payment for? To answer this question we must dip at least one toe in the dark waters of capital theory.

The marginal productivity of investment

In your first course in economics you learned to distinguish between consumption and investment. When all of income is consumed, the stock of capital goods remain the same size, as some items in the capital stock wear out each year and are replaced. When on rare occasions consumption is greater than income (this happened in the United States in 1933— the worst year of the Great Depression) not all of the capital goods which wear out are replaced. That is, the economy "disinvests." But in most years, the economy is characterized by "net investment." It invests (does not consume) some part of its income and the stock of capital goods grows. Therefore, beginning at some time in the future, the economy will have a greater income. In the language of capital theory, "capital is productive" because by not consuming income "now" in order to build capital goods, the economy can have more income "later."

Let ΔI denote an increment of income that is invested and ΔY the income that results from ΔI. Then $\Delta Y / \Delta I$ is the marginal productivity of investment in capital goods and an absolutely basic concept in economic analysis. Indeed, the fundamental theorem of interest states that:

    T11.1 Suppose that future events can be known with perfect certainty and capital goods and IOU's can be freely exchanged. Then the marginal productivity of investment in capital goods is always equal to the rate of interest on IOU's.

While there is a perfectly simple explanation of why the marginal productivity of investment must equal the rate of interest in a static economic model, it is often so cryptically expressed that it is not always grasped. So let us travel slowly at this point. To make clear the meaning of theorem

T11.1 we can invoke the aid of a famous pedagogical device—the Crusonia plant of Frank Knight. The Crusonia plant is the ultimate simplification in capital theory. Before Knight, many writers had attempted to illustrate the process of capital accumulation by having Robinson Crusoe, marooned on his island, increase his catch of fish first by sharpening a stick and then by building more sophisticated capital goods—a net, raft, boat, etc. Knight decided to go all the way in abstraction by assuming a kind of vegetation that supplies all human wants—the Crusonia plant.

Suppose that, when no part of the all-purpose Crusonia plant is consumed, it grows at a constant geometric rate—say 10 percent a year. Suppose further that everybody has his own particular Crusonia plant. In this example, the marginal productivity of investment is, of course, 10 percent a year. Should the owner of a 100 unit Crusonia plant allow it to grow for one year without any consumption, it will be a 110 unit plant at the end of the year. Thus the annual income of a 100 unit Crusonia plant is 10 units of Crusonia. Should the owner treat himself to an orgy once a year in which 10 units are consumed, a 100 unit plant will yield an annual income of 10 units of Crusonia "forever."

At the start of orgy day, the Crusonia plant stands at 110 units. Of this amount 10 units represents last year's income. Now our plant owner is in a position to trade off present consumption for more income in the future. Let him consume 9 units of last year's income on orgy day and invest (not consume) 1 unit. Then when orgy day comes around next year he will have a Crusonia plant of 111.10 units. In this example $\Delta I = 1$, $\Delta Y = 0.10$, and $\Delta Y/\Delta I = 0.10$.

On orgy day the plant owner could, of course, choose to invest more than 1 unit of last year's income. But a given condition of the problem is that the Crusonia plant, when not consumed grows at a constant rate of 10 percent a year; thus $\Delta Y/\Delta I = 0.10$ regardless of the amount of income invested. This is the case of "constant returns to investment."

When everybody has his own private Crusonia plant, there is no incentive to borrow or lend Crusonia. All we can say is that if any loan transaction does take place, it will be at an interest rate of 10 percent a year. This has to be true. Nobody will loan Crusonia for less than 10 percent a year. For if he wishes to add to his capital stock, he can do so by investing (i.e. not consuming) part of his income. But then nobody will pay more than 10 percent a year to borrow Crusonia. It would be cheaper for him to borrow from himself by consuming part of his income and, if necessary, part of his capital as well.

Because "capital is productive" everyone who (a) receives an income and (b) wishes to exhange a given amount of income "now" for more income "later" has two alternatives. He can set up shop as a money lender by buying other people's IOU's. Or he can invest his income directly, i.e. build capital goods. Unhappily, the complexity of the modern economic world conspires to disguise the existence of these two fundamental choices. Most of us do not become money lenders by becoming the loan shark of the office, barracks, or dormitory. Rather we become money lenders by putting our money in banks or buying stock in the Friendly Personal Finance Company. Nor do we not invest income directly by setting up a widget factory. We buy a part of a new stock issue of Acme Foundry or General Motors which then uses the proceeds to expand plant capacity.

Still, the fact remains that, for everyone who receives an income, buying other people's IOU's and building capital goods are alternative ways of increasing income over time. And arbitrage is always at work to make the return on direct investment equal to the rate of interest on IOU's of comparable risk and liquidity. In the static model we can forget about risk and liquidity and assert the truth of theorem T11.1. When future events can be known with perfect certainty, the marginal productivity of investment in capital assets is equal to the rate of interest.

In the uncertainty-plagued capital markets of the real world, there are a vast number of IOU's available for purchase. And they differ greatly both in the nominal rates of return that they promise and the credit ratings assigned to them by investors' services. Nevertheless, all of the interest rates of the real world are linked together by arbitrage. Ordinarily, United States Government bonds carry a lower yield than the bonds of private corporations because they are regarded by most people as both safer and more liquid. And when the yield on government bonds goes up, the yield on private bonds will also go up by the amount necessary to maintain what the bond market regards as the "right" differential. Hence economists in discussing the capital markets of the real world often talk in terms of *the* rate of interest instead of using the more accurate but more cumbersome phrase, the *set* of interest rates.

In microeconomic analysis the existence of an interest rate is important for two reasons above all others. First, it means that since all production takes time, an interest charge is always a part of cost of production. Second, it means that a stream of future income payments can be converted into a present market value. Indeed, we can go further and say: because the rate of interest "exists" a stream of future income payment *will* be converted into a present market value. That is, a stream of future income payments will be discounted at the rate of interest.

Three examples of discount

Consider the simplest problem of discount. Suppose that when the rate of interest per year is i, you have the chance to buy a gilt-edged IOU (say one co-signed by Nelson Rockefeller). The transaction will allow you to collect the sum Y_1 in exchange for this IOU one year from today. How much should you pay today for this IOU? To answer this question, simply ask: what sum V_1 would I have to invest today at i rate of interest per year in order to have Y_1 in one year's time? Since

$$V_1 + iV_1 = Y_1 \tag{11.1}$$

we have

$$V_1 = Y_1/(1+i). \tag{11.1a}$$

Now take a slightly more complicated problem of discount. The rate of interest per year is still i. But now you have a chance to buy a gilt-edged IOU that will pay you the sum Y_2 at the end of 2 years. (In this second example you get nothing at the end of the first year.) Again we ask: how much should you pay to buy the IOU. Again, we obtain an answer by finding V_2—the sum that, if invested at i rate of interest per year for 2 years, would grow to Y_2. Since

$$V_2 + iV_2 + i(V_2 + iV_2) = Y_2 \tag{11.2}$$

we have

$$V_2 = Y_2/(1+i)^2. \tag{11.2a}$$

Note that in the first year you earn interest only on the original principal; whereas in the second year you earn interest on the original principal *and* the interest earned during the first year.

Suppose that, when the rate of interest per year is i, you can buy a gilt-edge IOU that will pay you Y_1 at the end of one year and Y_2 at the end of the second year. Clearly, to buy this IOU you would pay an amount equal to the sum of its discounted future incomes, that is, an amount equal to $Y_1/(1 + i) + Y_2/(1 + i)^2$.

The perpetuity

One of the most useful notions in capital theory is that of the perpetual income or perpetuity—the income that goes on forever. Let an IOU promise an income of Y dollars every year for n years when the annual rate of interest is i. The present value of V_n of this IOU is given by

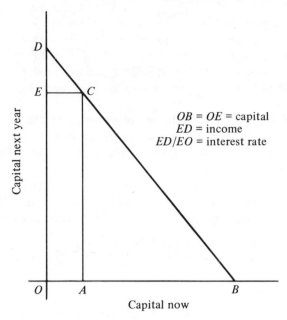

$OB = OE$ = capital
ED = income
ED/EO = interest rate

FIGURE 11.1

$$V_n = Y_1/(1+i) + Y_2/(1+i)^2 \ldots + Y_n/(1+i)^n. \tag{11.3}$$

When *n* goes to infinity, equation 11.3 can be written as

$$\operatorname*{Lim}_{n \to \infty} V_n = Y/i \tag{11.4}$$

or, for convenience, as simply

$$V = Y/i. \tag{11.4a}$$

We can enlist the aid of simple geometry to show why the present value of a perpetuity must equal its annual income divided by the rate of interest. In figure 11.1, OB gives the size of the capital stock "now." OD shows what the size of the capital stock will be one year from today if OB is invested for the whole year. In figure 11.1, $OE = OB$. Hence, $OD - OE$ or DE is the annual income of the capital stock OB. And the rate of interest (or marginal productivity of investment) is DE/OE.

If we divide annual income by the rate of interest the result is $DE \div (DE/OE)$ or OE. As we already knew, $OE = OB$.

In this connection, we might note that perpetuities really do exist in the real world. Many years ago (in the eighteenth century in fact) the British government began to sell bonds ("consols") of no face value. They simply obligate the government to pay to the owner a fixed sum each year presumably forever. Again, the preferred stock of a well-managed corporation is close to a perpetuity since it will pay a fixed annual income so long as nothing terrible (such as revolution or bankruptcy) happens to the corporation.

Still, in the real world perpetuities are rather rare. The important truth for our purposes is that every income stream of finite length has a perpetuity equivalent. For this reason, *every* investment can be viewed as an income in perpetuity.

Let an IOU promise to pay $100 at the end of the first year and another $100 at the end of the second year. Let the annual rate of interest i be 0.04. Then the present discounted value V of this income stream is

$$V = \$100/(1.04) + \$100/(1.04)^2 \qquad (11.5)$$

or

$$V = \$188.74 \qquad (11.5a)$$

There is a perpetual income N which has the same value as V. Since $V = N/i$, we have

$$N = \$188.74 \times 0.04 \qquad (11.6)$$

or

$$N = \$7.55. \qquad (11.6a)$$

Earlier in our discussion of interest we noted that when IOU's and capital goods can be freely traded in a market, not only *can* every stream of future income be discounted. Every stream of future income *will* be discounted. Moreover, every change in *expected* future income will, as soon as it is perceived, be immediately registered as a change in the present value of the income stream. This is the capitalization process. And no economist, investor, or public official can afford to forget its ubiquity in the real world.

Three examples of capitalization

A widow, aged 70 years, on the advice of an incompetent broker puts her entire estate into preferred stocks. She makes this investment when the rate of interest is 5 percent and so is able to obtain a portfolio of preferred stock which will pay dividends that total $2500 each year. The widow cannot live on her dividends; so, not planning to live beyond age 85 years, she plans to sell off $4000 worth of stock each year. If all goes as she planned, she will die nearly (but not quite) broke.

Immediately after the widow buys her preferred stock, the Federal Reserve System decides to fight inflation by putting the rate of interest up to 10 percent per year. This move spells disaster for the widow. True, she will still get the annual income promised by her preferred stocks; thus, in the first year; she will get $2500 in dividends. But now the present value of her future dividends is given not by $2500/0.05 but by $2500/0.10. Hence when the rate of interest goes from 5 percent to 10 percent, the value of the widow's portfolio falls from $50,000 to $25,000. If the Federal Reserve does not put the rate of interest back to 5 percent very soon or, if the widow does not die, she will be on welfare in a very few years.

A farmer makes an income after tax of $500 a year by cultivating his north forty acres. In order to improve the substandard local schools, his property tax is increased with the result that his net income falls to $495 from cultivation of this tract. Surely, no right thinking farmer will begrudge his impoverished local schools a mere 1 percent of his net income on the north forty acres. Or will he?

When the rate of interest is 5 percent, the value of the north forty is $500/0.05 before the tax increase. It is $495/0.05 after the tax increase. Thus, as a result of the modest rise in the property tax the value of the acreage falls from $10,000 to $9,900.

Moreover, the farmer pays the tax increase not while he owns the land but "for all time." A potential buyer, knowing of the tax, will not offer more than $9,900 for the property because, if he did so, he would not get a 5 percent rate of return. In the jargon of tax specialists, the tax has been "capitalized back" on the party who owns the property when the tax is first levied.

River City for fifty years has allowed only 100 taxicabs to operate on its streets, taxicab permits being transferable property rights. The only way that you can operate a taxicab in River City is by buying a permit from somebody who has one of the 100 permits outstanding. A cab with permit can be purchased for $21,000. Since by a generous estimate a secondhand cab is worth no more than $1000, $20,000 of this price is capitalized monopoly rent. If the rate of interest is 5 percent per year, this means that the market has valued the monopoly rent at $20,000 × 0.05 or $1000 a year.

A mysterious virus—call it free market fever—suddenly attacks the local politicians and the city council of River City votes to abolish all restrictions on the taxicab industry that have nothing to do with health and safety. As a result, a man who worked for 25 years in order to earn the $21,000 needed to buy a cab with permit finds that his investment has shrunk to a $1000 beat-up hack. He has been literally wiped out by the council's action.

We can generalize his fate. In the real world, the only people who profit from monopoly are those who get in on the ground floor. Johnny-come-lately's must buy their monopoly rents in a free market and hence must settle for a normal rate of return. But generally it is the Johnny-come-lately's who must bear the burden of any effort to "eliminate monopoly." For this reason, responsible governments are very loath to attack monopoly of long standing. Such monopoly has, in effect, been made respectable by the passing of time.

Rent and cost

The existence of an interest rate makes possible the capitalization of expected changes in future income. Such capitalization can seemingly do strange things to the cost functions of firms. In microeconomics, cost is defined to include only those outlays that are necessary to attract into industry resources needed for production. By this definition any rent or profit earned by the firm is not a part of cost. To accountants, statisticians, and econometricians, however, cost is defined to include all outlays that the firm must make in order to produce its output. Thus, their definition of cost includes expenses that microeconomics regards as economic rent. Indeed, the following generalization is justified. With the passing of time, the control of property changes hands by sale or lease. As these transactions occur, the usual system of cost accounting converts the rent realized by the original owners of the property into the fixed costs of later owners or lessees.

More specifically, as the control of property changes hands by sale or lease, two bookkeeping phenomena can be observed. First, average total cost *as defined by accountants* increases until it absorbs *all* rent. Second, the slope of the curve of average total cost *as defined by accountants* also changes. The way in which rent is capitalized into accounting cost is illustrated by figures 11.2 and 11.3.

Let figure 11.2 stand for the case of a Kansas wheat farmer who, in the 1880's pre-empted from the public domain an exceptionally fertile piece of wheat land. He farms his land to produce a commodity that is sold in a perfectly competitive market; and he maximizes economic rent by selling

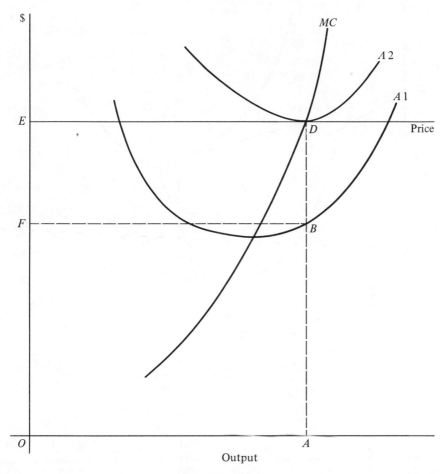

FIGURE 11.2

OA units at price *OE*. As figure 11.2 indicates, the original homesteader's ATC curve is *A*1. And he earns the rent *FBDE*. His marginal cost curve is labelled MC.

Now let the original homesteader lease his land to a tenant. The tenant will presumably be charged a rental equal to *FBDE;* so that, to the tenant, *FBDE* is a fixed cost of farming. Thus, when the tenant takes over cultivation of the land, his ATC curve is given by *A*2—the curve into which the original homesteader's rent has been capitalized.

In figure 11.2 note that capitalization appears to have changed the

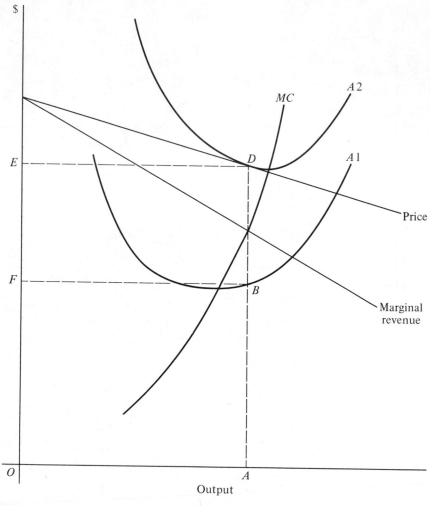

FIGURE 11.3

shape as well as the height of the ATC curve. When one looks at curve *A*1, the output of *OA* units is produced where average total cost is rising. When one looks at curve *A*2, the output of *OA* units is produced where average total cost is at a minimum. The moral is this. If one looks only at accounting data, most firms in perfectly competitive industries will appear to be operating at their optimum output. Note also that the capitalization of rent, since it creates a new fixed cost, has no effect whatsoever on variable cost and hence no effect on marginal cost.

Let figure 11.3 stand for the case of the electric power company that, in the 1890's obtained a perpetual and exclusive franchise to serve a small Kansas town. The original holder of the franchise has the ATC curve *A*1. Equating marginal cost to marginal revenue (we assume that this monopolist cannot practice price discrimination) he earns the monopoly rent *FBDE*. Now let the franchise be leased to a syndicate of latecomers. They must, of course, pay an annual rental of *FBDE* and so acquire the ATC curve *A*2 into which the monopoly rent of the original franchise owner has been capitalized.

Once again we observe that the capitalization of rent has changed the shape of the ATC curve. When the ATC curve is *A*1, at an output of *OA* units average total cost is rising. When the ATC curve is *A*2, at an output of *OA* average total cost is falling; and the firm appears to have excess capacity. The moral in this case? It is simply that, if one looks only at accounting data, most monopolies appear to be "decreasing cost" enterprises.

We are now in a position to set down a most useful theorem about average total cost.

T11.2 Let cost be defined to include all expenses that the firm must incur to produce its output. Then it is in the nature of average total cost, so defined, to equal average total revenue.

The proof of theorem 11.2 is virtually trivial. (Triviality of the proof does not, however, mean that the theorem is unimportant or that its truth is self-evident.) When resources are free to enter and leave an industry, a movement of resources will tend to remove any difference between average total cost and average total revenue. Resources will leave industries where losses are made and enter industries where profits are made. When resources are not free to move, any difference between average total cost and average total revenue will be capitalized. Whn ATC exceeds ATR, the ATC curve will move up; and when ATC is less than ATR, the ATC curve will move down.

Obviously "cost" means one thing to an economic theorist and something else to an accountant, statistician, or econometrician. All can agree that "cost is the sacrifice of alternatives," but there remains the question: whose alternatives are being sacrificed? We cannot say one viewpoint is "better" than others. We can only avoid confusion by recognizing that different viewpoints imply different definitions of average total cost.

Summary

In the real world, income can be increased, beginning at some time in the future, if some part of current income is used to build additional capital goods. Therefore, anyone who wishes to increase his income over time has two possible choices. He can build capital goods; or he can buy the interest-bearing IOU's of other people. Abritrage between the market for IOU's and the market for capital goods links the set of interest rates to the set of investment returns. In a static model where all assets are equally "liquid" and totally safe, there is only one rate of interest and only one rate of return on capital goods construction. In such a model arbitrage ensures that the marginal productivity of investment in capital goods is equal to the rate of interest.

The "productivity of capital" ensures the existence of an interest rate which, in turn, ensures that all economic rents will be capitalized. In fact, any difference between total revenue and total cost that cannot be capitalized is, by definition, not an economic rent. It is only a temporary profit or loss which the market believes will soon disappear. When all economic rents have been fully capitalized into cost curves, a firm operating in a perfectly competitive industry will appear to be producing at the minimum point on its ATC curve; whereas, a monopolist will appear to be producing where ATC is falling. In both cases, the ATC curve has been shifted by capitalization to a point of tangency with the AR curve.

REFERENCES

Alchian, A. A., and W. R. Allen, *University Economics* (Belmont, Calif., 2nd ed., 1967), chapter 13.

Dewey, Donald, *Modern Capital Theory* (New York, 1965), chapters 2, 3, and 4.

Fisher, Irving, *The Theory of Interest* (New York, 1930).

Friedman, Milton, *Price Theory: A Provisional Test* (Chicago, 1962), chapter 13.

Hirshleifer, Jack, *Investment, Interest, and Capital* (Englewood Cliffs, N.J., 1970), chapters 1, 2, 3, and 4.

Stigler, G. J., *The Theory of Price* (New York, 3d ed., 1966), chapters 15 and 17.

12
The Pricing of Factor Inputs

The derived demand for factor inputs

So far our concern has been mainly with the production and distribution of *final* products—those commodities which directly satisfy the needs (real or imagined) of consumers. We have assumed that producers of final products know how to combine the inputs of factors used in production in a way that minimizes the total cost of producing whatever output they wish to produce. We should, however, pause now to pay some attention to the forces which determine the supply of and demand for factor inputs. After all, the vast majority of people in this world obtain most of their incomes by renting out the factors that they own—that is, by selling the services of the factors that they own. Indeed, the sale of the services of one factor—labor—accounts for over three-fourths of all income received by American families each year. Labor income is equally important in most other industrially advanced countries. An eloquent bit of rhetoric in the Clayton Act (1914) which conferred a partial exemption from the antitrust laws on labor unions and agricultural cooperatives declared that "labor is not a commodity." But, of course, anything which is bought and sold in a market is a commodity and, by this test, the services of labor are certainly commodities. Presumably the authors of the Clayton Act wished to convey that people who sell labor services should be entitled to more "protection" from the law than people who provide other factor inputs in the production process.

Quotation marks enclosing "protection" are used because restrictions on the sale of labor services that benefit some workers usually harm other workers. Thus many states once had laws prohibiting the employment of women in certain jobs in order to protect their health and morals. No doubt these laws over the years did save some especially vulnerable women from dangerous machines and wily procurers but only by restricting the employment opportunities of other women who neither needed nor desired such protection. (Most state laws designed expressly for the protection of women have been rendered void by the Federal Civil Rights Act of 1964.)

Markets for factor inputs differ from the markets for final products in one important way. The demand for a factor input is derived from the demand for the products which the factor input can be used to produce. Nobody wants a ton of steel sitting around the house even as a conversation piece. We can, however, think of a great number of useful objects into which a ton of steel can be fashioned. The demand for a factor input can be derived directly from the demand for the final product when it directly produces the final product. Thus the demand of a barber shop owner for the services of journeymen barbers is directly derived from the demand for haircuts. But in the case of machinists who make the barber chairs that barbers use, the demand for their labor is only indirectly derived from the demand for haircuts. Fortunately, all we need to know about derived demand can be gained by examining the case where the demand for a factor input is derived directly from the demand for a final product.

A word on terminology is advisable before we move on. In this chapter our concern is with the pricing of factor inputs (services) and not with factor pricing. Why the verbal inelegance? The more awkward usage is justified because the difference is real. Factor pricing is, strictly speaking, a part, indeed the major part, of capital theory. An acre of farm land is an undoubted factor of production. In this chapter our concern is not with the determination of the market value of this acre but rather with the price that must be paid for its use during some interval of time.

Demand for a single variable factor input

Let us begin with the simplest case. We assume that

      A12.1 The firm both sells its final product in a perfectly competitive market and buys its factor inputs in a perfectly competitive market.

Let us use x to denote the output of the final product that is produced; p to denote the price of the final product. Let $MPP_1, MPP_2, \ldots MPP_n$ denote the marginal physical products of the inputs of factors, 1, 2, . . . n. The marginal physical product of a factor input is, of course, simply the amount by which the output of the final product is increased when (i) the amount of factor input is increased by one unit and (ii) the amount of every other factor input used to produce the final product remains unchanged. Finally, let w_1, w_2, . . . w_n denote the prices at which the inputs of factors 1, 2 . . . n can be hired.

We can now identify two conditions that must be satisfied if our firm (which, to repeat, both sells its final product in a perfectly competitive market and hires its factor inputs in perfectly competitive markets) is to maximize income.

$$\frac{MPP_1}{w_1} = \frac{MPP_2}{w_2} \cdots = \frac{MPP_n}{w_n} \tag{C1}$$

$$\left.\begin{array}{l} MPP_1 \times p_x = w_1 \\[4pt] MPP_2 \times p_x = w_2 \\ \quad \cdot \\ \quad \cdot \\ \quad \cdot \\ MPP_n \times p_x = w_n \end{array}\right\} \tag{C2}$$

The necessity that condition C1 be satisfied if income is to be maximized is virtually self-evident. Suppose that

$$MPP_1/w_1 > MPP_2/w_2.$$

Then clearly one dollar spent on inputs of factor #1 increases the output of commodity x by more than does a dollar spent on inputs of factor #2. The firm can increase its amount of physical output per dollar of expenditure by hiring more of factor #1 and less of factor #2. But as the firm changes the proportion of its two factor inputs in this way, MPP_1 will fall and MPP_2 will rise. When the ratio of the two factor inputs is such that $MPP_1/w_1 = MPP_2/w_2$, a dollar spent on each factor yields the same amount of physical output per dollar of expenditure. The firm no longer has an incentive to change the ratio of the two factor inputs.

Suppose that condition C2 is not satisfied because

$$MPP_1 \times p_x > w_1$$

Then by hiring the last (marginal) unit of factor #1 the firm has added more to its total revenue than to its total cost. For the addition to total revenue is $MPP_1 \times p_x$ while the addition to total cost is w_1. The firm can increase its income by hiring yet another unit of factor #1. But the law of variable proportions is not mocked. As more of factor #1 is hired (the amount of the other factors hired remaining the same), MPP_1 will fall.

Since the firm hires its factors in a perfectly competitive market by assumption A12.1, w_1—the price of an input of factor #1—does not change. The firm will continue to hire units of factor #1 until

$$MPP_1 \times p_x = w_1$$

When this equality is established, the firm cannot further increase its income by hiring additional units of factor #1.

Now let us go to the other extreme and assume that initially $MPP_1 \times p_x < w_1$. Clearly the firm is failing to maximize its income because it is spending too much on inputs of factor #1. It will move to correct its mistake by reducing the amount of factor #1 hired. As this happens, MPP_1 will rise until, finally, $MMP_1 \times p_x = w_1$. When this equality is established, the firm has no incentive to reduce further the amount of factor #1 hired.

When conditions C1 and C2 are both satisfied—that is, when the firm has maximized income—each term in condition C1 can be written as $1/p_x$. This is true since, by condition C2, $MPP_1 \times p_x = w_1$, $MPP_2 \times p_x = w_2$, ... $MPP_n \times p_x = w_n$. We can substitute for the w's in condition C1 and simplify. For example, $MP_1/(MP_1 \times p_x) = 1/p_x$. Thus when a firm hires its factors in perfectly competitive markets and sells its final product in a perfectly competitive market, it has maximized income when

$$\frac{MPP_1}{w_1} = \frac{MPP_2}{w_2} \ldots = \frac{MPP_n}{w_n} = \frac{1}{p_x} \tag{C3a}[1]$$

When perfect competition exists in the final product market, the firm that maximizes income will, of course, carry production to the level at which price is equal to marginal cost. Using mc_x to denote the marginal cost of the final product we can rewrite condition on C3a as

$$\frac{MPP_1}{w_1} = \frac{MPP_2}{w_2} \ldots = \frac{MPP_n}{w_n} = \frac{1}{mc_x} \tag{C3b}[2]$$

1. Mathematically, MMP_1 is simply the first partial derivative of total output with respect to inputs of factor #1, MMP_2 the first partial derivative of total output with respect to inputs of factor #2, etc.

Let the firm's production function be given by the continuous function, $x = \phi(q_1, q_2, \ldots q_n)$ where x is output of final product and $q_1, q_2, \ldots q_n$ the amounts of factor inputs $1, 2, \ldots n$ used by the firm. Then, given perfect competition in the markets for final product and factor inputs, the conditions for an equilibrium that maximizes the firm's income can be written as

$$\frac{\partial x}{\partial q_1} \bigg/ w_1 = \frac{\partial x}{\partial q_2} \bigg/ w_2 \ldots = \frac{\partial x}{\partial q_n} \bigg/ w_n = \frac{1}{p_x}$$

2. The truth that, given perfect competition in the markets for factor inputs and final products, income is maximized for the firm when condition C.3b is satisfied can also be demonstrated as follows.

Demand for a factor input with several inputs variable

It is true enough that the demand for a factor input is derived from the demand for the final product to whose production it contributes. However, the derivation of the demand curve for a factor input is beset with a number of complications not present in the kind of demand analysis so far encountered in this book. Fortunately, there is one situation in which deriving the demand curve for a factor input is simplicity itself. We shall consider it first.

Suppose that production is carried on with the inputs of two factors,

---

The production function is again given by $x = \phi\ (q_1, q_2, \ldots q_n)$ where x is final product output and $q_1, q_2, \ldots q_n$ the amounts of factor inputs used. To maximize income, the firm must minimize total cost subject to the constraint that x equals some constant x^*. (It does not do the firm any good to minimize total cost by producing zero output.) We therefore form the Lagrangean function

$$L = \sum_{i=1}^{n} w_i\, q_i - [\lambda\phi(q_1, q_2, \ldots q_n) - x^*].$$ (12.1)

In the above function, w_i is the price of the ith factor input; q_i is the amount of the ith factor input; and λ is a Lagrange multiplier. When $\partial L/\partial q_i = 0$, we have

$$w_i = \lambda \frac{\partial\phi}{\partial q_i}$$ (12.1a)

and

$$\frac{1}{\lambda} = \frac{\partial\phi}{\partial q_i} \div w_1$$ (12.1b)

$\partial\phi/\partial q_i$ is, of course, the marginal physical product of the ith factor input. And we can show that λ is equal to the marginal cost of final product output.

Let c denote the total cost of final product output; dc a small change in total cost; and dx a small change in final product output. Now

$$dc = \sum_{i=1}^{n} w_i\, dq_i$$ (12.2)

and

$$dx = \sum_{i=1}^{n} \frac{\partial\phi}{\partial q_i}\, dq_i$$ (12.3)

Marginal cost of final product output is, by definition, dc/dx. Therefore,

$$\frac{dc}{dx} = \frac{\sum_{i=1}^{n} w_i\, dq_i}{\sum_{i=1}^{n} (\partial\phi/\partial q_i)\, dq_i}$$ (12.4)

But from equation 12.1a we know that $w_i = \lambda \frac{\partial\phi}{\partial q_i}$.

Therefore we can substitute for w_i, simplify, and obtain

$$\frac{dc}{dx} = \lambda$$ (12.4a)

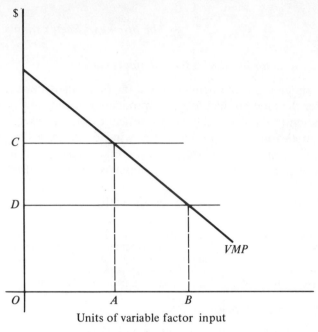

Units of variable factor input

FIGURE 12.1

one of which is fixed and the other variable. The fixed factor input can
be thought of as the services of a highly specialized piece of machinery,
and the variable factor input as the services of unskilled workers who are
hired by the hour.

Let MPP_v denote the marginal physical product of the variable factor
input and p_x the price at which the firm can sell each unit of its final product. Then we may define the value of the marginal physical product of
the variable factor input as the amount by the firm's total revenue is increased when one more unit of the variable factor is hired. Let us use
VMP_v to designate this value. VMP_v is, of course, the same thing as
$MPP_v \times p_x$.

By altering the amount of the variable factor that the firm employs, we
can generate a curve which relates VMP_v to different amounts to the
variable factor employed. This curve must have a negative slope since
MPP_v must decrease (and p_x must remain unchanged) as more units of
the variable factor input are employed. (figure 12.1). The lower the price
at which a unit of variable factor input can be hired, the greater the
quantity of it that will be demanded.

Figure 12.1 indicates two possible equilibria. When the price of a unit
of variable factor input is given by OC, then the firm maximizes income
by hiring OA units of the variable factor. Should the price of a unit of the

variable factor fall to *OD*, the firm would then maximize income by hiring *OB* units of variable factor.

Unhappily, when the firm uses more than one variable factor in the production process, the VMP curve of the variable factor is no longer the firm's demand curve for the input of this factor. For now a change in the price of the input of one variable factor will not only change the amount of this factor that the firm hires; it can also (and usually will) cause a change in the amounts of all other variable factors that the firm hires. This is true even though the prices of all other variable factor inputs remain constant as required by assumption A12.1 (perfect competition).

Consider the case where production is carried on with n variable factors ($n > 1$). Suppose that the price of an input of the *n*th factor falls while the prices of all other factor inputs remain the same. These other factors can be identified as complements, substitutes, or independent of the *n*th factor. If they are complements, the firm will hire more of them as it hires more of the *n*th factor. If they are substitutes, the firm will hire less of them as it hires more of the *n*th factor. And of course, when the amount of another factor that the firm wishes to use is independent of the price of the *n*th factor input, then its demand for such a factor is not affected by its increased use of the *n*th factor.

As the price of an input of factor *n* falls, the firm will hire more of it; this will serve to raise the VMP curves of all factor inputs that complement factor *n*. Why? Simply because each unit of these complementary factors has more units of factor *n* to work with. Therefore, the fall in the price of an input of factor *n* will induce the firm to hire more of the factors that complement factor *n*. But as the firm increases its use of the complementary factors, the VMP curve for factor n is raised; hence the firm is thereby induced to use still more inputs of factor *n*.

To the extent that a fall in the price of an input of factor n causes it to be substituted for another factor, the VMP curves of all other factor inputs (including factor n) are lowered. The firm will ultimately readjust its factor combination in response to the fall in the price of an input of factor n in a way that satisfies the equilibrium conditions C1 and C2. When this has been done, the new VMP curve for factor n will normally be above its old VMP curve. This is because, when the price of a single type of factor input falls, the firm will normally increase its expenditures on complementary factor inputs by more than it reduces its expenditures on substitute factor inputs. After all, most of the factor inputs combined in the typical production function are complements rather than substitutes. For example, if the price of leather were to fall, it is

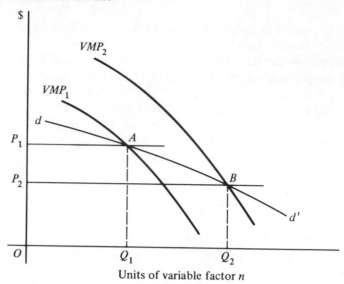

FIGURE 12.2

likely that shoe manufacturers would reduce the price of leather shoes and increase their output. It is easy to see that the increase in shoe output should cause shoe manufacturers to use more labor, shoe machines, office space, shoelaces, etc. It is difficult to think of anything for which leather would be substituted in the production function for leather shoes.

The effect of a fall in the price of an input of a single variable factor when two or more factors are variable is illustrated in figure 12.2. When the price of an input of factor n is OP_1, the VMP curve for inputs of factor n is given by VMP_1. The firm equates VMP to the price of factor inputs by hiring OQ_1 units. Now let the price of inputs of factor n fall to OP_2. And give the firm time enough to readjust its combination of factor inputs in the production function to ensure that its income is maximized. When this readjustment has taken place, the firm has a new VMP curve for inputs of factor n. This new curve is labeled VMP_2 in figure 12.2. And the firm, in its new equilibrium, maximizes income by hiring OQ_2 units of factor n.

In figure 12.2, A and B are two points on the firm's demand curve for inputs of factor n. This curve is dd' in figure 12.2. By lowering the price of inputs by small increments from OP_1 to OP_2 we can locate as many points on the demand curve dd' between A and B as we wish. We see then that when two or more factors are variable, the VMP curve for a single factor input *is not* the firm's demand curve for that factor input. However, the upward shift in the VMP curve that occurs as the price of the single factor input falls (the prices of all other factor inputs remaining unchanged) traces out the firm's demand curve for the inputs of that factor. Thus the firm's demand curve for the inputs of a variable factor is always "flatter" than the VMP curve for the factor input associated with any equilibrium factor combination.

Monopoly and the pricing of factor inputs

So far we have examined the firm's demand for a factor input on the premise that it sells its final product in a perfectly competitive market and buys its factor inputs in perfectly competitive markets. As you have every reason to expect, when the firm does not operate in this environment, it will observe different rules in its effort to maximize income. Let us assume:

A12.2 The firm hires its factor inputs in perfectly competitive markets but sells its final product in a market that it monopolizes.

Given this new assumption, the firm has, of course, a negatively inclined demand curve for its final product. Therefore, to the firm, price is no longer the same thing as marginal revenue. Let us denote the price of the final product by p_x (same notation as before) and its marginal revenue by mr_x. Since the monopolist hires his factors in perfectly competitive markets, he too will wish to arrange production so that

$$\frac{MPP_1}{w_1} = \frac{MPP_2}{w_2} \ldots = \frac{MPP_n}{w_n} \tag{C1}$$

But our monopolist has no interest whatever in ensuring that the price paid for a factor input is equal to its VMP. Rather he will wish to ensure that the price of a factor input is equal to the amount of additional revenue that an extra unit of the factor input adds to his total revenue. That is, when he uses n different factors, the monopolist, in order to maximize income, must arrange production so that

$$MPP_1 \times mr_x = w_1$$
$$MPP_2 \times mr_x = w_2$$
$$\vdots \tag{C4}$$
$$MPP_n \times mr_x = w_n$$

When conditions C1 and C4 are both satisfied—that is, when the monopolist has maximized income—each term in condition C1 can be written as $1/mr_x$ (since $MPP_1 = mr_x \times w_1$ etc.). Thus when the firm hires its factors in perfectly competitive markets but sells its final product in a market that it monopolizes, it maximizes income when

$$\frac{MPP_1}{w_1} = \frac{MPP_2}{w_2} \cdots = \frac{MPP_n}{w_n} = \frac{1}{mr_x} \qquad (C5)$$

When only one factor is variable, we can once again derive the firm's demand curve for the inputs of the variable factor without much difficulty. As we have seen, when MPP_v denotes the marginal physical product of the variable factor and p_x denotes the price at which MPP_v can be sold, the value of the variable factor's marginal physical product is simply $MPP_v \times p_x$. When the firm monopolizes the market in which its final product is sold is different, every increase in the amount of final product placed on the market lowers its price. This is merely another way of stating a truth we have known for some time: a monopolist's price is always greater than his marginal revenue. Thus when an additional unit of variable factor is hired, total revenue from the sale of final product will increase by an amount less than VMP_v. More specifically, when an additional unit of variable factor is hired, total revenue will increase by $MPP_v \times mr_x$. We can call this last magnitude *the marginal revenue product of variable factor input* and denote it MRP_v.

To maximize his income, the monopolist must equate the price that he pays for a unit of variable factor input to its marginal revenue product. That is, he must arrange production so that $MPP_v \times mr_x = w_v$. By changing the amount of the variable factor input employed with a fixed quantity of other factor inputs we can derive a MRP_v curve in the same way that the derived VMP_v curve. When only one factor is variable, the monopolist's MRP_v curve is, of course, his demand curve for the variable factor input. Examine figure 12.3.

When the price of variable factor input is *OC,* the monopolist maximizes income by hiring *OA* units. Should the price of variable factor input fall to *OD,* the monopolist, in the interest of income maximization, would increase his use of variable factor input to *OB.* In figure 12.3 it is apparent that a monopolist will always hire a variable factor at a price which is less than the value of its marginal physical product. This is obviously true: given monopoly power, the VMP$_v$ curve always lies above the MRP$_v$ curve. The inevitable discrepancy between VMP$_v$ and MRP$_v$ in a monopolized market has often led to the charge that a monopolist "exploits" the suppliers of the factors that he hires. The charge is made even more frequently against the firm that has power to affect the prices of the factors that it hires. This is the case where the firm has *monopsony power.* To avoid repetition, we shall examine the meaning of "exploitation" in connection with our discussion of monopsony.

When two or more factor inputs are variable, the MRP curve of a vari-

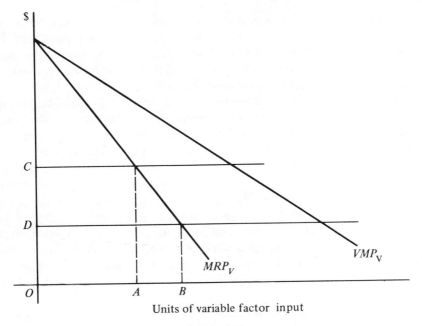

FIGURE 12.3

able factor is not the monopolist's demand curve for inputs of this factor. For, as in the case of perfect competition in which two or more factors are variable, a change in the price of one factor input will induce a change in the amount of other factor inputs used by the firm. This happens, as we have seen, even though the prices of these other factor inputs do not change. Thus a change in the price of one variable factor input ultimately brings about a new factor combination and a new MRP curve for that factor input.

Monopsony and the pricing of factor inputs

In any discussion of the markets for factor inputs, some mention should be made of monopsony.[3] When a seller can force up the price of whatever

3. Strictly speaking, a monopsonist is one who (i) is the only purchaser of a factor input in the market and (ii) does not fear that any economic rent that he earns will draw additional purchasers of that factor input into the market. However, economists usually describe anybody who has monopsony power as a monopsonist and we follow this usage. Having less interest in factor input markets than product markets, economists have not found it necessary to popularize the more accurate term, oligopsonist.

he sells by reducing the amount that he places upon the market, he is regarded as having monopoly power. As we noted in Chapters 6 and 7,
this power to influence price will not give the seller an economic rent unless he also has the power to keep other sellers from entering his market.
Hence the term monopoly power has a misleading connotation.

When a buyer can force down the price of whatever he buys by buying
less, he is regarded as having monopsony power. Here too the fact that
he has monopsony power will not allow him to earn an economic rent unless he also has the power to exclude other buyers from the market. As
we shall presently find, it is by no means certain that monopsony is of
much importance in real-world markets. However, for many years much
discussion of real-world markets (especially labor markets) has been
based upon the assumption that monopsony is an ever-present danger. In
fact, many of the most influential justifications offered for minimum wage
laws and government support for collective bargaining assume that most
labor markets are riddled with monopsony power exercised by employers.
It seems advisable to take a close look at monopsony and some of its
policy implications.

It is possible to imagine monopsony power being present in the market
for final products. (The Great Landlord, for example, might be the only
man for miles around who employs personal servants.) However, monopsony is usually viewed as more likely to occur in the market for factor
inputs. This is because the greater part of national income is organized
through private and public enterprises whose number is far smaller than
that of the persons who supply the factor inputs (mainly labor services)
used in production. For this reason, while monopsony can occur in the
market for any factor input, it is generally discussed in terms of a labor
market; and there is the widespread belief that workers are at a disad-
vantage in their dealings with employers. We shall respect tradition and
discuss monopsony on the assumption that the factor affected is labor.

We first examine monopsony with the aid of the following assumptions.

    A12.3 The firm produces a final product by combining a variable
            labor input with a fixed factor input (capital).

    A12.4 The firm sells its final product in a perfectly competitive mar-
            ket earning neither economic rent nor economic profit.

    A12.5 The firm enjoys monopsony power in the labor market.

In figure 12.4a, the wage that our firm must pay to attract different
quantities of labor is given by line FW. Since FW always has a positive
slope for a monopsonist, the marginal cost of labor to him is always above
the wage that he pays. In figure 12.4a, the marginal cost of labor curve is

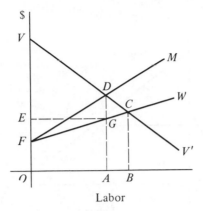

FIGURE 12.4a

the line *FM*. The firm's VMP_v curve is the line VV'. The firm maximizes its income by equating the marginal cost of labor to VMP_v. (Recall that when the final product is sold in a perfectly competitive market, VMP_v is always equal to the marginal revenue product of labor.) Thus in figure 12.4a the firm will employ *OA* units of labor at the wage *OE*. And, when *OA* labor is hired, the wage *OE* is less than the value of labor's marginal product which is *AD*.

Not a few economists are unhappy with any divergence between the wage and VMP_v in a market where the employer has monopsony power. They argue that both consumers and workers are exploited. Consumers are allegedly exploited because too little of the final product is produced. Workers are allegedly exploited because labor is not paid a wage equal to VMP. Hence it is often argued that economic welfare can be increased by labor union pressures and/or minimum wage laws which counteract the monopsony power of employers. Ideally, this pressure, so the argument goes, should be just enough to induce the employer to hire the quantity of labor which makes the wage equal to labor's VMP.

The implication of this argument for public policy is really quite startling. It is that union pressure and/or minimum wage laws can actually increase output and employment, as well as wages, in an industry whose employers have monopsony power in the labor market. But is it so?

Monopsony and labor unions

Suppose that the workers employed by our monopsonist-perfect competitor are organized by a labor union which succeeds in setting a mini-

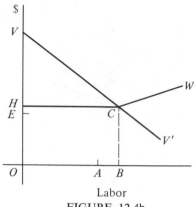

Labor
FIGURE 12.4b

mum wage which must be paid to all workers.[4] Let this minimum wage be *OH* in figure 12.4b. Since labor union success in winning a minimum wage affects neither the demand curve for the firm's final product nor the efficiency of its workers, the firm's VMP curve does not change. That is, the VMP curve, which is *VV'*, can be shifted without change from figure 12.4a to figure 12.4b.

Since the unionized firm must pay a wage equal to, or greater than, *OH,* the wage and the marginal cost of labor are the same for it so long as no more than *OB* labor is hired. The unionized firm of figure 12.4b will equate the marginal cost of labor to labor's VMP by hiring *OB* labor. Union pressure in setting a minimum wage at OH has apparently increased employment from OA in figure 12.4a to *OB* in figure 12.4b. But has it really?

Once again we must take care to distinguish between short-run and long-run effects. We know that in the short run—the period of time during which capital equipment is specialized to a particular use—a firm will continue to operate so long as total revenue is not less than total variable cost. We also know that in the long run the firm will not continue to op-

4. Labor unions generally bargain over wage rates, not over minimum wages. When the employer can hire all of the labor that he wishes at the negotiated basic wage rate—usually called the straight-time hourly wage rate—it usually becomes the minimum wage (also the maximum wage). However, when the employer needs additional labor in a hurry, he may face a "labor shortage," that is, he cannot get all of the labor that he wants at the negotiated basic wage rate. In this case, he must sweeten his offers to workers (which is most often done by promising overtime work at premium wages). Thus the average wage (defined as total worker compensation divided by total man-hours worked) rises above the negotiated basic wage rate.

erate unless total revenue is not less than total cost. For in the long run, specialized capital goods wear out. They will not be replaced unless investment in new machines promises to earn at least the normal rate of return on capital. (Recall that the normal rate of return on capital is simply the rate that it can earn in other industries, our assumption being that when capital is free to move it will tend to earn the same (normal) rate everywhere in the economy.)

Look closely at figure 12.4a. Before its workers are organized by the union, the firm has a total variable cost equal to the area *OADF;* this is the area under the marginal cost of labor curve when *OA* units of labor are hired. (By assumption A12.4 labor is the only variable factor and all variable cost is labor cost.) The total revenue earned by the firm when it hires *OA* labor is *OADV;* this is the area under the VMP curve. The difference between total revenue and total variable (wage) cost in figure 12.4a is the area *FDV*. The amount *FDV* is just sufficient to provide the fixed capital of the firm with a normal rate of return (since, by assumption A12.4, the firm earns no economic profit or economic rent).

After unionization, the firm's marginal cost of labor curve is line *HC* in figure 12.4b for the range of labor inputs between zero and *OB*. This is true because the labor union through collective bargaining has set the minimum wage that the firm must pay at *OH*. If the employer wishes to hire more than *OB* units of labor, he must pay a wage greater than *OH*. So long, of course, as the VMP curve is given by *VV'* in figures 12.4a and 12.4b, the firm has no incentive to hire more than *OB* units of labor and so force up the wage. After unionization, the firm will hire *OB* units of labor because at *OB* units the marginal cost of labor equals VMP. Thus the union by setting the minimum wage *OH* appears to have (i) raised the wage from *OE* to *OH,* (ii) increased employment from *OA* to *OB,* and (iii) made the wage equal to VMP and so ended the "exploitation" of labor.

Let us be careful here. Before unionization the firm paid a wage equal to *OE* (figures 12.4a and 12.4b) and earned zero economic rent. Unionization has raised its total wage bill from *OAGE* (which is the same as *OADF*) in figure 12.4a to *OBCH* in figure 12.4b. Therefore, after unionization has set the minimum wage at *OH,* the firm must be incurring a loss. Will it stay in business?

In the short run the firm definitely will stay in business. When the firm equates the marginal cost of labor to labor's VMP after unionization, it hires *OB* workers. (Figure 12.4b) When OB workers are employed, the firm's total variable cost (wage bill) is *OBCH* and its total revenue is

OBCV (which is the area under the VMP curve) when *OB* workers are hired. Since in figure 12.4b the firm's total revenue is greater than its total variable cost by the amount *HCV*, the firm will continue to operate in the short run.

In the long run the firm will close down when faced with a minimum wage *OH*. Before unionization, the firm earned a normal rate of return on its capital because total revenue exceeded total variable cost by the amount *FDV* in figure 12.4a. The result of the setting of the minimum wage at *OH* is, of course, to make the difference between total revenue and total variable cost less than *FDV*—the income necessary to give it a normal rate of return on capital.

In short, if a monopsonist sells his product in a perfectly competitive market (and earns no economic rent) it is only in the short run that he can be induced by union pressure to hire more workers at a higher wage. The success of the labor union in raising the wage against the monopsonist forces total revenue below total cost. Thus, the ultimate effect of union success is to cause our monopsonist-perfect competitor to discontinue production and shift his capital to another industry or another locality.

Labor leaders know well enough that strong pressure to raise wages applied to a single firm in a highly competitive, and largely non-union, industry is likely to kill the firm; hence the absence of "hard" collective bargaining in such firms, i.e. collective bargaining that involves time-consuming negotiations and the serious possibility of a strike. Contracts which give workers very few, if any, benefits that they could not have had without collective bargaining are sometimes denigrated as "sweetheart" contracts. Such contracts have often been negotiated by gangster controlled unions whose main interest was in collecting dues from members and shaking down employers who were prepared to pay blackmail in return for labor peace. But this contempt is quite undeserved by most labor unions which accept such contracts. Until a union has been able to organize most firms in an industry, the "soft" approach to collective bargaining is simply intelligent union behavior. It is all that the union can do for its members without causing them to lose their jobs. Even the relatively powerful automobile workers' union must operate under the constraints imposed by automobile imports from foreign countries. Some members once complained that the construction workers' unions were winning bigger wage increases. A leader of the UAW reminded them that while you cannot build Detroit office buildings in Tokyo, you can build cars there.

Now let us suppose that figures 12.4a and 12.4b stand not for a single firm but for all firms in the industry. Without union pressure, each firm

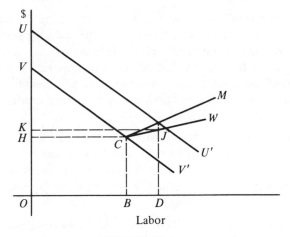

FIGURE 12.4c

hires *OA* labor and pays the wage *OE* (figure 12.4a). What will happen now to employment if the union succeeds in setting the minimum wage at *OH* (figure 12.4b)? Here again we must distinguish between the short-run and long-run effects of a wage increase.

In the short run, each firm expands employment from *OA* to *OB*. This is the same result we obtained when the minimum wage was applied to a single firm alone. In the long run the imposition of the minimum wage *OH* has a surprising result. Consider figure 12.4c.

Immediately after the minimum wage *OH* is imposed on the industry, each firm has *VV'* as its VMP curve; hence each firm hires *OB* units of labor. However, since total cost is below total revenue in every firm, some firms will leave the industry as their specialized capital equipment wears out. The effect of their exit is to raise the VMP curve for each firm that remains in the industry. Finally, a new equilibrium will be reached in which VMP is equal to the marginal cost of labor in each firm that survives.

In figure 12.4c, *UU'* is the VMP curve of each surviving firm in the new equilibrium. That is, as some firms exit from the industry, the VMP curve facing each remaining firm moves up from *VV'* to *UU'*. In the new equilibrium, each firm equates the marginal cost of labor to VMP by hiring *OD* workers. But in order to obtain *OD* workers the firm must pay the wage *OK* (or *DJ*). And the wage *OK* in the new equilibrium is actually greater than the minimum wage *OH* set by the union. (Figure 12.4c) The explanation of this surprising outcome is quite simple. The exit of some firms as a result of the union's success in setting the minimum wage at *OH* restores to the firms that remain in the industry some of the monopsony power that union pressure had taken away.

To sum up. If the labor union succeeds in imposing a minimum wage equal to VMP on a set of monopsonists who sell their final products in perfect competition with one another, the following results come to pass in the long run.

> Some firms will leave the industry. Total employment in the industry will decrease. A new equilibrium will be reached in which the wage actually paid by the firms that remain in the industry is above the minimum wage set by the union. In the new equilibrium labor's VMP is again greater than the wage.

The process by which the labor union seeks to counteract the monopsony power of employers described above can be repeated ad infinitum. But so long as monopsonists sell their final products in a perfectly competitive market, the union can never, in the long run, get VMP equal to the wage. Its efforts will lead to successive falls in total employment in the industry.

Monopsony plus monopoly

We can now draw an obvious but important conclusion from our discussion of monopsony. If the upward pressure on wages that a labor union applies to a monopsonist is not, in the long run, to cause unemployment, then the monopsonist must also have the monopoly power in the market for his final product that earns him an economic rent. (Recall from Chapter 6 that a monopolist who earns no economic rent is a logical possibility.) Let us strike out assumption A12.4 and replace it with the following.

> A12.6 The firm sells its final product in a market that is not perfectly competitive and earns an economic rent.

In figure 12.5a the VMP curve of the monopsonist-monopolist is given by *VV'* and his MRP curve by *VR*. Remember that MRP is short for *labor's marginal revenue product* and that, for a monopolist, MRP is always less than VMP. In the absence of a labor union, the wage that the firm must pay in order to employ different amounts of labor is given by *FW*. The marginal cost of labor to the firm is given by *OM* in figure 12.5a. The firm maximizes economic rent by equating the marginal cost of labor to MRP. Hence, in the absence of a labor union, our monopsonist-monop-

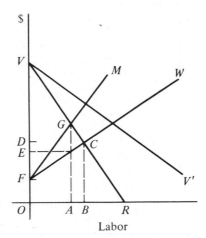

FIGURE 12.5a

olist will employ *OA* units of labor and pay the wage *OE* in figure 12.5a.

Suppose now that a labor union organizes the workers and by collective bargaining sets the minimum wage at *OD*. (Figures 12.5a and 12.5b) After unionization, the monopsonist-monopolist has a labor supply curve given by *DCW* and a marginal cost of labor curve given by *DCM'*. As figure 12.5b indicates, he can hire *OB* units of labor or less by paying the minimum wage *OD;* but he must pay more than this minimum if he wishes to hire more than *OB* units of labor.

The success of the labor union in getting a minimum wage *OD* had deprived the employer of his power to force the wage below *OD* by employing less than *OB* units of labor. Therefore, if the employer equates marginal cost of labor to MRP, after unionization he will hire *OB* units of labor (figure 12.5b). Before unionization, he employed the smaller quantity of labor *OA*. But will the employer remain in production after unionization that sets the minimum wage at *OD?*

In the short run, he will obviously remain in production; in fact, he will increase employment from *OA* to *OB* as a consequence of unionization. Since labor is a variable input and capital a fixed input, we know that, when *OB* labor is hired, the employer's total revenue from the sale of his output is equal to the area *OBCV* in figure 12.5b. That is, when *OB* labor is hired, total revenue is equal to the area under *VR* which is the MRP curve. The employer's total variable cost is his wage bill. This is area *OBCD* in figure 12.5b. Since area *OBCV* is greater than area *OBCD* the

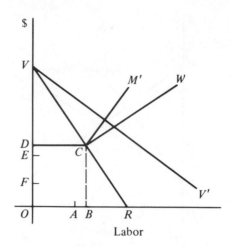

FIGURE 12.5b

monopsonist-monopolist will, in the short run, stay in business and hire *OB* labor.

Will he continue to hire *OB* units of labor in the long run? On the basis of the information provided by figure 12.5b, we cannot say for sure. There are, however, only two possibilities.

(i) Suppose that when the monopsonist-monopolist hires *OB* labor at wage *OD*, his total revenue is equal to or greater than his total cost. In this case he will continue to hire *OB* labor indefinitely. Here labor union success in placing the minimum wage at *OD* has merely diverted some or all of the economic rent earned by the firm from employer to workers. But labor union success has not made it worthwhile for the employer to transfer his capital to another industry where only a normal rate of return can be earned.

(ii) Suppose that when the monopsonist-monopolist hires *OB* labor at wage *OD*, his total revenue is less than his total cost. In this case he will, of course, close down in the long run.

Since figure 12.5a does not provide information on the size of the economic rent that was earned before unionization, we cannot be specific about what will happen to employment in the long run. We can say only this: If the monopsonist-monopolist, before the coming of the labor union, earned an economic rent, then the union, within limits, can both raise the wage and increase employment even in the long run.

One final point. We noted that some economists view labor as being

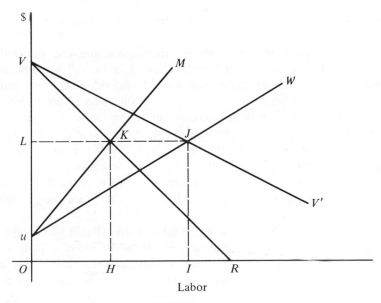

FIGURE 12.6

"exploited" whenever it does not receive a wage equal to VMP. Figure 12.5b indicates that the union may be able simultaneously to raise the wage from *OE* to *OD* and raise employment *OA* to *OB*. However, when *OB* workers are hired, the wage *OD* is below VMP. Hence in figure 12.5b, union success in setting a minimum wage has not ended the "exploitation" of labor—only reduced it.

In order for a labor union which bargains with a monopsonist-monopolist to be able to equate the wage to VMP, two conditions must be satisfied. First, the labor union must be able to specify not only the minimum wage but also the minimum amount of labor that must be hired. Second, the wage bill that the monopsonist-monopolist must pay when collective bargaining has made the wage equal to VMP must not be so great that total revenue is driven below total cost. Consider figure 12.6.

Once again *VV'* is the firm's VMP curve and *VR* is its MRP curve. In the absence of a labor union, the firm's labor supply curve is *UW* and its marginal cost of labor curve *UM*. Suppose that the firm in figure 12.6 could, if compelled to, accept a wage bill equal the area *OIJL* and still earn an economic rent. That is, a wage bill equal to area *OIJL* will not cause the firm to shut down even in the long run. Now suppose that a labor union organizes the firm's workers and manages to set the minimum wage at *OL* (or *IJ*) in figure 12.6 but lets the firm hire as much (or as little) labor as it wishes.

Figure 12.6 indicates that, before unionization, the firm equated the marginal cost of labor to MRP by hiring *OH* labor. After unionization, its marginal cost of labor curve becomes *LJ* (provided no more than *OI* labor is hired). Hence, after unionization, the firm continues to hire *OH* labor. However, if the firm is compelled by the union both to pay a minimum wage *OL* and to hire a minimum amount of labor *OI,* then the firm will hire *OI* labor. And when *OI* labor is hired, "labor is paid a wage equal to the value of its marginal product." In short, any effort to end the "exploitation of labor" by equating the wage to VMP requires that the union bargain with the monopsonist-monopolist over both the wage and the amount of labor to be hired.

Of course, there is no reason why a labor union should be content with a wage bill that exactly equates the wage to VMP when it deals with a firm that earns an economic rent. In this situation the object of intelligent union policy is simply to capture the whole of this economic rent for its members.

Monopsony in practice

How useful is the concept of monopsony for analyzing the determination of wages in the real world? Many (probably most) economists would answer about as follows: The concept of monopsony is essential to an understanding of wage determination in the short run. Its significance for wage determination in the long run is certainly debatable and probably small.

Let us suppose that a textile firm located in a small Alabama town (population 2000) wishes to increase its output by 50 percent. (This example is not unrealistic; the southern states contain a great many small towns where a substantial part of the local labor force is employed in a single textile firm.) If the firm wants to raise output by this amount within the space of, say, 10 days, it must obtain the necessary additional manhours almost entirely from its own workers. Since each remaining hour of leisure becomes more valuable to a worker as the length of the work week increases, the textile firm must raise the *average* wage in order to persuade his work force to put in longer hours. (The average wage is usually raised by paying premiums for night work, week-end work, and, in general, work beyond 40 hours per week.) In this very short run, the textile firm has very considerable monopsony power.

If the textile firm is able to spread a 50 percent increase in output over several months, it has time to bid experienced workers away from other firms and train the untrained. Yet, in a small labor market, even this method of expanding the work force is likely to result in some rise in the wage. Still, it is a cheaper way of increasing output than paying premium rates for extra effort from experienced workers.

When the textile firm can spread the increase in production over many months, it has the option of building another plant in another town—preferably one with a labor "surplus." Indeed, its out-of-town expansion may have no effect whatever on the local wage. If so, the firm does not behave as a monopsonist in the long run.

If monopsony power were economically significant in the long run, we would expect that wages would be lower in labor markets where a few employers do most of the hiring than in labor markets where many bid against one another to attract workers. This does not seem to be true. One systematic study of this relationship found that there was virtually no association between the wage paid for a labor skill and the degree of employer concentration in American labor markets.[5]

Professional sports (especially baseball) where players are bought and sold by teams after they have signed their first contract are often cited as an instance where wages are depressed by the monopsony power of employers. This apparent peonage is made possible by the so-called reserve clause in sports contracts. In its pure form (now found only in professional baseball) the reserve clause permits the athlete to play only for the team that owns his contract.[6] Still, it is not clear that the average wage of a professional athlete would rise if the reserve clause were to be relaxed. Highly successful athletes would benefit and unsuccessful or unproven athletes would lose from a relaxation of the reserve clause. Stars would be even better paid than at present; the bonuses paid to merely promising high school athletes who sign professional contracts for the first time would fall. Nobody really knows what would happen to the lifetime earnings of the "average" player if the reserve clause were eased. The impact of a change on the average player would probably vary from sport to

5. Robert Bunting, *Employer Concentration in Local Labor Markets* (1962).
6. In professional sports other than baseball, e.g. football and basketball, the player is allowed to "play out his option"—that is, to sever his connection with his team by giving a year's notice and continuing to play under terms no better than those of his old contract. The favored treatment of owners of baseball teams can be traced to a series of very peculiar Supreme Court decisions which held that baseball was a "sport" while all other professional games were "commerce." Baseball alone has received a nearly total exemption from the federal antitrust laws. Most sports observers believe that baseball as exemption will not endure indefinitely and may well be modified by an agreement with the players' union in the very near future.

sport. The outcome would depend in part on the elasticity of substitution of average players for star players in the team's production function.

Analyzing the possible consequences of changing the reserve clause in professional sports is made even more difficult by the possibility that any change will trigger changes in the rules of the games. Thus professional football by allowing unlimited substitution of players during a game has completely eliminated the economic value of the star triple-threat specialist of an earlier era. It seems likely that the great Red Grange (for details consult a male professor over age 50) would have to make it as a modestly paid punt return specialist in modern professional football.

Summary

In this chapter we have examined certain features of the market for the factor inputs of the production process. If the firm is to maximize income it must simultaneously equate marginal cost to marginal revenue and combine factor inputs in a way that minimizes the cost of its output of final product.

When the firm both sells its final product in a perfectly competitive market and hires its factor inputs in perfectly competitive markets, income is maximized when

$$\frac{MPP_1}{w_1} = \frac{MPP_2}{w_2} \ldots = \frac{MPP_n}{w_n} = \frac{1}{p_x} \tag{C.3a}$$

Recall that for the inputs of factors 1, 2, . . . *n, MPP* denotes marginal physical product of factor input, *w* the price of factor input, and p_x the price of final product.

When the firm monopolizes the market for its final product but hires its factor inputs in perfectly competitive markets, price (p_x) is no longer equal to marginal revenue (mr_x). In this situation, the condition for income maximization is written as

$$\frac{MPP_1}{w_1} = \frac{MPP_2}{w_2} \ldots = \frac{MPP_n}{w_n} = \frac{1}{mr_x} \tag{C4}$$

When only one factor input is variable in the production function, the firm's demand curve for that input is simply the curve of marginal revenue product of that input (MPP_v). When the variable factor input is hired in a perfectly competitive market, this MRP_v curve is the same as the curve which gives the value of the marginal physical product of the variable factor input (VMP_v). Recall that MPP_v is simply $MPP_v \times mr_x$ and VMP_v is $MPP_v \times p_x$.

We saw that when two or more factor inputs in the production function are variable, the MRP curve of a factor input *is not* the firm's demand curve for that input. The reason, as we noted, is that a change in the price of a single variable factor input can (and probably will) induce the firm to change the amount of other variable factors that it uses in the production process.

Economists have long been intrigued by the case where the firm has monopsony power—the power to vary the price of a factor input by varying the amount that it hires. We examined the widely held view that a labor union which deals with a monopsonist can both compel him to pay a higher wage and induce him to hire more labor at this higher wage. We found that labor union pressure exerted through collective bargaining may produce this result in the short run. But in the long run it cannot have this result unless the firm has monopoly power in the final product market that gives it an economic rent.

REFERENCES

Becker, Gary, *Economic Theory* (New York, 1971), chapter 8.
Leftwich, R. H., *The Price System and Resource Allocation* (5th ed. 1970), chapters 14 and 15.
Mansfield, E., *Microeconomics: Theory and Applications* (New York, 1970), chapters 12 and 13.
Rees, Albert, "The Effects of Unions on Resource Allocation," *Journal of Law and Economics* 5 (1963), 69-78.
Russell, R. R., "On the Demand Curve for a Factor of Production," *American Economic Review,* 54 (1964), 726-32.

13

Increasing Economic Welfare

Forward from positive economics

So far our concern has been with what is usually called positive economics (as distinct from normative or welfare economics). We have constructed certain economic models, set them in motion, and observed that certain results follow. So far we have tried to refrain from asserting that some results are better than others. For example, we found that if an industry can be organized either as (a) a perfectly competitive industry or (b) a monopoly that cannot practice price discrimination, then price will be higher and output lower under non-discriminating monopoly than under perfect competition. But so far we have refrained from asserting that perfect competition is "better" than non-discriminating monopoly. After all, common sense advises a little caution where these "welfare" judgments are concerned. Nobody objects to the only moderately profitable monopolies that are created by city ordinance for blind sellers of newspapers at major street intersections in New York City. And (almost) nobody objects when the provision of telephone service is entrusted to a single firm in his town. It is bad enough to have one firm tearing up the streets at frequent intervals to install or repair telephone lines.

Nevertheless, most of us have the gut feeling that, in most situations, competition (perfect or otherwise) is preferable to monopoly (discriminating or non-discriminating). We *do* make welfare judgment about monopoly and, indeed, about a very wide range of economic issues. For that matter, most of us study economics in the first place precisely because we wish to improve our capacity to make "good" judgments about economic issues. All of us are welfare economists at heart and this is to our credit.

To choose wisely among economic policies we obviously need information; yet information alone is not enough. We also need a concept of economic welfare—or if you prefer, a vision of the good life. In response to this need there has developed the very considerable subject known as welfare economics. One truth we shall freely concede at the outset: Economic welfare as defined by economists is only a part of the sum total of social welfare—"that part of social welfare that can be brought directly or indirectly into relation with the measuring-rod of money."[1] Still, it is both an important part of this larger welfare and a means to realizing other ends. If we can devise a way to produce five different models of four-door sedans with fewer resources, we can use the released resources in a great number of ways, e.g. to produce more models of four-door sedans, to build more hospitals, or to support more artists-in-residence at our favorite college or university.

It is fashionable in many circles to sneer at the emphasis on "economic materialism." But this affectation, while mostly harmless, is rather foolish. Virtually all legislative programs designed to improve the quality of life have one thing in common. They will be costly to implement.

Two traditions

In the history of welfare economics two traditions are clearly visible. The first is concerned with the welfare gains and losses that will result if a specific economic change is carried out (building a bridge, changing a rate charged by an electric power company, providing free milk for children). Economists who work in this pragmatic tradition have no grand design for maximizing economic welfare. They are content to devise criteria by which we can tell whether a small change in economic arrangements is likely to increase or decrease economic welfare.

The second tradition in welfare economics has aimed at greater generality by seeking to identify the conditions that must be fulfilled if an economy is to achieve an optimal allocation of resources. Many of the economists who have worked in this more ambitious tradition have been concerned with the problem of devising price and investment policies for a wholly socialist economy. In this chapter we shall consider some of the work which has been done in the first tradition. The chapter that follows examines the more ambitious tradition in welfare economics.

1. A. C. Pigou, *The Economics of Welfare* (London, 4th ed., 1932), p. 11.

The basic assumptions

The foundation stones of modern welfare economics are two value judgments that almost nobody (economist or non-economist) will accept without attaching at least a few qualifications. (More on this later.) They are:

A13.1 The individual is the proper judge of how his own actions or the actions of others (including the State) affect his economic welfare.

A13.2 No economic policy can be said to increase economic welfare unless it can (not necessarily will) make somebody better off without making anybody else worse off.

Assumption A13.1 is obviously inapplicable to very young children and adults who suffer from serious emotional or mental disability. And collectively we demand that the State through legislators and civil servants make many decisions that involve choices where our information is poor. For example, we quite properly regard it as a form of consumer protection when we are deprived by law of the chance to buy potentially dangerous drugs about which we know very little. But here again we have an assumption whose use is justified because it is preferable to the alternatives. Since we do not wish to assume that Big Brother knows best in all cases, and since it is too much trouble to list in detail all of those special situations where he really does know best, we take the easy way out. We assume that individuals are the best judge of their own interests.

In a world of perfect justice it might be desirable to insist that those persons who benefit from a change in economic policy pay full compensation to those who lose from the change. In the real world it is obviously impossible to compensate fully every victim of economic change. The whole subject of welfare economics would be made trivial if we concerned ourselves only with cases where full compensation will be paid. Therefore, assumption A13.2 does not require an income transfer from gainers to losers. It merely states that it must be *possible* for those who gain to compensate those who lose (and still be better off).[2]

2. Welfare economists have long recognized that an irritating complication arises when an economic policy is carried out without payment of compensation to those who are hurt by it. A change in the allocation of resources *may* change commodity prices and factor prices; which is to say that it *may* change the distribution of real income. Hence if compensation is not paid to losers, they may be so badly injured that they will be willing to bribe the gainers to return to the original distribution of resources.

In the absence of compensation one could conceivably have an endless oscillation between two "economic states." Therefore some welfare economists propose a two-fold test for judging economic policy: (i) People who gain from the change must be

Note that assumption A13.2 accepts as "correct" whatever distribution of income happens to prevail. It excludes the possibility that economic welfare can be improved by transferring income from rich to poor, from bachelors to widows with children, or from boorish peasants to sensitive artists. This is not to say that economists who use the basic assumptions of welfare economics to screen economic proposals are not concerned with the distribution of income. (Most of them do have this concern.) Rather they regard the "correct" distribution as a political question to be decided before consumer preferences are allowed to guide the allocation of resources. One can favor progressive income taxation to make the distribution of income more equal simply because one prefers more equality. The fact that the poor who benefit cannot compensate the rich who lose is not relevant.

It is sometimes argued that assumption A13.2 and the compensation test that it implies must be accepted by economists because "one cannot make interpersonal comparisons of utility," i.e. that we cannot say that Jones is happier than Smith. This statement is not really correct. In the real world, of course, we constantly do make interpersonal comparisons of utility. The statement that Jones is happier than Smith is not a nonsense statement as logicians understand the term, i.e. in the sense that it transmits no information from speaker to listener. Even the statement that Jones is 3.2 percent happier than Smith is not complete nonsense. The difficulty is that although economists and laymen alike, can agree in a vague way on what constitutes human happiness, they cannot agree on the rules that should be followed in measuring it. Hence the refusal of welfare economists to make interpersonal comparisons of utility rests not upon the fact that they cannot be made but rather on the judgment that, in view of the paucity of hard information about what makes people happy, such comparisons should not be made.

Technical efficiency versus welfare efficiency

Provided that assumptions A13.1 and A13.2 are accepted, we may readily distinguish two types of economic efficiency—technical efficiency and welfare efficiency. Technical efficiency presents no problem.

---

able to compensate people who lose and still be better off; (ii) people who, in the absence of compensation, lose from the change must not be able to bribe potential gainers from carrying out the change. Fortunately, a small change in economic policy is not likely to have any great effect on income distribution; so that in appraising piecemeal economic change we need not bother with this refinement. That is, in most cases it is enough if we are satisfied that gainers could pay full compensation to losers and still be better off after the change.

Suppose that, at a given set of factor prices, X amount of factor input yields more of commodity A when organized through the beta production technique than when organized through the alpha production technique. Then economic welfare is greater when beta rather than alpha is used to produce commodity A. If alpha is the old technique and beta the new, and (a most important qualification) if there is no cost of changeover, the economy can shift from alpha to beta and pay compensation to anyone who is hurt by the transition. (There may well be 70-year-old machinists who cannot or will not cope with the new technology.) After the shift from alpha to beta there is simply more output to be divided. For this reason technical progress almost always increases economic welfare as defined above.

Now suppose that, at existing factor prices, commodity A is being produced in what is technically the most efficient manner; and the same is true of commodities B, C, and D. It is still possible that economic welfare can be increased by changing the *amounts* of commodities A, B, C, and D that are produced. After all, who wants buggy whips today no matter how efficiently they are produced? In short, technical efficiency is not enough. We must also see that the "right" mix of commodities is being produced.

Unfortunately the interactions between technical efficiency and welfare efficiency are fiendishly complex. The correct choice of production technique depends upon the prices of factor inputs; yet any change in the mix of commodities produced will change the prices of factor inputs. For this reason, there are a great many loose ends in welfare economics. Before commenting upon a few of the more troublesome loose ends, let us first see how the welfare approach has been applied to three classic policy problems—public works to be financed out of taxes, correct price policy for public utilities, and private cost versus social cost.

Dupuit's bridge

The intellectual father of modern welfare economics was Jules Dupuit (1804-66), an engineer in the employ of the French government.[3] Dupuit faced a very practical problem. When should public funds be used to build a bridge?

3. Jules Dupuit, "De la mesure de l'utilité des travaux publics," *Annales des Ponts et Chaussées* (2nd series, VIII, 1844). Translated by R. H. Barback as "On the Measurement of the Utility of Public Works," *International Economic Papers,* 2 (1952), 83-110.

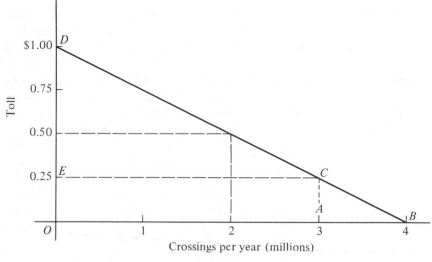

FIGURE 13.1

Imagine that a bridge can be built in virtually no time at all; that once built it will last forever and have no upkeep costs; that it can always accommodate all traffic without congestion;[4] and that the demand curve for the services of such a bridge is given by *DD'* in figure 13.1. Suppose, finally, that there is a rate of interest of 5 percent per annum at which public funds can be borrowed or invested.

From figure 13.1 it is clear that, if the bridge is operated as a non-discriminating toll facility, the profit-maximizing toll is 50 cents and the bridge has two million crossings per year. When a toll of 50 cents is charged, marginal revenue is equal to marginal cost (which is zero since the bridge has no upkeep costs). Thus the maximum income that can be collected each year without price discrimination is $1 million. A non-discriminating toll bridge could be viewed by private investors as a perpetuity of $1 million per year. Recall from Chapter 11 that the formula for the present value *V* of a perpetuity is $V = I/i$, where *I* is annual income and *i* is the

4. The assumption of instant bridge construction and no upkeep costs is used to simplify the numerical computation. When construction is instantaneous we have no need to reckon interest on capital used during the "period of production." When the bridge has no upkeep cost, we do not have to reckon with depreciation as a cost.

By assuming that the bridge never becomes congested even at a zero toll, we avoid yet another problem. Any congestion caused by a zero toll would be an economic cost imposed upon travelers. This cost would have to be taken into account in setting the "correct" (i.e. welfare maximizing) toll.

rate of interest. Therefore, a private investor not able to practice price discrimination would build the bridge provided that its cost of construction was no greater than $1 million/0.05, that is, no greater than $20 million.

Should Government in deciding whether or not to build the bridge with public funds use the same investment criteria as a private investor? As an engineer who believed in building bridges, Dupuit argued vigorously against such a narrow market test. By his analysis, the economic benefit to the public is the area under the demand curve in figure 13.1. This benefit is $2 million. Thus, when the rate of interest is 5 percent per annum, the bridge should be built provided that its cost does not exceed $40 million. If the cost were greater than $40 million, the public would not be getting a 5 percent return on its bridge investment and should use its funds for some other purpose.

The next question that Dupuit faced was: if the bridge is built, should a toll be charged? If so, what toll? Dupuit's answer was that no toll should be charged. Remember that we assume that the bridge can handle without congestion all of the traffic that would cross at a zero toll. There is, of course, a case for a toll whenever it is necessary to achieve the "correct" (i.e. welfare maximizing) amount of traffic congestion because such congestion is a cost that travelers must bear.

Why no toll on Dupuit's bridge? Suppose that a toll of 25 cents is charged, bringing the State $750,000 per year. If we assume that each traveler will receive his toll payments back from the State in the form of public services that he values as much as his bridge crossings (schools, free abortions, police, art museums, etc.) then the $750,000 paid to the State in bridge tolls represents no loss of economic welfare. However, the 25-cent toll reduces the crossings by one million per year and so causes a *deadweight loss* of economic welfare of $125,000. The toll of 25 cents reduces use of the bridge for no good reason. The bridge could handle all traffic without congestion at a zero toll. In figure 13.1 the deadweight loss resulting from the 25-cent toll is the area of the triangle *ABC*.

One final point. You will note that in deciding whether or not to build the bridge, Dupuit would have the State use the same criterion as would a private monopolist who could practice perfect price discrimination. For reasons that we have already developed, perfect competition and monopoly that practice perfect price discrimination result in the same output. The only difference is that, under perfect competition, all of consumer surplus is collected by consumers; whereas, under perfectly discriminating monopoly, all of it goes to the monopolist.

If consumers (acting through the State) are themselves the perfectly discriminating monopolist, the objection to price discrimination presumably disappears. On strictly welfare grounds (we ignore administrative and political considerations for the moment) there is a case for building bridges and other public projects out of taxes and then making them "free" to all users (so long, of course, as congestion does not result). There is an equally good case for financing such projects by selling bonds which are to be paid off out of highly discriminatory user charges. But on welfare grounds (and again we ignore administrative and political considerations) there is no case for financing projects by bond sales which are to be paid off out of non-discriminatory tolls. On strictly welfare grounds there are two, and only two, valid reasons for charging for the use of State-owned facilities—(1) to reduce congestion and (2) to implement price discrimination.

The public utility with decreasing average total cost

Dupuit's bridge has no upkeep costs and never imposes inconvenience costs on travelers by becoming congested. Thus, as we have emphasized, the bridge has a zero marginal cost. Many years after Dupuit's work appeared economists were to generalize his results in their study of the regulation of so-called public utilities (railroads, gas, electric, water companies etc.).

In most states, government commissions that regulate public utilities purport to restrict them to a "fair rate of return on a fair valuation of investment." In the language of economists (state utility commissions are, of course, run by lawyers) this roughly translates into the belief that the price of a commodity should equal average total cost. Is this "average cost pricing" a proper goal of regulation? Most welfare economists now argue that it is not. Following Dupuit they contend that price should equal marginal cost on the ground that price measures the value of a unit of the commodity and marginal cost measures the value of the additional resources used to produce it.

Clearly, economic welfare is increased by compelling a profitable public utility to equate price to marginal cost. For the welfare gain awarded to consumers by imposing "marginal cost pricing" on the utility is greater than the extra cost imposed on the utility. We assume that, in the absence of regulation, the utility would equate marginal cost to marginal revenue.

But what do we do with a utility which (a) has decreasing average total cost "over the relevant range of output" and (b) will incur a loss if com-

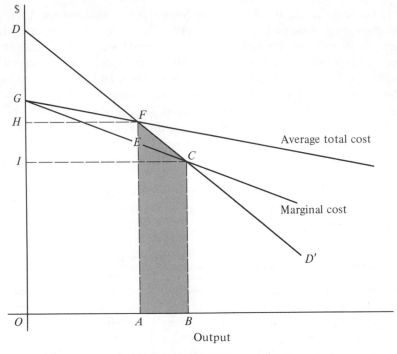

FIGURE 13.2

pelled to equate price to marginal cost? The geometry of such a firm is given by figure 13.2. The firm's demand curve is *DD′* in this diagram. Should we relent and let the utility equate price to average total cost, i.e. practice average cost pricing? Or should we pay a subsidy out of taxes to the utility so that it can equate price to marginal cost and still break even? A careful look at figure 13.2 will show that we should insist on marginal cost pricing and pay the necessary subsidy.

If regulators allow the utility to practice average cost pricing, price will be *OH* and output will be *OA*. If it is compelled to use marginal cost pricing, price will fall to *OI* and output will rise to *OB*. Should regulation force a shift from average cost pricing to marginal cost pricing, the welfare gain to consumers would be the shaded area *ABCF* in figure 13.2. But the addition to total cost imposed by this shift to marginal cost pricing would be the smaller included area *ABCE*.

Recall that since marginal cost is the first derivative of total cost with respect to total output, total cost is given by the area under the marginal cost curve. Thus in figure 13.2 when output increases from *OA* to

OB, total cost increases from *OAEG* to *OBCG.* And the addition to total cost from this increase in output is *ABCE.* Assuming that taxpayers and the public utility's customers are the same people, it will pay to give a subsidy out of taxes to the utility in order that it can produce output *OB.*

We might note that the case for subsidizing decreasing cost utilities when necessary to get price equal to marginal cost does not depend upon who owns the utilities. That is, the case would in no way be changed by assuming that the utility is government-owned or some form of consumer cooperative.

Economic theory and externalities

So far in this book we have deliberately ignored the possibility that production and consumption are characterized by externalities. For our purposes, an externality exists when some activity of party A imposes a cost or confers a benefit on party B for which party A is not charged or compensated by (through) the price system. Read this definition carefully. We shall presently see that an externality can be charged or compensated for through "side-bargains" outside the price system, i.e. through a private deal between beneficiaries and victims of the externality.

In the real world, production and consumption are obviously riddled with externalities and their existence has long troubled economists. This is because externalities were seen as posing a threat to all efforts to generalize about economic efficiency on the basis of market prices and market costs. Does it matter whether or not a firm is producing an output at which price is equal to average total cost (and average total cost is minimized) if, at the same time, this firm is madly polluting the water, fouling the air, and slowly killing its employees with lead poisoning? But if we cannot use market prices and market costs as a basis for judging economic efficiency, what is to be done?

Over the years one tradition (the "Pigouvian" tradition) in welfare economics sought to put the subject on a firm foundation by building on a distinction between private cost and social cost. (An analogous distinction was drawn between private benefit and social benefit.) Social cost is usually held to be the "true" total cost of producing a commodity, i.e. the value of all resources devoted to its production. Private cost is usually held to be the part of total cost that falls directly upon the producer. Thus social cost is the sum of (i) private cost and (ii) costs that fall on persons other than the producer (usually his workers and the general public).

The firm, of course, has no interest in social cost or social benefit. Its object is to maximize private income which is the difference between total cost and total revenue. Given this narrow business goal, many economists have concluded that there is an inevitable "failure of the market" whenever externalities are present. By their logic, one necessary condition for achieving maximum welfare is that the marginal social cost of a commodity be equal to its marginal social benefit. They argue that when the firm can shift some part of the cost of producing a commodity to other parties, marginal social cost will exceed marginal private cost. The result? Too much of the commodity will be produced. Conversely (so the argument goes), when the firm creates a thing of value for which it cannot charge a price, too little of it will be produced.

Textbooks are full of examples of the supposed divergence between private çost and social cost. One hoary illustration is the smoke nuisance. If there are no controls on pollution of the atmosphere, it is likely that some of the costs of producing steel will be borne by housewives who live near the mill; they will have to spend more time and money to keep their homes acceptably clean. A not quite so hoary example of the uncompensated externality is the apiary-orchard illustration. A by-product of apple-growing is pollen which is appropriated by bees and used to make honey. Thus apple growers provide beekeepers with a free input.

At this point we should proceed slowly. Externalities which give rise to a discrepancy between private cost and social cost obviously exist. But what is their significance for economic welfare? Let us try to answer two closely related questions. (1) Is economic welfare as modern welfare economists define the term reduced when private cost does not equal social cost? (2) Can economic welfare be increased by making private producers bear the complete cost of production? Let us be careful to note that these two questions are not quite the same. It may be possible that economic welfare suffers because private and social cost diverge; yet more harm than good will result if we try to close the gap (because gap-closing has a cost).

No doubt your first reaction is to say amen to both of the above questions. Resist the temptation for the moment. It will take you down the wrong road. And it should be no consolation that this road in the past was traveled by not a few distinguished economists, most notably the great English economist, A. C. Pigou (1877-1959).[5]

5. Pigou's years of work culminated in *The Economics of Welfare* (London, 4th ed., 1932). For his treatment of private cost versus social cost see especially chapter 9.

Ranchers versus farmers: Coase's problem

The problem of private versus social cost was given the following formulation in a memorable article by Ronald Coase of the University of Chicago.[6]

Let us suppose that a farmer and cattle-raiser are operating on neighboring properties. Let us further suppose that, without any fencing between the properties, an increase in the size of the cattle-raiser's herd increases the total damage to the farmer's crops. I shall assume that the annual cost of fencing the farmer's property is $9 and that the price of the crop is $1 per ton. Also I assume that the relation between the number of cattle in the herd and the annual crop loss is as follows:

Number in herd (steers)	Annual crop loss (tons)	Crop loss per additional steer (tons)
1	1	1
2	3	2
3	6	3
4	10	4

In the first instance let us have the laws of liability drawn up by a state legislature dominated by damage-conscious farmers. Cattle-raisers are liable for every last penny of damage done by their straying steers to farm crops. Here obviously none of the costs of cattle-raising can be shifted from ranchers to farmers.

The cattle-raiser must now treat liability for damage done by his herd to crops as a cost of production; and it will play a part in determining how many steers he will graze. Of course, if his decision is to maintain a herd of four steers or more, there is no problem. He will spend $9 a year on a fence and reduce the damage done by his wandering critters to zero. But for a herd of three steers or less, it is cheaper to pay damages than to build a fence.

For a herd of three steers or less, the cattle-raiser will follow a simple rule. Add another steer so long as the value of the additional meat produced is equal to or greater than additional costs incurred. One of these additional costs is the need to pay more in damages to the farmer whose crops are damaged when the extra steer is added.

Now let the state legislature pass into the hands of cattlemen who proceed to rewrite the laws of liability in their own favor. The straying of

6. Ronald Coase, "The Problem of Social Cost," *Journal of Law and Economics*, 2 (1960), 1-44.

a steer becomes an "act of God" and the cattle-raiser is relieved of all liability for damage done by his herd to neighboring crops. Will the economy's resources be misallocated and economic welfare decreased because cattle-raisers, finding that they can shift some of their costs to farmers, decide to raise more steers?

If the herd consists of four steers or more, once again there is no problem. The cost of maintaining a fence—$9 a year—is promptly dropped by the cattle-raiser and picked up by the farmer. But suppose that before cattlemen rewrote the legal code our cattle-raiser maintained a herd of two steers.

At first glance it might seem that he has a new incentive to add one or two additional steers. He can now add a third steer without paying another $3 to the farmer for damage done. However, we know that the third steer will not add more than $3 to his income; otherwise, he would have added it even before the law of liability was changed by the cattlemen.

Consider the impact of the law's change from the farmer's standpoint. It will now pay him to bribe the cattle-raiser to keep his herd at two steers. The inducement?

If the herd goes from two steers to three, the farmer will suffer an additional crop loss of $3. Provided always that he is not blinded by a hatred of cattlemen, he will pay up to $3 in order to prevent this loss. Thus the "true" additional cost of adding the third steer is $3 to the cattle-raiser regardless of how the law of liability is written. If he is not liable for crop damage and the farmer will pay him $3 to keep his herd at two steers, then he will lose $3 by ignoring the farmer's offer and adding the third steer.

In short, in Coase's example, the output of cattle and crops *will not* be affected by exempting cattle-raisers from liability for damage done by their steers to the crops of neighboring farmers. Such a change in the legal code will increase the incomes of cattle-raisers at the expense of farmers. But it will not increase economic welfare as we have defined the term. For the cattle-raisers are not so much better off after the change in the legal code that they can compensate farmers for the loss suffered and still be better off.

Who should bear the cost of crop damage—or, for that matter, of water pollution, air pollution, and aesthetic pollution (in the form of unsightly buildings)? This is purely and simply a matter of public opinion as expressed in the legal code. Economic analysis has nothing to say about how property rights should be assigned in this world. It can only explore the consequences that follow after they have been assigned.

Competition with prohibitive contract costs: fisheries

The implication of Coase's example is that, under some rather extreme assumptions, the distinction between private cost and social cost is entirely without significance for economic welfare. Does it follow that the enormous volume of writing by A. C. Pigou and his followers designed to show how economic welfare could be increased by closing the gap between private cost and social cost was simply wrong? Or can something be salvaged from the Pigouvian tradition?

We note, first of all, that Coase considers only a single farmer and a single rancher. In his example it is reasonable to suppose that the contract cost of arranging a deal between the two is negligible. Hence we can assume that a deal will be made because it is in the interest of both parties. But suppose that the farmer is damaged by the straying steers of many ranchers or that the steers of one rancher trample the crops of many farmers. Where an externality affects many parties, the contract costs of negotiating a deal may be so great that it cannot be arranged. Indeed, in fairness to Pigou and his followers, we should note that they seem to assume that the contract costs of dealing with externalities by side-bargains are prohibitive.

The way in which prohibitive contract costs prevent the "internalizing" of externalities is illustrated by the problem of over-fishing in international waters. A particularly tasty variety of fish, say tuna, can be eaten by other fish or by human beings. In the absence of commercial fishing, some quantity of tuna each year would be eaten by other fish and die of old age, and each year would see some natural increase in tuna population. In a biological equilibrium, tuna loss would equal tuna replacement and the tuna population would have a zero growth rate. Thus, in biological equilibrium, there is maximum sustainable yield of tuna—the maximum amount that can be taken from the sea each year without causing this yield to be lower in some future year. Provided that commercial tuna fleets take no more than the maximum sustainable yield each year, over-fishing is no problem. But should their annual catch exceed this amount, then the sustainable yield of tuna must fall below the maximum.

Unfortunately, certain economic characteristics of the tuna industry ensure that over-fishing will occur in the absence of international agreements to limit the catch. The scale of efficient production is small and entry is easy. Hence so long as price is greater than average total cost, investment in fishing will increase irrespective of what the maximum sustainable yield happens to be. When the demand for tuna is price inelas-

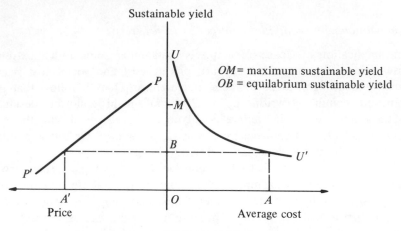

FIGURE 13.3

tic, the perverse effect of near-perfect competition (all that one ever gets in the real world) is even worse. Now the total value of the annual catch actually goes up as sustainable yield goes down.

Moreover, as the tuna population declines, and more boats compete for fewer fish, the average total cost of landed tuna goes up. This process will continue until average total cost becomes equal to price. In this equilibrium, annual catch is equal to sustainable yield; but this sustainable yield is less than maximum sustainable yield.[7]

Equilibrium for our tuna industry is illustrated in figure 13.3. Sustainable tuna yield is measured from point O upward with OM designating maximum sustainable yield. The average total cost of tuna is measured from point O to the right and is given by curve UU'. Price is measured from point O to the left and is given by the demand curve PP'. When sustainable yield is at its maximum OM, price exceeds average total cost and investment (and hence output) will increase in the industry. Sustainable yield will fall until it reaches OB. At level OB, average total cost is equal to price (OA being equal to OA' in figure 13.3).

From figure 13.3 it is also clear that technological progress in tuna catching can have a perverse welfare effect. If some innovation in fishing technique moves curve UU' downward and to the left, sustainable yield will fall even further. (The limit case of perverse technological progress

7. For the economic problems of fisheries, see H. Scott Gordon, "The Economic Theory of a Common-Property Resource: The Fishery," *Journal of Political Economy*, 62 (1954), 124-42; and J. A. Crutchfield and Giulio Pontecorvo, *The Pacific Salmon Fisheries: A Study of Irrational Conservation* (Washington, D.C., 1969).

occurred in the last century when it led to the complete extermination of some species of animal and plant life, e.g. the passenger pigeon.)

In the above case, competition has certainly not produced a welfare optimum. A condition of "many firms" and unrestricted entry has led to an equilibrium with too little tuna being caught at too high a cost. Yet it would obviously be self-defeating for any single fishing fleet or even any single fishing nation to restrict tuna fishing on its own. Other fleets and nations would promptly move into the vacuum. Even though less fishing this year would mean more and cheaper tuna in future years, this goal cannot be reached unless all fishing nations agree to restrict catch. (This proposition must of course be qualified to the extent that a nation can control fishing within its own territorial waters and such fishing is a significant fraction of international fishing effort.) As yet, international diplomacy has been inadequate to the task of bringing about anything close to optimal exploitation of international fisheries. Given the large number of nations involved, the technical complexities of the problem, and the difficulties of enforcement, this is hardly surprising.

Politics and externalities

Let us accept that, in the real world, there are many malign externalities which the victim cannot avoid by paying a bribe. Does it follow that economic welfare can be increased if the State intervenes to reduce the output of the commodity whose production gives rise to an offending externality? This the State could do directly by limiting the output of the commodity or indirectly by taxing each unit of output and so raising its marginal cost.

We cannot exclude the possibility that we can increase economic welfare by substituting State action (politics) for the market. But there is no assurance that the substitution will have this beneficial result. There are, in fact, two reasons for believing that there may often be no way to improve upon the "bad" distribution of resources brought about by a price system which generates externalities not accompanied by side bargains between beneficiaries and victims.

1. The political process has its own externalities. An all-wise and totally benevolent dictator might try to arrange things so that, in every industry, private marginal cost is equal to social marginal cost. But if we assume that individuals acting through the political process are motivated by the same desire to maximize personal welfare that they exhibit in the market, then securing this equality will be neither the object nor the result of political action.

Consider the simple case where all decisions are taken by a majority vote of the population affected by them. The object of an individual motivated by self-interest is to maximize the net benefits accruing to himself through political action. To do this, he must be part of a winning majority which means that he must be prepared to indulge in political log-rolling. (I'll vote for your bill if you vote for mine.) Thus farmers damaged by straying cattle may join with the construction lobby to obtain a public works project that provides them with free fences. This is good for farmers and fence builders. But, to say the obvious, a policy of free fences for farmers may flunk the welfare test; that is, it may not produce a rearrangement of resources that could make everybody better off (if compensation to losers were paid). For politics to guarantee better results than pricing in dealing with externalities, we would have to assume that individuals show a nobler side of themselves when acting through politics than when acting through the market.

2. Suppose that the control of externalities can be turned over to an all-wise and totally benevolent dictator. Suppose also that he has the power to grant subsidies to industries producing benign externalities and levy taxes on those producing malign externalities. His goal is to bring about a distribution of resources which makes private marginal cost equal to social marginal cost in all industries. There still remains the matter of administrative costs. For example, if taxes are to be used to improve the distribution of resources, some resources have to be used to levy and collect them. It may be cheaper to live with a particular "market failure" than to do something about it.

It is, of course, possible that whenever externalities are not accompanied by side-bargains between beneficiaries and victims (because contract costs are prohibitive) economic welfare can be increased by substituting politics for pricing. In a locality plagued by mosquitos, the discomfort can be dealt with by letting every citizen buy his own fly swatter. By almost universal consent, a better solution is to devote some fraction of public tax revenue to mosquito control. However, when pricing and politics are alternative ways of coping with externalities, the question of which method is best is one for empirical investigation. The fact that private cost demonstrably diverges from social cost in a particular industry should never be taken as conclusive evidence that the sum of economic welfare is reduced by the divergence. The divergence can suggest but does not prove that resort to political action may increase economic welfare.[8]

8. The high contract costs that may justify the substitution of politics for pricing can often be traced to the complexity of the law and the slowness of the courts. Com-

Welfare optimum versus welfare optima

So long as we do not ask too much of welfare economics it does good service for us most of the time. If we are content to make small incremental changes in economic policy there is a strong presumption that we should accept a change which would allow gainers to compensate losers and reject a change which cannot meet this test. And so long as we deal in specific proposals—another bridge across the Hudson River, a new sewage plant for Yonkers—it is usually possible to estimate a range for possible gains and losses that most people will accept. But many economists are inveterate generalizers. Some, not content to evaluate bridges and sewage plants, have aspired to specify the conditions that a complete economic system must satisfy if economic welfare is to be maximized. These "macro" efforts are examined in the next chapter. We shall comment here on only one feature of the problem.

We have noted that one of the two fundamental assumptions (assumption A13.2) of modern welfare economics is that no change can be said to increase economic welfare unless it can (not necessarily will) make at least one person better off without making anyone else worse off. Economists sometimes describe the case where no such change is possible anywhere in the economic system as a *Pareto optimum* (after the Italian economist and sociologist Vilfredo Pareto (1848-1923) who laid the foundations for much of modern welfare economics). It is often asserted that in an economic model (i) composed entirely of perfectly competitive commodity and factor markets and (ii) having no externalities of production or consumption, a Pareto optimum would exist.

For nearly self-evident reasons, perfect competition in this case would bring about a Pareto optimum. In equilibrium, price would equal both private marginal cost and private average total cost; private marginal cost would equal social marginal cost; and every consumer would be on his highest indifference curve. Nevertheless, the unqualified identification of perfect competition (with no externalities) with a welfare optimum is misleading in two very important respects.

---

menting on the problem of saving the central business district from further decay, the mayor of Selma, Alabama, complained:

"Some downtown buildings are tied up in estates owned by as many as 32 people scattered all over the country. It makes it almost impossible for them to get together and carry out renovations that are necessary. As a result, the upper floors—the ones which were occupied by lawyers, doctors, and dentists—are now all vacant. They're unusable." Quoted in a *New York Times* article on the problems of urban renewal, February 8, 1972.

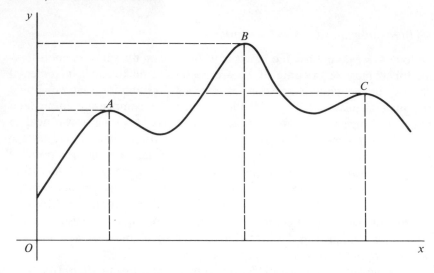

FIGURE 13.4

First, it implies that there is only one welfare optimum, which is not so. To make this truth clear we can resort to a mathematical analogy. In your calculus course you learned to distinguish between a global maximum and a local maximum. In figure 13.4 the variable y is shown as a function of the variable x. Points A, B, and C all represent maximum values for the function $y = f(x)$ in the sense that $dy/dx = 0$ and $d^2y/dx^2 < 0$. However, points A and C are merely local maxima while point B is a global maximum.

Likewise, in welfare economics we can distinguish between a local optimum and a global optimum. Consider the problem of making a welfare judgment about the standard railroad track gauge of most Western countries. For more than one hundred years most trains have operated on a track width of 4 feet, 8½ inches. Is this an optimal width?

In one sense this standard gauge is obviously not optimal. If it were wider we could operate bigger, faster, more comfortable, and generally more efficient trains. It is our tough luck that nineteenth-century railroad builders chose the present standard gauge instead of a wider one. Yet if the narrow tests of welfare economics are applied, the standard gauge is clearly optimal. In order to change to a wider width we would have to scrap most of the existing rolling stock of the railroads, re-lay the whole track system, and rebuild every station. Almost nobody would contend that the gains of a wider gauge would exceed the cost of changing to it.

We find it cheaper to live with many of the engineering mistakes of the past than to correct them.

By the same token, we may regret that a particular industry has evolved over the years into a non-discriminating monopoly. But now there may be no way of restructuring it into a perfectly competitive industry without making somebody worse off. In the real world there is always a cost of change-over in the short run, and often in the long run as well. And change-over costs may be "prohibitive." Perfect competition (without externalities) is a unique welfare optimum only when it is possible to move to it *without cost* from a situation that falls short of perfect competition (without externalities).

We might put the matter in this way. If we had inherited a perfectly competitive economy (without externalities) from our ancestors we would not be able to change it without inflicting welfare losses that could not be compensated out of welfare gains. However, because we did not inherit a perfectly competitive economy, it does not necessarily follow that we can improve upon what we did receive. To repeat: only some of the mistakes that have come down from the past are worth correcting.

The conservative bias of modern welfare economics

You now know enough about modern welfare economics to realize that it incorporates a rather astounding conservative bias. It takes the distribution of income as "given," assumes that people are the best judges of their own interests, and comes perilously close to asserting that, wherever the market is allowed to operate, "whatever is is best." Welfare economists do not invariably come down against intervention by the State to alter the distribution of resources realized through the market. For since contract costs do exist in this world, it is possible that the substitution of political decisions for market decisions will increase economic welfare. Welfare economists do insist that since State intervention also has its costs, it may be cheaper to live with existing evils than to remove them.

Objections to welfare economics

This chapter began by asserting that almost nobody (economist or non-economist) accepts the fundamental assumptions of welfare economics without some qualification. Nor is there any reason why he (or she) should. One can reasonably argue that improving economic welfare by changing the allocation of resources cannot become a legitimate policy goal until the State has brought about the correct (and presumably less unequal) distribution of income. Or one can argue that greater economic welfare should be the policy goal only to the extent that consumers have the information needed for intelligent decisions. If the market indicated that most consumers of ice cream, in common with a distinguished Columbia University dean, prefer strawberry to tutti-frutti, so be it. But if, in their ignorance, they prefer expensive, unsafe cars to cheap, safe cars, there is no reason why they should be allowed to persist in error. Whether he knows it or not, the consumer will "really" be better off if he is forced or led to drive a safe, cheap car.

We close our discussion of the limited, pragmatic tradition in welfare economics with two comments. In the real world, policy decisions are made on the basis of incomplete information; and proponents of particular views have a well-developed capacity to believe what they want to believe. Nobody can tell in advance whether another bridge across the East River in New York City could make someone better off without making anybody else worse off. People who want another bridge will so believe; people who do not want it will vehemently deny the possibility.

Second, in much of our economic behavior most of us have at least a touch of schizophrenia. We may behave one way when we make our decisions through the market and quite another way when we make them through the political process. As voters we may support laws to curtail the sale of booze and then, as consumers, patronize bootleggers. Left to our own devices we will neglect buying automobile liability insurance and yet support compulsory insurance laws. When politics and pricing give different answers for the same set of people, which way is "best"? This question you will have to answer on your own.

Does welfare economics really matter considering the difficulty of applying it to real-world problems? Yes, it really does matter. Without a clear-cut definition of economic welfare we are at the mercy of every crackpot, self-canonized saint, and special interest group that wants to make economic policy for us. But having said these kind words about welfare economics, the fact remains that the views of reasonable men (and women) differ greatly about the respective merits of politics and pricing as alternative ways of making economic decisions.

Summary

In this chapter we have, for the first time, paid explicit attention to the role of value judgments in economics. What are the criteria that should be used to distinguish a "good" economic policy from a "bad" one? We made the acquaintance of an important tradition in modern economics which commands the respect, though not always the affection, of most economists. As we saw, modern welfare economics rests upon two fundamental assumptions. (a) Every individual is the sole judge of whether an economic change makes him better off or worse off. (b) No change can be said to increase economic welfare unless it can (not necessarily will) make somebody better off without making anybody else worse off. That is, there is no increase in economic welfare unless those who gain from change could fully compensate those who lose from change and still be better off themselves.

We distinguished between technical efficiency and welfare efficiency in the use of scarce resources. Developments that increase technical efficiency and so allow more income to be obtained from a given quantity of resources almost always increase economic welfare as the term is defined above. The tough problems of welfare economics involve proposals to increase welfare efficiency by using economic policy to bring about a different allocation of resources.

The tools of welfare economics were then applied to three classic issues —the choice of criteria for screening public work projects, price policy for a decreasing cost public utility, and the meaning of private versus social cost. Finally, we noted that the task of making value judgments about economic policy is complicated by a certain troublesome inconsistency in human behavior. The same person will often, so to speak, vote one way when spending his income in the market and quite another when making economic decisions through the political process. When this schizophrenia is present, it is a matter of personal opinion whether decisions should be left to politics or to the market.

REFERENCES

Bator, F. M., "The Anatomy of Market Failure," *Quarterly Journal of Economics,* 92 (1958), 351-79.

Buchanan, J. M., "Politics, Policy, and the Pigouvian Margins," *Economica* (n.r.) 29 (1962), 17-28.

Coase, Ronald, "The Problem of Social Cost, *"Journal of Law and Economics,* 2 (1960), 1-44.

Mishan, E. J., *Welfare Economics: Ten Introductory Essays* (New York, 2nd ed., 1969), especially chapter 4.

Nath, S. K., *A Reappraisal of Welfare Economics* (London, 1969), especially chapter 5.

Nicholson, Walter, *Microeconomic Theory: Basic Principles and Extensions* (Hinsdale, 1972), chapters 21-25.

Pigou, A. C., *The Economics of Welfare* (London, 4th ed., 1932), especially parts I and II.

Regan, D. H., "The Problem of Social Cost Revisited," *Journal of Law and Economics,* 15 (1972), 427-37.

Whitcomb, D. K., *Externalities and Welfare* (New York, 1972), especially chapter 1.

14
Maximizing Economic Welfare

An alternative tradition in welfare economics

In the last chapter we mentioned that a second tradition in welfare economics has aimed higher than the one so far considered which simply seeks to determine whether an incremental economic change will increase welfare. Work in this second tradition attempts to set down the conditions that must be fulfilled if an economy is to achieve the optimal allocation of economic resource that maximizes economic welfare. In economics, as in mathematics, the most general results are the most elegant; but the elegance of generality, like everything else in this world, has its cost. The principal cost of employing the more ambitious approach to welfare economics is the neglect of contract costs and the costs of altering whatever allocation of economic resources has been inherited from the past. When these costs are assumed to be zero, it is possible to identify the conditions that must be satisfied if the economy as a whole is to have an optimal allocation of resources. Once again we define an optimal allocation of resources to be one in which it is not possible to make any change in the distribution of resources without making somebody worse off. As we noted in the last chapter, this is usually called a Pareto optimum.

The conditions necessary for Pareto optimality

We can show that the following five conditions must be realized before an optimal distribution of resources can exist.

C14.1 The marginal rate of substitution between any two commo-

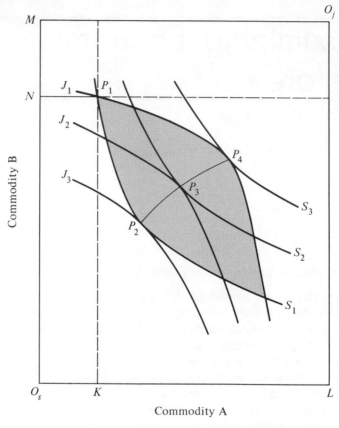

FIGURE 14.1

dities must be the same for any two consumers of these
commodities.

Condition C14.1 is merely another way of saying that it must not be
possible for any two consumers to make themselves better off by engaging
in additional trade with each other. That is, any pair of consumers must
be on their "contract curve." We have already demonstrated in Chapter 2
the necessity that this condition be satisfied before the mutual gain from
trade is exhausted. We did so with the aid of the Edgeworth box diagram
which is reproduced, for ready reference, in figure 14.1.

Once again we have Smith and Jones dealing in commodities A and B.
In figure 14.1, the "width of the box," which is equal to the horizontal
distance O_sL gives the total amount of commodity A that is owned by

both Smith and Jones. The "height of the box," which is equal to the vertical distance O_sM, gives the total amount of commodity B that is owned by both Smith and Jones.

The amount of commodity A that Smith alone owns (before trade) is measured horizontally from the origin O_s at the lower left corner of the box. The amount of commodity B that Smith alone owns (before trade) is measured vertically from the origin O_s. Therefore, any interior point in the box diagram also indicates a possible combination of commodities A and B in the possession of Smith and Jones. Look at point P_1 again. It indicates that Jones has $(O_jM\text{-}O_sK)$ units of commodity A and $(O_jL\text{-}O_sN)$ units of commodity B. Three of Smith's indifference curves are given in figure 14.1. They are S_1, S_2, and S_3. Three of Jones's indifference curves are also given. They are J_1, J_2, and J_3. Remember that the amount of commodity A owned by Jones is measured horizontally to the left of point O_j; while the amount of commodity B owned by Jones is measured vertically and downward from point O_j.

Smith's economic welfare will increase as he moves from points close to O_s upward and to the right toward point O_j. Likewise, Jones's economic welfare will increase as he moves from points close to O_j downward to the left toward point O_s. To repeat, point P_1 in figure 14.1 represents the initial division of commodities between Smith and Jones before they begin to trade with each other.

Given the initial division of the two commodities between them, Smith is on indifference curve J_1. If the two consumers are free to trade with each other, some amount of trade will obviously make both better off, i.e. move each to a "higher" indifference curve. Recall in figure 14.1 for Jones "lower is higher" since we have turned his set of indifference curves upside down. Smith will gain by giving up some part of his stock of commodity B in exchange for some part of Jones's stock of commodity A. Jones becomes better off by parting with some part of his stock of commodity A in order to get part of Smith's stock of commodity B.

We do not know exactly how much trade will take place between Smith and Jones because we do not know their respective bargaining strengths. We do know, however, that they will engage in trade until they have reached a point on the contract curve that runs from P_2 through P_3 to P_4. Recall that the contract curve contains all points at which (i) the indifference curves of Smith and Jones are tangent and (ii) trade benefits both parties. In figure 14.1 the shaded area includes all combinations of commodities A and B that Smith and Jones both prefer to the combination represented by point P_1. However, when trade is possible, only those points in the shaded area which lie on the contract curve are equilibrium points.

Once Smith and Jones have reached a point on the contract curve P_2P_4, they have exhausted the possibilities of a mutual gain from trade. Further trade can only make one party better off by making the other worse off. At any point on the contract curve, the slopes of the indifference curves of Smith and Jones are equal. For example, at point P_3, the slope of J_2 is equal to the slope of S_2. Hence Smith and Jones will not have exhausted the gains of trade until condition C14.1 has been satisfied.

> C14.2 The marginal rate of transformation between a factor input and a commodity must be the same for any two firms that use the factor input to produce the commodity.

C14.2 is really saying that the marginal physical product of the factor input must be the same in both firms. This is practically self-evident. Suppose that firms M and N use a given factor input to produce the same commodity and the marginal physical product of this input is 6 units in firm M and 2 units in firm N. Obviously there will be a net increase in commodity output of 4 units if 1 unit of the factor input is transferred from firm N to firm M.

Condition C14.2 is sometimes expressed by saying that the marginal rate of substitution between any two factor inputs must be the same for any two firms that use both to produce the same commodity. If the marginal physical product of every factor input is the same for both firms, then the marginal physical product of input x divided by the marginal physical product of input y must be the same ratio for the two firms. And this ratio is the marginal rate of substitution between inputs x and y.

> C14.3 A firm that produces more than one commodity must allocate its factor inputs in such a way that the marginal rate of technical substitution of any two factor inputs is the same in the production of any two commodities.

We can demonstrate the necessity of this condition by using a modification of the Edgworth box diagram. (The box diagram was not Edgeworth's only contribution to economics but it was certainly the most popular.) In figure 14.2 the width of the box now indicates the total amount of labor input available to the firm and the height of the box indicates the amount of capital input available to it. The firm can use these inputs to produce various combinations of commodities A and B.

The concave and convex curves in figure 14.2 are commodity isoquants. Thus all points on curve A_2 represent the same amount of commodity A. The amount of commodity A is measured to the right from the vertex O_A.

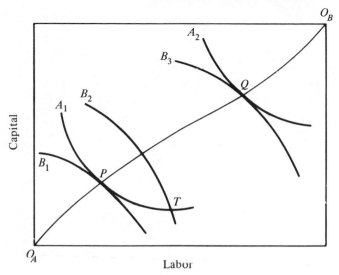

FIGURE 14.2

Thus every point on curve A_2 represents a greater amount of commodity A than every point on curve A_1.

Likewise every point of curve B_1 represents the same amount of commodity B. The amount of commodity B being measured to the left from the vertex O_B, every point of curve B_1 represents a greater amount of commodity B than every point on curve B_2.

Clearly, the firm in figure 14.2 will only produce a combination of commodities A and B at which an A isoquant is tangent to a B isoquant. Two such combinations of commodities are given by points P and Q. Suppose that the firm, for some reason, is producing the combination represented by point T in figure 14.2. By shifting labor to the production of commodity B and capital to the production of commodity A, the firm can move to point P. And point P represents more of commodity B than T and the same amount of commodity A. Thus point T represents a technically inefficient way of producing commodities A and B.

      C14.4 The marginal rate of transformation between any two commodities must be the same for any two firms that produce both commodities.

Condition C14.4 requires that the optimal degree of specialization among firms be achieved. Suppose that firm M can produce 4 more units of commodity A by producing 1 less unit of commodity B. Whereas firm N can have 1 more unit of commodity A by producing 1 less unit of commodity

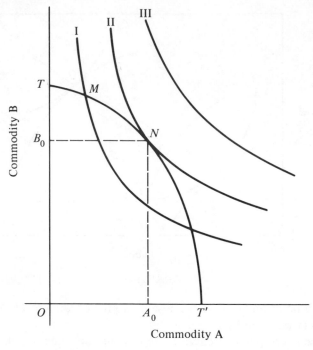

FIGURE 14.3

B. Now it will pay firms M and N to enter into a contract whereby M increases its output of commodity A and offers some part of the increment to firm N in exchange for some amount of commodity B. In the language of the business world, it will pay firm M to subcontract some part of its requirements for commodity B to firm N. Likewise it will pay firm N to subcontract some part of its requirements for commodity A to firm M. Condition C14.4 requires that a firm, like a nation, should specialize in the production of that commodity in which it has the greatest comparative advantage.

> C14.5 The marginal rate of substitution between any two commodities for an individual who consumes both must be the same as the marginal rate of transformation (for the community) between them.

Condition C14.1 says that a welfare optimum is never reached until individuals have exhausted all possible gains from trade. Conditions C14.2, C14.3, and C14.4 say that whatever combination of commodities is produced must be produced in the most technically efficient way.

Condition C14.5 says that a welfare optimum is never reached until the "right" combination of commodities is produced.

The necessity for condition C14.5 can be illustrated with the aid of figure 14.3. In the interest of simplicity, let us suppose that the economy consists of a single individual who wishes to consume commodities A and B. Let three of his indifference curves be given by curves I, II, and III. The curve TT' in figure 14.3 is a transformation curve that shows the various combinations of commodities A and B that the economy can produce when its resources are fully employed. The marginal rate of transformation of commodity A into commodity B (and vice versa) is given by the slope of TT' (which is, of course, different for every combination of A and B). Curve TT' can be regarded as a production-possibility frontier.

Obviously the individual is on his highest indifference curve (II) when OA_o units of commodity A and OB_o units of commodity B are produced. This combination is given by point N in figure 14.3. At point $N,$ the slope of the consumer's highest attainable indifference curve, which is curve II, is equal to the slope of the commodity transformation curve TT'. Hence, the marginal rate of transformation of commodity A into commodity B (and vice versa) is equal to the individual's marginal rate of substitution for these two commodities.

Pareto optimality and perfect competition again

What kind of an economic system satisfies all five of the conditions above and so makes possible maximum economic welfare? The answer, in a word, is a perfectly competitive system which contains no externalities. In such a system, market price would everywhere be equal to marginal social cost and it would not be possible to make somebody better off without making somebody else worse off.

At this point, it is advisable to recall the caution offered in the last chapter. Because perfect competition without externalities represents a welfare optimum, it does not follow that, in the real world, a departure from perfect competition and/or the presence of externalities represent a welfare loss. In the real world, it is not always possible to achieve the conditions necessary for a close approximation to perfect competition without externalities in a given industry. And, as we shall presently note in our discussion of the "theory of the second best," even when these conditions can be created by political action, the costs of creating them may exceed the welfare gains that they will bring. Likewise, the costs of correcting the externalities of perfect competition may exceed the welfare gains to be had.

The social welfare function

When the distribution of income among individuals is taken as given, it is easy enough to write down the conditions that must be satisfied for a welfare optimum. After all, the five conditions that we listed above are merely a precise way of saying that economic welfare is maximized when the economic system produces the combination of commodities that people want and does it in the way that is technically most efficient.

In the real world, of course, we do not accept whatever distribution of income is brought about by the price system. To say the obvious, we insist that income be redistributed in favor of people who would starve to death if compelled to rely on the incomes that they could earn in the marketplace. Indeed, most of us would now prefer that progressive income taxation and government assistance programs carry the redistribution of income well beyond the point necessary to rescue our most unfortunate neighbors from absolute destitution.

Moreover, in this world, there are certain goals that cannot be achieved through the market alone. There are public goods—commodities and services for which markets cannot be organized because they become freely available to all individuals as soon as they are made available to one. (Some conventional examples of public goods are national defense, weather forecasting, lighthouses, "pure" scientific research, and mosquito control.[1]) Smith and Jones may be able to move on to higher indifference curves by exchanging commodities A and B. But Smith cannot get more police protection by buying some from Jones in exchange for his (Smith's) right to walk in Central Park. Decisions about public goods are necessarily political decisions.

The unreality of discussing economic welfare without reference to income distribution and public goods has led many economists to insist that the problem of maximizing economic welfare be discussed in terms of a social welfare function. Let us do so with the aid of figure 14.4. We remain

---

1. The definition of public goods given above will suffice for our purpose. We merely wish to make the point that individuals have preferences which cannot be satisfied through the market. However, in the real world there is usually no hard-and-fast dividing line between public and private goods. Policeman have been known to accept "gratuities" in return for keeping a close watch on certain business properties and so converted police protection from a public good into a private good. Highways are usually regarded as a public good not because they could not be provided through a market (toll roads have a long history) but because federal policy decrees that they must be toll free. A citizen cannot be charged for the pleasure he gets from viewing the Bronx Botanical Garden from the outside; he can be (and sometimes is) charged for the pleasure of walking in the Garden.

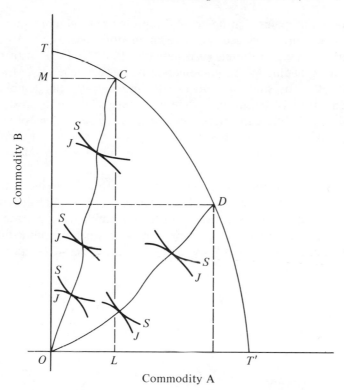

FIGURE 14.4

in the world of Smith and Jones and the possibility of dividing scarce economic resources between the production of two commodities, A and B.

The economic welfare (utility) of Smith and Jones depends upon two
things: (i) the combination of commodities A and B that is produced
(more of commodity A always meaning less of commodity B, and vice
versa, when resources are fully employed); and (ii) how the combination
actually produced is divided between Smith and Jones (more for Smith
always meaning less for Jones, and vice versa). Curve TT' in figure 14.4
is simply the commodity transformation curve reproduced from figure
14.3. Recall the curve TT' shows the combinations of commodities A and
B that can be produced when all economic resources are fully employed.
The utility levels attained by Smith and Jones depend upon how a given
combination of commodities is divided between them. Hence every point
on TT' implies a unique Edgeworth box diagram and a unique contract
curve for Smith and Jones.

Suppose that point C in figure 14.4 represents the combination of commodities actually produced. (This combination consists of OL units of commodity A and OM units of commodity B.) The Edgeworth box diagram corresponding to this combination is the rectangle $OLCM$. And the contract curve of Smith and Jones corresponding to this combination is OC. (In figure 14.4 selected indifference curves of Smith are labelled S and selected indifference curves of Jones are labeled J.) As we know, every point on the contract curve OC represents a "state" in which Smith cannot be made better off unless Jones is made worse off (and conversely).

Now let the combination of commodities actually produced be represented by point D in figure 14.4. By changing the division of this new combination of commodities between Jones and Smith we can trace out the new contract curve OD. Clearly, by moving down the commodity transformation curve from point T to point T' we can generate a set of contract curves for Smith and Jones.

FIGURE 14.5

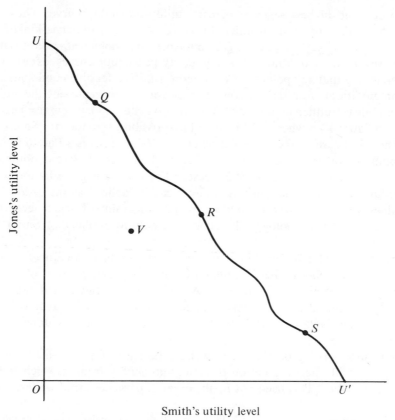

Smith's utility level

FIGURE 14.6

The information provided by the set of all contract curves that can be created in this way allows us to construct a *utility-possibility frontier* for an economy consisting of Smith and Jones. Each contract curve implies a *utility-possibility curve* which shows the respective utility ranks that Smith and Jones can achieve for every combination of commodities represented by a point on the commodity transformation curve *TT'*. Four such utility-possibility curves are drawn in figure 14.5, these curves being *AA'*, *BB'*, *CC'*, and *DD'*. A utility-possibility curve must, of course, have a negative slope since Smith can only increase his own utility at the expense of Jones's utility (and vice versa).

Assume that only four possible combinations of commodities can be produced. On this assumption, the heavy line *DA'* in figure 14.5 incor-

porates the highest segment of each utility-possibility curve. Thus *DA'*
is the utility-possibility frontier. In figure 14.5 this frontier is kinked because curves *AA'*, *BB'*, *CC'*, *DD'* intersect one another at several points.
However, we can draw as many utility-possibility curves as we wish
(assuming that any point on *TT'* in figure 14.4 is a feasible combination of
commodities). For this reason, it is customary to represent the utility-
possibility frontier as a continuous function, i.e. smooth curve. This we
do in figure 14.6 where *UU'* is the utility-possibility frontier for Smith and
Jones. In figure 14.6 every point on curve *UU'* represents a Pareto welfare
optimum for Smith and Jones. Three such points of Pareto optimality
are *Q*, *R*, and *S*. Which point is "best"? The answer is given by the social
welfare function which, in this context, can be defined as the ordering of
values which determines (subject to the constraint of scarce economic
resources and technology) the economic welfare (utility) of Smith and
Jones.

A social welfare function strongly biased in favor of Jones against
Smith would choose the distribution of resources and division of income
that yields point *Q* in figure 14.6. A social welfare function that is relatively indifferent to the claims of Jones and Smith would favor point *R*.
And a social welfare function biased in favor of Smith against Jones would
favor point *S*.[2]

In most writing on the social welfare function it is assumed that the
function will select a point on the utility-possibility frontier which is *UU'*
in figure 14.6.[3] This need not be the case. A perverse social welfare func-

2. When speaking loosely, we are likely to say that the social welfare function in
the above example allocates economic welfare between Smith and Jones. However,
recall that in Chapter 2 we accepted the restrictions implicit in an ordinal definition
of utility. We do not presume to compare the utilities of Smith and Jones. And we
can only rank levels of economic welfare (utility) for each individual. For example,
in figure 14.6 suppose that a change in the social welfare function moves Smith and
Jones from point *R* on the utility-possibility frontier to point *S* (the utility possi-
bility-frontier being curve *UU'*). As regards Smith, we can only say that this change
has raised him to a higher level of economic welfare (utility). We cannot say by
how much his economic welfare has been increased. Thus, in figure 14.6 distance
from the origin at point *O* along the *x*-axis does not really measure Smith's economic
welfare (utility). It merely indicates the level of economic welfare (utility) that he
has reached.
3. Some writers conceive of the social welfare function as a set of social indifference
curves that relate the welfare rankings of Smith and Jones. By this view, the slopes
of these social indifference curves determine the point at which the highest social
indifference is tangent to the utility-possibility frontier (one such frontier is frontier-
curve *UU'* in figure 14.6). The objection to this view is that it makes the social welfare function incorporate the preference that any point on the utility frontier is to be
favored over any interior point. This is a wildly inaccurate view of the social welfare

tion is a logical possibility; indeed, in the real world, it is virtually a political certainty. It is possible that the social welfare function will allocate to Smith and Jones the utility ranks represented by point V in figure 14.6. In this case, the social welfare function is perverse in the sense that, since point V lies inside the utility-possibility frontier, UU', a change in the distribution of economic resources could make both men better off.

We can think of any number of reasons why society does not want Smith and Jones to reach the utility-possibility frontier UU'. Maybe Smith and Jones are hard-working atheists who live in a society that believes that religious holidays should be scrupulously observed. If so, the interior point V in figure 14.6 might represent the levels of economic welfare that Smith and Jones are allowed to achieve by a social welfare function that keeps them idle against their will. Or it may be that Smith and Jones are at point V because a law against usury forbids contracts that they would be willing to enter. Smith could be a frustrated loan shark and Jones a luckless gambler who usually needs $100 to carry him to his next payday. The social welfare function keeps them apart and so off the utility-possibility frontier.

Deriving a social welfare function from individual preference

The concept of a social welfare function is quite concrete since some ordering of preferences obviously does determine the individual and social choices made in an economic system. That is, a social welfare function undoubtedly "exists" in every economic system of the real world. The concept of "maximizing a social welfare function" is a much more rarefied thing since maximizing involves identifying and ranking the preferences that make up the function. The task of describing the content of a social welfare function of the real world is generally left to sociologists and anthropologists. (Quite legitimately, workers in these fields use a different terminology, e.g. they generally prefer to speak of a "value system" rather than a social welfare function.) In the history of economics most interest in the social welfare function has centered on the questions: Using only the preferences expressed by individuals, is it in principle possible to con-

---

functions that determine social choice in the real world. A good part of social legislation in the form of restrictions on freedom of contract is designed to ensure that Smith and Jones are kept from reaching their utility-possibility frontier. The *raison d'être* for this restraint is simply that any decision to place Smith and Jones on the utility-possibility frontier would require the sacrifice of values which the social welfare function wants respected.

struct a social welfare function that does not allow one man to impose his preferences on another? Or must the social welfare function always contain preferences which are imposed without the consent of some individuals?

In the real world, obviously every social welfare function does contain imposed preferences. But we can still ask if this need be true. For economists—and indeed for all persons who place a high value upon respect for individual preferences—the question raises fundamental issues about the nature of the good society. If a social welfare function could be constructed from individual preferences, presumably all persons with a bias in favor of individualism would wish it to be done mainly in this way. If no such function can be constructed from individual preferences, then people with such a bias (and this set includes most economists) must rethink their philosophical position.

As discussed by economists, the question of a social welfare function is generally framed in the following way: Using only the preferences of individuals and certain reasonable assumptions about human behavior, is it possible to construct a social welfare function that satisfies certain reasonable conditions? As you might expect, the answer turns upon what is meant by "reasonable." In a famous early investigation of this problem, Kenneth Arrow returned a negative answer (and thereby went a long way toward gaining his Nobel prize). Let us assume that two conventional axioms of utility analysis hold.

a.1 The preferences of every individual can be ranked. When an individual is faced with choices x and y, he prefers y to x; he is indifferent between y and x; or he prefers x to y.

a.2 The ordering of every individual's preferences is transitive. If he prefers x to y and y to z, then he must also prefer x to z. Likewise, if he is indifferent between x and y and between y and z, he must also be indifferent between x and z.

Using these two axions, Arrow was able to show that, in general, it is not possible to construct a social welfare function that does not violate at least one of the following five conditions.

c.1 The social welfare function must incorporate unanimous preferences. If every individual prefers a "state" where at least 1 percent of national income is spent on cancer research, then at least 1 percent of national income must be so spent.

c.2 The social welfare function must not respond perversely to changes in individual preferences. Suppose that one individual's preferences change in a way that causes him to prefer a state

TABLE 14.1

X_1X_2	Y_1X_2	I_1X_2
X_1Y_2	Y_1Y_2	Y_1I_2
I_1I_2	X_1I_2	I_1Y_2

that accords a higher rank to alternative x. In the revised social welfare function, alternative x must rank either higher or at least not lower than in the initial ordering.

c.3 The social welfare function must incorporate only those preferences that are capable of being realized. Thus the relative rank assigned to train travel should not be affected by the fact that somebody prefers to fly at a speed of 5000 miles per hour if air travel at this speed is not yet possible.

c.4 The social welfare function must not be "imposed" by custom or State constitution. That is, it cannot require that alternative x be preferred to alternative y regardless of individual preferences.

c.5 The social welfare function is not the creation of a dictator. One individual's preferences must not be allowed to determine the content of the function.

Suppose that the problem is to construct a social welfare function for two individuals who must choose between two alternatives, x and y, and to do it in a way that satisfies Arrow's five conditions. Let X denote a preference for x over y. Let Y denote a preference for y over x. And let I denote indifference between x and y. With two individuals and these alternative ways of ranking x and y, we have the nine possible combinations of individual preferences given in table 14.1.

While we have nine possible combinations of rankings of x and y for our two individuals, only a combination that lies in the *unshaded* boxes of table 14.1 can provide a basis for a social welfare function that satisfies Arrow's five conditions. For example, $W(X_1, X_2) = X$ is an acceptable social welfare function because both individuals prefer x to y. So also is $W(X_1, I_2) = X$ an acceptable social welfare function because individual #1 prefers x to y and individual #2 is indifferent between x and y. However, $W(Y_1, X_2) = Y$ is not an acceptable social welfare function; it allows individual #1 to impose his preference for y on individual #2. Likewise $W(Y_1, X_2) = X$ is not acceptable because it allows individual

#2 to impose his preference for x on individual #1. In the case of I_1, I_2, the social welfare function must contain some agreed-upon rule for resolving the tie between x and y. (One such rule might require that a tie be broken by tossing a coin.)

Arrow's impossibility theorem

We have, in effect, demonstrated that in a world consisting of two individuals and two alternatives to be ranked, it *may* be possible to construct a social welfare function from individual preferences. Indeed, as table 14.1 shows, the odds are 7 to 2 that it can be done in the case of two individuals and two choices. It was Arrow's achievement to show that when individual utility functions rank three or more alternatives, it is generally impossible to construct a social welfare function that satisfies his five conditions. The proof of Arrow's "impossibility" theorem is a subtle (but not difficult) exercise in set theory.[4] We prove it with the aid of the notion of a decisive set.

Suppose that the social welfare function ranks three alternatives—let these alternatives be y, z, and x—in the following order of importance: *xyz*. Thus in the social welfare function x is prefered to y. A set which is decisive for x against y in the social welfare function consists of all persons who prefer x to y. Likewise a set which is decisive for y against z consists of all persons who prefer y to z.

Now suppose that the social welfare function contains some ranking of x, y, and z which satisfies all of Arrow's five conditions. From the sets of all individuals that are decisive for social choices among x, y, and z, select a set M such that it has no subsets that are decisive. Such a set M must exist. Since the social welfare function is assumed to satisfy all five conditions, the set of all individuals in the population must be decisive. From this universal set, we can remove individuals one at a time in a way that leaves a decisive set. When this can no longer be done, we have a "minimally decisive" set M.

This set M must contain at least two individuals. For should it contain only one individual, he would be a dictator who has written his own rank order for x, y, and z into the social welfare function. And a dictator is ruled out by condition c.5.

Let A designate an individual who is removed from set M. Let B designate the set that remains after individual A has been removed. And let M designate the set of all persons not in M. Thus set A contains ex-

4. William Vickrey, *Microstatics* (New York, 1964), pp. 277-78.

actly one person, and set *B* contains at least one person. Set *M* may be an empty set.

Suppose that the individuals in set *B* prefer the ranking *yzx* while *A* prefers the ranking *xyz*. Suppose that all members of set *M*, if it is not empty, prefer the ranking *zxy*. By definition, the individuals in *A* and *B* together make up the decisive set *M*. Hence the social welfare function must rank y above z. The single individual who is in set *A* cannot constitute a decisive set. But if x is at least as high as y in the social welfare function and y outranks z, then x must also outrank z. Now *A* is the only individual who prefers x to z. However, in the social welfare function, x must not outrank z. For if x does outrank z, then *A* is a dictator and condition c.5 is violated.

Therefore, it follows that, in the social welfare function, x must outrank z and must not outrank z. This is a contradiction. It shows that we cannot construct a social welfare function that satisfies the five conditions.

Social choice as expressed in the activities of the State has always contained an authoritarian element. So far the main policy implication of theoretical work on the social welfare function has been the demonstration that, however much we may wish to respect individual preferences in social choice, the authoritarian element cannot be reduced to zero. The practical significance of this demonstration, however, is rather limited.[5] The economic issues of the real world turn upon whether the economy should make a little more or a little less use of the market in its decision making. Economic policy, except in the case of a revolution carried through by Utopians, is a matter of incremental changes, not a quest for a welfare optimum.

The problem of the "second best"

In the real world it never happens that an economic system—or even a particular industry—satisfies the conditions necessary for a walfare optimum. It is also true that these conditions are capable of being more closely approximated in some parts of the system than in others. We cannot have anything resembling perfect competition in the production of electricity from atomic power plants. But we can have a reasonable facsimile thereof in the production of wheat, nylon carpet, or paper envelopes. Should "as close to perfect competition as possible" be the goal of economic policy? The (possibly) surprising answer is: not necessarily. Because we

5. See, for example, Gordon Tullock, "The General Irrelevance of the General Impossibility Theorem," *Quarterly Journal of Economics*, 81 (1967), 256-70.

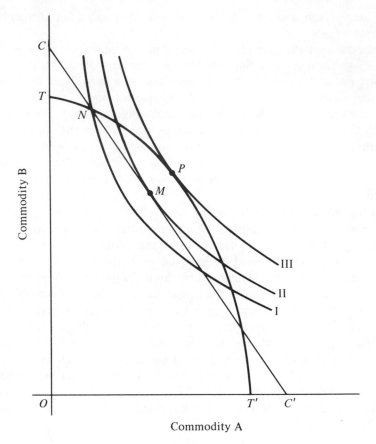

Commodity B

O   T'   C'

Commodity A

FIGURE 14.7

cannot have all of the results that perfect competition would produce, it does not follow that the second-best solution is to secure as many of these results as we can.[6] While the formal proof of this theorem is rather involved, the reasoning behind it can be conveyed with the aid of figure 14.7.

In figure 14.7, TT' gives the production-possibility frontier that would exist in a two-commodity world if conditions c.2, c.3, and c.4 were satisfied. Recall that these are the conditions necessary for *technically* efficient production. Curves I, II, and III are three social indifference curves implied by a social welfare function that wishes to maximize economic wel-

6. Kelvin Lancaster and R. G. Lipsey, "The General Theory of Second Best," *Review of Economic Studies*, 24 (1956-57), 11-32.

fare. (As we have noted, the social welfare functions of the real world most emphatically *do not* incorporate this goal.)

The highest attainable social indifference curve is curve III in figure 14.7. It is reached when the economy produces the combination of commodities A and B given by point *P*. However, for curve III to be tangent to *TT'* at point *P,* it is necessary that every pair of consumers be on their contract curve. That is, for point *P* to be reached, condition c.1 must be satisfied. Now suppose that some natural impediment—say the search costs that consumers must incur in order to exchange commodities A and B with one another—makes it impossible for the economy to reach point *P*. This impediment to exchange in the form of consumer ignorance we represent by line *CC''*.

Nature says that we cannot have point *P* in figure 14.7. Should we nevertheless insist that the economy achieve the technical efficiency represented by an attainable point on the production-possibility frontier *TT'?* If we so insist, point *N* is the attainable point that lies closest to *P*. However, *N* lies on indifference curve I which is below indifference curves II and III and so represents "less welfare." By staying inside its production-possibility frontier the economy can reach point *M* and so attain indifference curve II. Clearly we should not insist that production be at a point *TT'* in figure 14.7 if our goal is to maximize economic welfare.[7]

The enforcement history of the American antitrust laws provides many instances of the unwisdom of myopically concentrating on a single way in which an industry departs from perfect competition. The most frequent instances of this myopia involve the effort to "increase competition" through trust busting—that is, by increasing the number of firms in the industry with no attention to the consequences for technical efficiency in production and marketing. The ultimate absurdity came some years ago when the Antitrust Division of the Justice Department sought to break up

7. It can be shown that even within the framework of static economic theory, "as close to perfect competition as possible" is not necessarily the second best when perfect competition is not attainable. A possibly more telling criticism of the preoccupation with perfect competition was offered some years ago by the late John Maurice Clark. He pointed out that in any real-world industry, the rule is not movement to equilibrium but constant change under great uncertainty. Hence, economic policy ought to aim at creating the conditions necessary for the kind of dynamic competition that brings about the right kinds of economic progress. And this goal, Clark argued, is incompatible with making competition as perfect as possible. For example, much real-world competition involves product innovation which would obviously be retarded by an effort to impose product standardization on firms in order to promote the product homogeneity that perfect competition requires. J. M. Clark, *Competition as a Dynamic Process* (Washington, D.C., 1961), especially chapter 3.

the Great Atlantic & Pacific Tea Company even though it accounted for less than 7 percent of the country's retail grocery sales.[8]

Still, we should be careful about the inferences we draw from a study of the problem of the second best. The principal lesson is not that a government policy designed to make the economy more competitive in some limited way is stupid but rather that the welfare consequences of adopting such a policy are a matter for empirical investigation. Happily, the enforcement history of the American antitrust also contains many instances where the myopic concentration on a single aspect of competition probably did increase economic welfare. By almost any welfare test, the government attacks on industries which use patents of doubtful validity to construct cartels that restrict output have increased economic welfare.[9]

Summary

In the history of economics, an influential tradition has sought to discover the conditions that must be satisfied if a Pareto welfare optimum is to be realized—a state in which it is not possible to make somebody better off without making somebody else worse off. Work in this ambitious tradition ultimately established that Pareto optimality is synonymous with the allocation of resources that would characterize a perfectly competitive economy (with no externalities) in long-run equilibrium. It also showed that every different distribution of personal income can imply a different allocation of resources consistent with Pareto optimality. Since every economic system of the real world makes social choices which involve preferring one man's welfare to another's welfare, economists have been led to investigate the social welfare function. This work led in turn to the disconcerting discovery that, in general, it is not possible to construct a social welfare function from data supplied by individual preferences unless some people are permitted to impose their preferences on others. The practical significance of this demonstration is open to question, since politics almost by definition is a struggle in which individuals and groups seek to impose their preferences and the costs of realizing them on one another. It would appear that policy makers have more to learn from the more modest tradition in welfare economics (examined in Chapter 13) which is content to assess the welfare consequences of small incremental

8. United States v. New York, A & P Tea Co., 67 F. Supp. 626 (E.D., Ill. 1946).
9. Two infamous cases involving price-fixing cartels based on patents are United States v. Trenton Potteries Co., 273 U.S. 392 (1927); and Hartford-Empire Co. v. United States, 323 U.S. 386 (1945).

changes in economic policy. Finally, we noted that whenever an economy cannot realize all of the conditions necessary for an equilibrium of perfect competition, it has the problem of choosing the second best; and that second best does not necessarily involve realizing all of those equilibrium conditions of perfect competition which are attainable.

REFERENCES

Arrow, Kenneth, *Social Choice and Individual Values* (Edinburgh, rev. ed., 1963).
Bergson (Burk), A., "A Reformulation of Certain Aspects of Welfare Economics," *Quarterly Journal of Economics,* 52 (1938), 310-34.
Mishan, E. J., *Welfare Economics* (New York, 2nd ed., 1969), chapter 4.
Nicholson, Walter, *Microeconomic Theory* (Hinsdale, Ill., 1972), chapters 20, 21, and 22.
Reder, M. W., *Studies in the Theory of Welfare Economics* (New York, 1947), chapters 1, 2, and 3.
Tullock, Gordon, "The General Irrelevance of the General Impossibility Theorem," *Quarterly Journal of Economics,* 81 (1967), 256-70.
Vickrey, W. S., *Microstatics* (New York, 1964), chapter 5 and 6.
Vickrey, W. S., "Utility, Strategy, and Social Decision Rules," *Quarterly Journal of Economics,* 74 (1960), 507-35.

15
Profit and Decision Making

Profit and uncertainty

So far in this book we have stayed strictly within the confines of *static* economic analysis. We have assumed that all parties who make economic decisions make them on the basis of complete information and hence always achieve what they intended—never more, never less. Static analysis is an immensely powerful tool when applied to those economic activities of the real world where information, if not complete, is at least "very good." Static analysis, for example, lets us learn, with a minimum of effort, all that we wish to know about the phenomenon of arbitrage in organized securities and commodities markets. For trading in such markets generates an enormous volume of accessible data every trading day. The price of wheat in Chicago today, the price of wheat in Kansas City today, and the cost of shipping a bushel of wheat from Kansas City to Chicago are "facts" easily discoverable by almost anybody. Therefore, with the aid of static analysis, we can confidently assert that, most of the time, the price difference on a bushel of wheat between the Chicago and Kansas City markets cannot exceed the cost of shipping a bushel between these two points.

When we turn to those economic activities where the information in the possession of most participants is poor, the limitations of static analysis soon become apparent. Thus one of the most important economic phenomena of the real world is fashion and style change; and, until the present time, nobody has figured out a way to apply static analysis to it with useful results. For better or worse, we cannot predict the future length of women's skirts or the future width of men's ties. Whereas arbitage holds no surprises for the economist, fashion and style change holds nothing but surprises for him. Admittedly, decision making on the basis of incomplete information—that is, under conditions of uncertainty—is a messy subject. Still, if only to preserve our intellectual self-respect, we have to say something about it.

Let us begin by taking a sharp look at the venerable proposition of economic textbooks which asserts that "every businessman seeks to maximize his profit." We note for the record that it is economists who usually advance this proposition. Businessmen hardly ever use the verb "to maximize" in any form (unless, of course, they are recent economics majors fresh from college or business school). Businessmen prefer to say that their goal is to "increase profits" or to "reduce losses." As we shall presently see, this semantical difference is not without economic meaning. But to continue. What can we say about "maximizing profit"?

No profit in the static state

The first point worth making is nearly self-evident. In strictly static analysis the term "profit" has no distinctive meaning. As we have seen, in an economic model with complete information, average cost (as defined by accountants) will equal average revenue (as defined by accountants). When resources are free to move from one employment to another, resource movement brings about this equality. When resources are not free to move—or, when for some reason they will not move—an economic rent is created. But, as the ownership of resources changes hands by lease and sale, economic rent is capitalized in the way that we have already examined (Chapter 11). Specifically, the capitalization of economic rent boosts and skews the curve of average total cost (as viewed by the firm) until it is tangent to the curve of average total revenue. What we call economic rent some call profit (usually "monopoly profit"). Since the term "profit" is also applied to other things as well, this usage has nothing to recommend it. If profit cannot exist in a world where all things are certain, an obvious conclusion follows. Profit exists because uncertainty exists.

Profit as an accounting term

Before we probe for the connection between profit and uncertainty, a second truth should be set down. The term "profit," as used by businessmen, accountants, labor leaders, economic forecasters, and incautious economists is an accounting term. The profit of their vocabulary is always defined with reference to some accounting period (usually the fiscal year). And it is always the difference between revenue and the sum of (a) fixed contractual expenses—wages, rent, fire insurance, etc. and (b) depreciation on the capital equipment used to generate the revenue. Actually, in the published statistics on national income, the term "profit" is used only in connection with the activities of firms that are organized as legal corporations. These statistics contain an entry *corporate profits before tax* and another entry *corporate profits after tax*. The taxes referred to are state and federal income taxes. The other taxes paid by corporations are treated as costs of doing business. For business firms and farms that do not take the corporate legal form, the national income statistics contain an entry *net income of unincorporated enterprises*. This entry roughly corresponds to what is often called "the profits of small business."

In short, the calculation of profit is always governed by some set of accounting rules, a fact which by itself should make us careful about attaching too much importance to published profit statistics. Two results of cost accounting are especially worth noting. First, other things being equal, the greater the number of fixed contractual expenses that a firm incurs, the smaller its accounting profit. Suppose, for example, that a firm can finance a $1 million plant expansion either by selling bonds ("going into debt") or by selling additional common stock ("taking in more partners"). If bonds are sold, payments to bondholders each year will be a fixed contractual expense until the bonds are retired. If common stock is sold, dividends paid to the stockholders are a part of accounting profit.

Second, the size of the profit entry in a firm's annual report is affected by the rules for reckoning depreciation that it follows. Suppose that the firm buys a machine that will last between five and fifteen years (its actual length of useful life being determined by rate of use, the cost of repairs, and the cost of new machines). If the firm intends to remain in business for more than five years, depreciation must be charged. That is, the firm must set aside funds that will allow it to replace the machine when it (the machine) is no longer economically useful. The machine ceases to be economically useful when the amount that its operation adds to total revenue becomes less than the amount that its operation adds to total cost.

Should the firm amortize the machine over a period of five years? Ten years? Fifteen years? If the decision is to amortize over five years, how much depreciation should be charged to the first year? The second year? These matters are usually left to accountants. For our purposes, the important point is that the more rapidly the machine is amortized, the smaller the accounting profit "now" and the greater the accounting profit "later."

We should also remember that, during the accounting period, the firm may make economic gains or losses that do not show up in its annual income statement. The firm may own a piece of real estate whose market value has gone up because its location has suddenly become more attractive to potential buyers. Such a rise in asset value ("asset appreciation") will not be reflected in the firm's statement until it is actually sold.

The ambiguity of "economic profit"

We could multiply *ad nauseam* the pitfalls that lie in wait for anyone who uncritically accepts profit data that come to him from accountants. However, we have gone far enough to know that the profit reported by a firm in any given fiscal year is no more than a crude index of the "success" of the firm in that year. If by profit we mean accounting profit, then the statement that every businessman seeks to maximize profit is clearly wrong. A businessman can no more deliberately seek to maximize accounting profit than he can seek to "maximize good luck." He may hope for good luck and give thanks when it comes to pass. But good luck (like bad luck) is a phenomenon which, by definition, is beyond the control of the recipient.

Is it possible to frame an economic definition of profit that would make valid the statement that every businessman seeks to maximize profit? The answer is: probably not. No economist has yet succeeded in this task. And there are good reasons for believing that it cannot be done.

While economists have long recognized that profit defined as a difference between "revenue" and "cost" is related to uncertainty, they have traveled two different roads in their efforts to establish a precise connection. The first road has sought to equate profit with "payment for uncertainty-bearing." The second road has sought to equate profit with "payment for organizing production in the face of uncertainty." In the case of a small merchant or manufacturer who operates and totally owns his own business, there is no need for this distinction. The same individual performs both functions. He can be regarded as hiring factors of production "now" at known price in order to fashion a product or service that will be sold "later" at a price that cannot be known in advance. In his case his costs incurred during the period of production are mainly of three sorts: (i) his fixed contractual expenses; (ii) the interest forgone because he used his capital in his own business instead of investing in, say, government bonds; and (iii) the wages forgone because he used his own labor in his own business. Should any residual remain after these explicit and implicit costs have been deducted from revenue, it could reasonably be regarded as "economic profit."

In the case of the large corporation, the economic function of organizing production in the face of uncertainty is partly (but only partly) performed by hired managers; while the economic function of uncertainty-bearing is partly (but only partly) performed by inert stockholders. In a world of uncertainty where decisions are made on the basis of incomplete information, everybody—manager, stockholder, bondholder, worker, and consumer—must both bear some uncertainty and play some part in organizing production in the face of uncertainty. The influence of uncertainty is so ubiquitous that it affects all incomes received in the real world. It is this obvious truth that has defeated all efforts to equate profit with "payment for uncertainty-bearing."

For some purposes, it may be useful to treat both uncertainty-bearing and the entrepreneurship devoted to organizing production in the face of uncertainty as separate factors of production. (Any classification of the factors of production is, of course, arbitrary; the question is always whether the classification is useful.) But no good purpose is served by trying to equate something called "economic profit" with payment to some specific factor of production. It is not surprising that one noted economist (Milton Friedman) has tried to expunge the very term "profit" from the economist's vocabulary.[1]

Decision making and uncertainty

We can easily satisfy ourselves that businessmen do not seek to maximize anything that closely resembles the profit entry of a firm's income statement. But they do not usually make decisions by casting dice or consulting fortune tellers. Businessmen have goals and methods of operation which (in their opinion at least) are designed to achieve these goals. The coward's way out is to say that a businessman tries to maximize his "utility

1. Friedman prefers to speak of "non-contractual costs"—the difference between total receipts and total contractual costs. This difference can in turn be divided into the expected part (usually called economic rent or quasi-rent) and the unexpected part ("pure" profit). Milton Friedman, *Price Theory: A Provisional Text* (Chicago, 1962), pp. 68-73.

It is not clear that economists would gain much by adopting Friedman's terminology since the individual decision-maker would have to remain the judge of whether an *ex post* difference between revenue and contractual costs was expected or unexpected. In this situation, businessmen with good foresight earn economic rents, and businessmen with bad foresight earn "pure" profits or losses.

function." This is not much of an answer because a completely defined utility function would have to include everything that influences his decision in any way—everything from his desire for more income to his mild disapproval of salesmen who wear bow ties. The problem is to identify those elements in the utility function of the businessman that allow us to explain most of his behavior.

We have a problem only because decisions must be made under conditions of uncertainty. Therefore, let us assume that the decision maker in business has only two goals in life. (i) He wishes to employ his capital in a way that gives him the greatest income during some finite planning period. (ii) He wishes to employ his capital in a way that minimizes the uncertainty that surrounds the earning of this income. Thus we give the decision maker a two-goal mix or, if you prefer, a utility function with two variables.

Let the problem that the decision-maker must solve be a very simple one: invest $10,000 in the way that, given his two goals, is "best" for him. Finally, let us suppose that, rightly or wrongly, he believes that he has only four investment alternatives. They are:

1. Invest $10,000 in United States Government Bonds.
2. Invest $10,000 in machines.
3. Invest $10,000 in additional advertising.
4. Invest $10,000 in a manpower training program that raises the productivity of his workers.

When decisions are made upon the basis of incomplete information, the decision maker must necessarily form a *subjective* estimate of the possible payoffs of his investment alternatives. Why do we italicize "subjective"? Simply to emphasize that, *at the time the decision is made,* we have no basis for passing judgment on the rationality of his decision. Such a basis exists only when there is complete information about the possible payoffs and the probability that each payoff will be realized. This possibility is ruled out by our assumption that the decision maker acts on the basis of incomplete information. We may believe that the decision maker is a fool or an ignoramus or both. The passing of time may seem to show that our estimate is correct. But when a decision is made under conditions of uncertainty nobody can know for sure what the outcome will be. Only the decision maker can determine the course of action that is rational from his viewpoint.

In order to make what from his own viewpoint is a rational choice among alternatives, the decision maker must assign a set of possible payoffs to each of the four investment alternatives and a probability coefficient

TABLE 15.1

investment alternatives	outcome	probability	expected payoff	minimum gain
*bonds	7	1	7	7
*advertising	40 20 0	⅓ ⅓ ⅓	20	0.0
*machines	90 60 −15	⅓ ⅓ ⅓	45	−15
†manpower training	29 0 −20	⅓ ⅓ ⅓	3	−20

* rational choices
† irrational choice

to each possible payoff. Let his estimates—his *subjective* estimates we emphasize again—be given by table 15.1. The possible outcomes of each of the four investments are expressed as rates of return. The subjective estimate that any outcome will, in fact, be realized is given by a corresponding rational fraction.

For a reason that will soon be made clear, in table 15.1 the minimum payoff that the decision maker assigns to each investment alternative is also entered separately. Thus, when $10,000 is invested in advertising, he believes (rightly or wrongly) that three outcomes are possible; they are 40, 20, and 0.0. respectively. The *expected* payoff from investing $10,000. in advertising (or if you prefer, the *mathematical value* of this investment) is ⅓ (40 + 20 + 0) or 20. Thus minimum possible payoff from the advertising investment is thought to be 0.0.

Which of these four possible ways of investing $10,000 is the economically rational choice for the decision maker whose only goals are to increase his income and avoid uncertainty? Actually, any of the first three alternatives in table 15.1—bonds, advertising, or machines—is economically rational in the sense that "more is preferred to less." This is true because each of these three alternatives represents "more utility."

Investment in machines promises the highest expected (subjective) estimate of future income (45). Investment in bonds promises the greatest avoidance of uncertainty as measured by the highest minimum payoff (7). Investment in advertising is best for the decision maker who will willingly bear some amount of uncertainty provided that no part of his $10,000. principal is endangered. In an uncertainty situation there would be a single best (economically most rational) alternative if, and only if, one choice promised both the greatest possible payoff and the least uncertainty as measured by every index of uncertainty that can be applied to the data.

It is this last test that rules out the fourth investment alternative—investment in a manpower training program—as an economically rational choice in table 15.1. An investment in manpower training is clearly inferior to expenditure on machines in every respect. The maximum possible gain from machines is 90 as against 29 from manpower training. The expected payoff from machines is 45 as against 3 from manpower training. And the minimum possible payoff from machines is −15 as against −20 from manpower training.

The truth is that it is difficult to say anything very precise about decision making under conditions of uncertainty. As we have seen, the reason is simply that "rational" behavior in this context can only be defined in terms of the information available to the decision maker and his (subjective) estimate of the cost and benefit of securing additional information. When we presume to say that somebody's decision made on the basis of incomplete information is "irrational," all that we can mean is that it is irrational on the basis of information available to us. Obviously the decision maker thinks he knows something that we do not know. Only time will tell whether he is correct in this estimate. And often there cannot even be an appeal to "history" after the decision is made since, even in retrospect, there may be no way of telling how much a successful outcome was due to the decision maker's foresight and how much to blind good luck.

Perhaps the most important lesson that we can learn from our brief examination of decision making and uncertainty is the unwisdom of supposing that we can ever achieve the power to completely predict economic developments. Given uncertainty about future events, there is no reason why businessmen in objectively similar circumstances should behave in the same way. For instance, faced with increasing competition from the invasion from abroad of small foreign-made cars, an automobile manufacturer in Detroit has a number of options. To cite a few of the obvious: (1) he can bring out his own line of small cars; (2) he can try to merge with a foreign competitor; (3) he can advertise his big cars more heavily; (4) he can spend resources on a public relations campaign aimed at securing tariff protection against the foreigners; or (5) he can go out of business. Given our incomplete information about future consumer demand for cars, there is no reason why all Detroit manufacturers should choose the same response to foreign competition. And we have no basis for saying that one response is more rational than another.

Summary

It is often said that "businessmen try to maximize profit," with "profit" being implicitly defined as the difference between revenue earned and cost incurred by the firm in some accounting period. When this difference is negative, the firm is presumed to "minimize loss." The phrase "profit maximization," however, is an unfortunate choice of words, being both inaccurate and misleading.

When economic decisions are made on the basis of complete information, there can be no permanent difference between cost and revenue in the firm. When firms are free to enter and leave an industry, most or all of the difference between cost and revenue will, sooner or later, be wiped out by the entry of new firms or the exit of old firms. Any difference between cost and revenue that cannot be eliminated by the entry or exit of firms becomes an economic rent earned by the firm. It will be capitalized into a higher curve of average total cost for the firm as its ownership changes hands. In fine, when information is complete—that is, when no uncertainty confronts the decision maker about the outcome of his actions—there can be no permanent "profit" in the firm.

It follows that if there exists some permanent component of income that is not economic rent, it must be related to the "fact" of uncertainty in the real world. We noted that, in the real world, profit is an accounting term; and that its computation is governed by a set of rules which are necessarily "arbitrary." From the economist's viewpoint, the profit entry of the accountant is a catch-all category. It partly records implicit interest on the firm's own capital and partly implicit wages (especially in the case of individually owned firms). Moreover, the profit entry of the accountant does not pick up all of the consequences of uncertainty. It may miss, for example, many of the capital gains and losses experienced by the firm during the accounting period. Whatever businessmen try to maximize, it obviously *is not* the profit entry of the firm's annual income statement.

We also noted that nobody has yet been able to rewrite the accountant's definition of profit in a way that makes it acceptable to economists. The basic difficulty is that any surplus of revenue over cost in the firm is not a homogeneous entity. It includes quite a few things, most notably a payment to stockholders for uncertainty bearing, a payment to management for organizing production in the face of uncertainty, and a "pure" capital gain which by definition is not payment for any service rendered.

As an alternative to the idea of profit maximization, we made use of a simple model of decision making under conditions of uncertainty. We gave the decision maker a utility function consisting of (i) a preference for more income rather than less income and (ii) an aversion to uncertainty. And we gave him a set of investment alternatives. We found that, in this choice situation, there was no single, objectively determined "best" investment. The economically national choice for the decision maker who must choose when outcomes are uncertain is partly a function of his willingness to accept the danger of greater loss in order to gain the chance of a greater payoff.

REFERENCES

Cohen, K. J., and R. M. Cyert, *Theory of the Firm: Resource Allocation in a Market Economy* (Englewood Cliffs, N.J., 1965), chapter 15.

Fellner, William, *Probability and Profit* (Homewood, Ill., 1965), especially chapters 4 and 5.

Hirshleifer, Jack, "The Bayesian Approach to Statistical Decision: An Exposition," *Journal of Business* 34 (1961), 471-89.

Kirzner, I. M., *Competition and Entrepreneurship* (Chicago, 1973), chapters 1 and 2.

Knight, F. H., *Risk, Uncertainty and Profit* (London, 1948).

Lamberton, D. M., *The Theory of Profit* (Oxford, 1965), especially chapters 2 and 3.

Shackle, G. L. S., *Decision, Order and Time in Human Affairs* (Cambridge, 2nd ed., 1969), especially chapter 28.

APPENDIX TO CHAPTER 15
FULL-COST PRICING

As we have seen, the premise that businessmen behave in ways that they believe will maximize their incomes is, to some extent, unrealistic. Being human, businessmen are not so single-minded. They can—and do—trade off some amount of prospective income in order to reduce uncertainty, spend more time with the wife and kids, and work with congenial associates in pleasant surroundings. However, for our purposes, the important issue is: does the hypothesis that businessmen seek to maximize income provide a better basis for predicting business behavior than any discernible alternative hypothesis? Most economists do not doubt that the income maximizing hypothesis outperforms all rivals when judged by this test. However, this feeling is not universal. By one persistent minority view, the first step in framing an hypothesis about business behavior is to ask businessmen how they "really" go about setting prices. And this view holds that the answers indicate that businessmen are not maximizers but merely "satisficers." They do not seek maximum profits but only "satisfactory" profits.

In the last forty years economists, with the aid of case studies, have assembled a very extensive literature on pricing in action.[1] As you should expect by now, the most conspicuous feature of this literature is its astounding diversity. There are as many methods of setting prices as there are prices to be set. But the economist is not (or ought not to be) concerned with the multiplication of "facts" about pricing. He has to ask: Is there any unity in this diversity? Happily, an affirmative answer seems to be justified. Virtually all of the case studies of pricing do have one result in common.

Almost all businessmen when asked will say that "prices are based upon costs"—that the price of a commodity is set so that, "in the normal course of business," price is equal to average total cost plus a fixed markup. Remember that to a businessman dividends paid to suppliers of equity capital (stockholders) are not a cost, i.e. he uses a narrower definition of cost than does an economist who makes it "the sacrifice of alternatives." The avowed object of this method of setting prices is to yield the firm some target rate of return on its investment. This method of setting prices goes under various names. The most common are full-cost pricing, average-cost pricing, administered pricing, target pricing, cost-plus pricing, and rule-of-thumb pricing.

In many textbooks on managerial economics this method of pricing—let us call it full-cost pricing—is illustrated with a break-even chart. The firm is presumed to have a normal or customary rate of output (sometimes called the standard volume) which is at or near the rate at which average total cost is minimized. The firm is then presumed to choose a price which, provided that it operates at this normal rate, will yield the target rate of

1. See, for example, A. D. H. Kahn, J. B. Dirlam, and R. F. Lanzillotti, *Pricing in Big Business: A Case Approach* (Washington, D.C., 1958); or D. C. Hague, *Pricing in Business* (London, 1971).

return on investment—usually somewhere between 10 and 20 percent per annum. Thus price is equal to "full cost plus a fixed markup."

So long as the prices of its factor inputs do not change, the firm is presumed to stick with the price derived with the aid of its full-cost formula. An increase in demand will not cause it to raise price. A decrease in demand will not cause it to lower price.

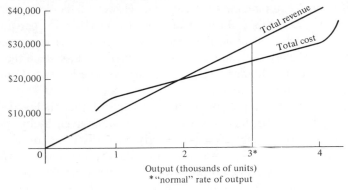

FIGURE 15.1

Figure 15.1 is a hypothetical break-even chart for commodity X. It assumes:

(i) For every output from 1000 through 4000 units, total variable cost is directly proportional to output, e.g. increase output by 2 percent and you increase total variable cost by 2 percent.[2]

(ii) The firm's normal (standard) rate of output is 3000 units.

(iii) The firms target is a profit of $5000 when its normal output of 3000 units is sold.

(iv) The firm can earn its target profit with the sale of its normal output (3000 units) *provided that a price of $10 per unit is charged.*

Note that a price of $10 yields the target profit of $5000 for the firm only when 3000 units are sold, i.e. only when production is "normal." At a $10 price the firm will incur a loss whenever output falls below 2000 units—the break-even point. And, at a $10 price the firm's profit will rise above the target profit of $5000 as sales expand from 3000 to 4000 units.

2. Case studies indicate that most firms (at any rate in manufacturing which is the sector of the economy most intensively studied) really do believe that, most of the time, they operate within a range of output in which changes in total variable cost are roughly proportional to changes in output.

Figure 15.1 can be used to illustrate an important difference in the terminologies of business and economics. A sale of 2000 units (at a \$10 price per unit) is a break-even point for the businessman because, at this output the total revenue just suffices to cover the firm's contractual expenses and depreciation. No worker or supplier will sue for non-payment for services rendered; and the firm earns the revenue needed to replace each piece of capital equipment as it wears out. However, the economist takes a different view. When 2000 units are sold (at a \$10 price per unit) the firm's stockholders collect no dividends. To an economist this means that the firm is not really breaking even. It is incurring a loss since the capital supplied by the stockholder could be earning positive interest if employed somewhere else in the economy.

Some economists, impatient of any criticism of their beloved income maximizing hypothesis, have dismissed the answers given by businessmen to questions about their pricing methods as self-serving or even self-deluding rhetoric. Certainly we have no difficulty in showing that businessmen, like other people, do not always practice what they preach. The Bureau of Labor Statistics regularly publishes statistics on price changes for a wide range of commodities based upon price information obtained from questionnaires returned each month by a sample of producers. One study showed that, for the years 1956-59, the Bureau reported a total of 127 price changes for 30 selected commodities.[3] But data obtained from a sample of large firms which bought these same 30 commodities in this period showed a total of 236 price changes. If the sample of buyers had been larger, even more price changes would have been detected for the 30 commodities. Clearly, the firms supplying information to the Bureau of Labor Statistics were sending along their "official" prices—not the prices at which transactions were actually concluded. This result should surprise nobody. After all, in many industries, "everybody knows" that an official price is merely a point of departure for bargaining—the firm's opening offer which is not to be taken too seriously.

Does the undoubted discrepancy between official prices and transaction prices mean that businessmen are having fun at the expense of gullible, plodding economic researchers when they stoutly maintain that prices are equal to full cost plus a fixed markup? Probably not. There are at least four good reasons for paying careful attention to the answers of businessmen.

3. H. E. McAllister, Staff Paper No. 8 in "Price Statistics of the Federal Government" printed as *Government Price Statistics* by the Joint Economic Committee (Washington, D.C., January 21, 1961).

1. Price quotations cannot be pulled out of the air. They have to be based upon something. And it is quite reasonable to expect firms to use cost as a reference point in setting prices. This is because the firm has more and better information on costs than it does on the demand for its commodity. Fixed costs are, by definition, a known magnitude. And, when the firm can buy factor inputs at known prices, it can closely estimate how its total cost would be affected by, say, a 10 percent increase or decrease in output. It may have only a very hazy idea about how output changes of this amount would affect total revenue.

2. In many markets (e.g. the cigarette market of the United States) the number of competing firms is small and the rivals employ much the same technology and buy factor inputs at the same prices. Full-cost pricing is one way of stabilizing such oligopoly markets. For since costs are very nearly the same for all, full-cost pricing—provided that a common markup is used—will eliminate the sudden and sharp price cuts that can trigger a mutually unprofitable price war.

3. Full-cost pricing is a kind of stayout pricing. There is usually no point in being greedy for short-run profits if the result is to attract additional firms into the market or to encourage customers to embark upon a search for new sources of supply.

4. Finally, price changes are not without cost to firms in the imperfectly competitive markets of the real world. When prices change, salesmen must be briefed, advertising altered, catalogues rewritten, and customers placated. It simply may not pay the firm to vary price in response to a small change in demand—especially when the firm believes that the change is merely a short-lived departure from the normal.

Let us accept that businessmen are telling if not the whole truth at least a good part of it when they aver that price is equal to cost plus a fixed markup. Does this behavior subvert the usefulness of the hypothesis that their behavior can be studied on the assumption they are income maximizers? Of course not. In an economic model the decision maker needs no rule-of-thumb in pricing because he has complete information. The businessman needs such a rule precisely because his information is limited and can only be increased at some cost to himself. To reconcile the income maximizing hypothesis with full-cost pricing it is only necessary to suppose that businessmen are capable of learning from experience; that they will shift from one rule-of-thumb (full-cost formula) to another when they have reason to believe that the switch will increase profits. The considerable literature on full-cost pricing indicates that firms sometimes switch too soon and sometimes too late as market conditions change.

But it leaves no doubt that they do switch. Full-cost pricing formulas are made for businessmen, not vice versa.

Does the use of full-cost pricing by businessmen in pursuit of profit have any economic significance? Or should we treat full-cost pricing with no more respect than a literary critic accords to the "fact" that Shakespeare wrote his plays with a quill pen? In a microeconomics course, where the main object is to understand how markets operate, full-cost pricing is of very marginal interest. Full-cost pricing merely means that firms using it respond more rapidly to changes in cost than to changes in demand. But respond they do; and in basic microeconomics we are not interested in the speed of response—only in the final results.

Public officials and civil servants who seek to keep the economic system behaving properly through monetary and fiscal policy cannot afford so much abstraction. They know that competitive industries in which all firms are price takers will respond more quickly to their carrots and clubs than will oligopolists who follow pricing formulae. They know also that an oligopolist is more likely to make a determined effort to pass the full amount of any wage or other cost increase on to his customers. Even if this effort fails "eventually," it can affect the economy's expectation of inflation over a period of weeks or months. Many economists (and even more businessmen and labor leaders) believe that the widespread use of full-cost pricing is a fact that should be allowed for in monetary and fiscal policy. Unfortunately, our present understanding of the short-run impact of macro-policy changes on particular firms and industries is so limited that nobody knows for sure.

REFERENCES (APPENDIX)

Hague, D. C., *Pricing in Business* (London, 1971).

Hall, R. L. and C. J. Hitch, "Price Theory and Business Behavior," in *Oxford Studies in the Price Mechanism* ed. T. Wilson and P. W. S. Andrews (Oxford, 1951), pp. 107-38.

Kahn, A. D. H., J. B. Dirlam, and R. F. Lanzillotti, *Pricing in Big Business: A Case Study Approach* (Washington, D.C., 1958).

Scherer, F. M., *Industrial Market Structure and Economic Performance* (Chicago, 1970), chapter 6.

Stigler, G. J., *The Organization of Industry* (Homewood, Ill., 1968), chapter 19.

16
Oligopoly with Limited Information

Oligopoly as a "dynamic" phenomenon

In previous chapters we found that the assumptions employed in "static" economic analysis give results that are both elegant and convincing when applied to three market forms—perfect competition, monopoly, and pricing designed to block the entry of rival firms. In these three cases, the firm knows precisely what it must do in order to maximize income. And in all three cases, the firm need not worry about the behavior of other firms in the industry.

In the case of monopoly, there are no other firms to worry about. In the case of perfect competition, other firms are so numerous that it is pointless to worry about them—that is, in perfect competition, one firm knows that it is so unimportant that, acting alone, it cannot affect the price at which its commodity sells. When pricing is used to block entry, the firm can, in the static model, calculate the price that is just low enough to discourage the entry of other firms; it maximizes income by charging that price.

In the real world, most firms are not able to operate in total disregard of what other firms do. The representative firm of the real world is not the sole seller in its market. Neither is it one of a "very large number of firms" in its market. To survive the representative firm must develop a marketing strategy that takes account of the marketing strategies of at least some actual or potential rivals.

We have previously used the term *simple oligopoly with free entry* to describe the market form where:

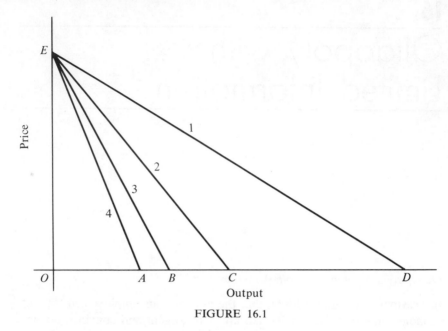

FIGURE 16.1

(a) the market consists of a small number of sellers;
(b) sellers are prevented by Law or Nature from merging or form-
     ing a profit-sharing cartel;
(c) all sellers are of equal size;
(d) every seller exactly matches the price and output of every other
     seller.

In one sense the term *simple oligopoly with free entry* is misleading
since it is applied to a situation where each firm has perfect knowledge
about how all other firms will react to a price or output change on its part.
As figure 16.1 indicates, once the firm knows the market demand curve
and the number of other firms in the market it also knows its own demand
curve. Thus, when the market has one firm, its demand curve is *ED*. When
the market has two firms, the demand curve for each firm is *EC*.

In microeconomics, the term "oligopoly" is generally used to describe
a market form where (i) firms are so few that a sense of interdependence
—a sense of being rivals—is present and (ii) no firm can predict with complete accuracy how other firms will behave. Thus, the term oligopoly usually denotes a market form where business decisions are made on the basis
of incomplete and/or inaccurate information. And it is the presence of uncertainty about the behavior of rivals that takes the analysis of oligopoly

out of "statics" and makes it a part of "dynamics" in economics. In short, "true" oligopoly is *interdependence plus uncertainty*.

The uncertainty ingredient in oligopoly must be emphasized. When rival firms have a sense of interdependence but can predict one another's behavior, they can calculate the unprofitable consequences of their rivalry and take steps to restrict it. If no new firms can enter the market and it is possible to organize a cartel or multiplant firm, oligopoly will evolve (or degenerate) into monopoly. If new firms can enter and the industry cannot cartelize or organize a multiplant firm (that will practice stayout pricing) then the best that its member firms can do is to learn to play follow-the-leader. Here the result will approximate what we have called simple oligopoly with free entry. As we have seen, the distinctive feature of this market form is an equilibrium where each firm produces an output at which average total cost is falling. Recall that in Chapter 10 we concluded that this result is economically wasteful when it can be traced to man-made restrictions on mergers and cartels and merely unfortunate when it can be traced to "natural" causes (e.g. diseconomies of scale in the firm).

If fewness of sellers in the market is to lead to something other than monopoly or the mechanical price leadership of simple oligopoly, we must introduce the following assumption:

A16.1 Firms make their price and output decisions on the basis of information which is inaccurate and/or incomplete.

Cournot's solution

The most famous of all treatments of oligopoly is historically the earliest, having been offered in the nineteenth century by the French economist Augustin Cournot (1801-77).[1] Cournot began with duopoly—the case of two producers and the simplest possible form of oligopoly. In Cournot's model, the commodity sold is homogeneous mineral water that has no cost of production. Each duopolist can supply all mineral water that the market will take at a zero price. Arbitrage is so effective that the outputs of the duopolists always sell at the same price. And the aggregate demand curve for mineral water is known to both parties. Finally, Cournot specified his famous behavioral rule.

A16.2 One duopolist in selecting his output always assumes that the second duopolist will continue to produce whatever he (the second) is presently producing.

1. A. A. Cournot, *Récherches sur les principes mathématiques de la théorie des richesses* (Paris, 1838). Translated by N. T. Bacon as *Researches into the Mathematical Principles of the Theory of Wealth* (New York, 1897).

We note immediately that Cournot's duopolists delude themselves. Precisely because each assumes that he can act without provoking a reaction from the other, each will act and so provoke a reaction. However, assumption A16.2, in effect, specifies that neither duopolist ever learns from experience. The result, of course, is persistent and unending miscalculation. Nevertheless, Cournot was able to show that, in his model, his duopolists will approach an equilibrium.

Let the aggregate demand function for mineral water be given by

$$p = 10 - \tfrac{1}{2}q \tag{16.1}$$

where p denotes price and q output.

Suppose that production of mineral water is first begun by duopolist #1. Since duopolist #2 is producing nothing when production begins, duopolist #1 assumes that duopolist #2 will continue to produce nothing. Hence duopolist #1 takes the aggregate demand function as his own personal demand function. Since cost of production is zero in Cournot's model, duopolist #1 maximizes profit by maximizing total revenuer. We can also write his total revenue as $10\,q_1 - \tfrac{1}{2}\,q_1^2$. Marginal revenue is, of course, dr/dq_1 or $10 - q_1$. Marginal cost is zero, and total revenue is maximized when marginal revenue is equal to marginal cost, hence total revenue is maximized for duopolist #1 when

$$10 - q_1 = 0 \tag{16.2}$$

or when

$$q_1 = 10 \tag{16.2a}$$

and

$$p = 5 \tag{16.2b}$$

Now imagine that duopolist #2 comes to life. He begins production by assuming that his rival will continue to produce 10 units of output. Therefore, duopolist #2 believes that the "unused" segment of the aggregate demand curve is all his own. So believing, he views his personal demand function as

$$p = (10 - 5) - \tfrac{1}{2}q_2 \tag{16.3}$$

or

$$p = 5 - \tfrac{1}{2}q_2 \tag{16.3a}$$

Note that in equation 16.3a the intercept of the demand curve and the price axis is 5 rather than 10 as in equation 16.1. This is because duopolist #2 assumes that his rival will continue to produce 10 units. So believing, he maximizes his total revenue which is $q_2(5 - \frac{1}{2}q_2)$ or $5q_2 - \frac{1}{2}q_2^2$. Here too his total profit and total revenue are always equal since his mineral water also has no cost of production.

The total revenue of duopolist #2 is maximized when

$$5 - q_2 = 0 \tag{16.4}$$

or when

$$q_2 = 5 \tag{16.4a}$$

and

$$p = 2.5 \tag{16.4b}$$

Duopolist #1 receives a nasty jolt as price falls from 5 to 2.5 because his rival has entered the market. But, in Cournot's model, he shrugs it off and decides that his rival's output will remain forever at 5 units. Therefore, he concludes that henceforth his own personal demand curve will be

$$p = (10 - 2.5) - \frac{1}{2}q_1 \tag{16.5}$$

or

$$p = 7.5 - \frac{1}{2}q_1 \tag{16.5a}$$

Firm in this faith, duopolist #1 maximizes total revenue when

$$7.5 - q_1 = 0 \tag{16.6}$$

or when

$$q_1 = 7.5 \tag{16.6a}$$

and

$$p = 3.75 \tag{16.6b}$$

After duopolist #1 revises his output, dupolist #2 receives a pleasant surprise; price rises from 2.5 to 3.75. (Since arbitrage is perfect, the outputs of the two duopolists always sell for the same price.) Duopolist #2 believes that his rival's output will stay at 7.5; and he believes his new demand function to be

$$p = (10 - 3.75) - \frac{1}{2}q_2 \tag{16.7}$$

or

$$p = 6.25 - \frac{1}{2}q_2 \tag{16.7a}$$

The total revenue of duopolist #2 is now maximized when

$$6.25 - \tfrac{1}{2}q_2 = 0 \tag{16.8}$$

or when

$$q_2 = 6.25 \tag{16.8a}$$

and

$$p = 3.115 \tag{16.8b}$$

And so forth ad infinitum. With pencil and paper (and maybe an algebra book) you can easily verify the following generalizations. As each of our duopolists continues to misread the other's intentions, the combined output of the two expands by the geometric progression

$$10 \left[1 + \tfrac{1}{4} + (\tfrac{1}{4})^2 + (\tfrac{1}{4})^3 \ldots + (\tfrac{1}{4})^n \right]$$

When n goes to infinity, the sum of this progression approaches the limit $10/(1 - \tfrac{1}{4})$ or 13.334.

As each duopolist miscalculates, the output of duopolist #2 expands by the geometric progression

$$5 \left[1 + \tfrac{1}{4} + (\tfrac{1}{4})^2 + (\tfrac{1}{4})^3 \ldots + (\tfrac{1}{4})^n \right]$$

When n goes to infinity, the sum of this second progression approaches the limit, $5/(1 - \tfrac{1}{4})$ or 6.667.

In short, in Cournot's duopoly model, an equilibrium will be approached in which (i) output is divided equally between the two sellers and (ii) their combined output is equal to two-thirds of the output that the industry would produce if it were perfectly competitive.

The second truth is not self-evident but consider: Under perfect competition price would equal average total cost in the long run. Cournot's mineral springs have no costs of production and can supply all the market will take at a zero price. Hence, if production were in the hands of perfect competitors, price would also be zero in the long run. The aggregate demand function in our problem is

$$p = 10 - \tfrac{1}{2}q \tag{16.1}$$

When $p = 0$, $q = 20$. As we have seen, the equilibrium output in Cournot's duopoly is 13.334.

Cournot did not stop with two sellers. Indeed, he was able to show that when Q_n designates the combined output of n oligopolists and Q_c the output of the industry if organized by perfect competitors, then

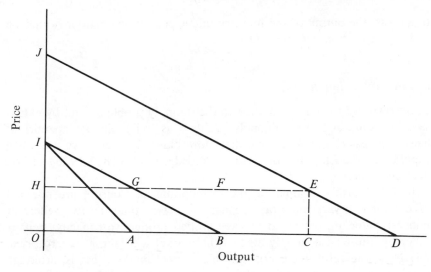

FIGURE 16.2

$$Q_n = nQ_c/(n + 1) \qquad\qquad (16.9)$$

It can be demonstrated that equation 16.9 holds for both linear and non-linear demand curves.[2] But we will limit our proof to the simpler case of the linear demand curve.

More than two sellers

Suppose that we wish to find equilibrium output in Cournot's model when the number of oligopolists is three. We make this determination with the aid of figure 16.2 where aggregate demand is given by the line *JD*.

> Step 1. Divide *OD* into $n + 1$, or 4 segments of equal length; and label the division points *A, B,* and *C*.
> Step 2. Draw line *HE* parallel to *OD* and equal to *OC*.
> Step 3. Divide line *HE* into three equal parts; and label the division points *G* and *F*.
> Step 4. Draw line *IGB* and line *IA*.

In figure 16.2 *IGB* is, of course, parallel to *JD*. And *IGB* is the demand curve for each of the three oligopolists. The marginal revenue curve corresponding to *IGB* is *IA*. The output of a single oligopolist is *OA*. And the combined output of all three oligopolists is *OC*. Since there are no produc-

2. W. S. Vickrey, *Microstatics* (New York, 1964), pp. 307-8.

tion costs, the output of the industry under perfect competition would be *OD*. By inspection, *OC* = ¾ *OD*.[3]

Edgeworth's solution

In his own age Cournot's solution to the duopoly problem (and by extension his solution to the oligopoly problem as well) did not go unchallenged. A less elegant but somewhat more plausible alternative was early supplied by the English economist, F. Y. Edgeworth (1845-1926) of box diagram fame.[4]

In Edgeworth's formulation the assumptions of Cournot are retained except for two very important changes. (i) This time the two sellers of mineral water are presumed to have limited productive capacity; neither seller by himself can supply all that the market will take at a zero price. (ii) Now mineral water is not sold in a perfect market; that is, arbitrage is sufficiently sluggish that, in the very short run, two different prices for mineral water may be quoted in the market.

Sluggish arbitrage makes possible the construction of a "price variation" model of duopoly. Cournot's model is generally termed a "quantity variation" model because, the market being perfect, there is a single market price which an individual seller can affect only by varying output.

Edgeworth, using a price variation model, could assume:

3. For many years Cournot's pioneer work on oligopoly was treated as a mathematical curiosity having little or no significance for the study of markets in the real world. Some critics objected that Cournot made the wrong assumptions about how oligopolists behave. Others held that there was no such thing as an oligopoly problem since, if sellers were few they would very soon join together to act like a monopolist. In recent years, however, William Vickrey has shown that the Cournot model is a more interesting and possibly more powerful tool of analysis than was previously supposed.

Vickrey framed the duopoly problem in this way. Suppose that the two sellers of costless mineral water are, in the first instance, totally ignorant of one another and, indeed, ignorant of the aggregate demand function itself. How much information can a duopolist collect by experimenting with different output policies? If the duopolists could experiment by producing a large number of different outputs and then pool their statistical data on sales, they could figure out the aggregate demand function for mineral water. They could then cooperate to behave as would a monopolist. But if the duopolists cannot pool sales data, a monopoly solution is not possible. Vickrey showed that each duopolist, acting alone, would ultimately collect sales data which, when analyzed, would lead him to behave as would a Cournot duopolist. See W. S. Vickrey, *Microstatics* (New York, 1964), pp. 306-8.

4. F. Y. Edgeworth, "La teoria pura del monopolio," *Giornale degli Economisti*, 15 (1897), 13-31. Translated in his *Papers Relating to Political Economy* (London, 1925), Vol. I, pp. 111-42.

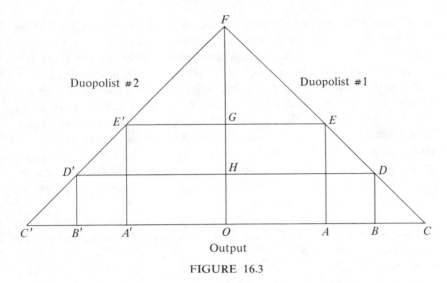

FIGURE 16.3

A16.3 One duopolist in selecting the price at which he will sell always assumes that the second duopolist will continue to charge whatever price he (the second duopolist) is presently charging.

Consider Edgeworth's geometry in figure 16.3. Edgeworth assumes that, in the long run, when the duopolists charge the same price they will divide the market equally. In figure 16.3 price is measured along the vertical axis. The output of duopolist # 1 is measured from point O along the horizontal OC. The output of duopolist #2 is measured from point O along the horizontal line OC'. Thus FC is the demand curve for the output of duopolist #1; and FC' is the demand curve for the output of duopolist #2. To repeat, both FC and FC' are constructed on the assumption that both sellers charge the same price.

In figure 16.3, OB represents the maximum amount of mineral water that duopolist #1 can produce. Likewise, OB' represents the maximum amount of mineral water that duopolist #2 can produce. Now if the two sellers cooperated to maximize joint profits, the first would produce output OA and the second output OA'. Price would be OG and joint profit would equal the area $A'AEE'$ in figure 16.3.

In Edgeworth's model, as in Cournot's model, the sellers are persistently greedy and incapable of learning from experience. When price is OG duopolist #1 believes that by cutting price a little below OG, he can take customers away from his rival who will continue to charge OG. So duopolist #1 cuts price by, say, 10 percent. Duopolist #2 upon finding that his customers are leaving him, cuts price 15 percent below *OG*. The price war continues until price reaches *OH*. At this level, neither party will cut further because they lack the productive capacity to handle new business.

Is this the end? By no means. Duopolist #1 now believes that he can increase his profit by raising price above *OH*. This rise may price a few customers out of the market. But it will not cause any to desert to duopolist #2 because duopolist #2 already has all of the customers that he can handle at price *OH*. Duopolist #2, observing that his rival is earning a greater profit at a higher price, raises his own price above *OH*. Ultimately, price reaches *OG;* and once again one seller has an incentive to steal his rival's customers by price cutting.

Thus in figure 16.3 price will endlessly move between the upper limit *OG* and the lower limit *OH*. There is no unique equilibrium price and no unique equilibrium output.

In the imperfect markets of the real world one often observes the kind of price cuts and rises described by the Edgeworth model. But the reasonable man's objection to the Edgeworth model is the same as his objection to Cournot's. Both assume that there is no ability to learn from experience about the greater profits to be had by cooperating with one's rival to restrict output and maintain price.

Oligopoly as a game

In the present century, the most ambitious effort to construct an all-purpose theory of oligopoly has been inspired by the collaboration of economist Oskar Morgenstern and mathematician John von Neumann in the "theory of games."[5] A vast number of games are possible. We will limit our consideration to two simple types which will indicate both the advantages and limitations of treating oligopoly as a "game."

Suppose that a business game has two players—duopolists A and B. Suppose that the profit that one can earn depends partly upon the market strategy followed by the other. Suppose further that, for some reason, duopolists A and B are unable to exchange information and devise a common strategy that will maximize their joint profits. Finally, suppose that duopolists A and B may choose from among three market strategies.

We label the strategies open to duopolist A as A1, A2, and A3 and the strategies open to duopolist B as B1, B2, and B3. The possible profits of

5. John von Neumann and Oskar Morgenstern, *Theory of Games and Economic Behavior* (Princeton, 2nd ed., 1947).

duopolist A are given in table 16.1a. The possible profits of duopolist B are given in table 16.1b.

The profit payoff that seller A can collect depends both upon the strategy that he adopts and the strategy that seller B adopts. The same is true for seller B. As tables 16.1a and 16.1b indicate, every move by A or B has three possible profit payoffs. In game theory, however, the players either cannot or will not assign probability coefficients to these possible payoffs. How should the duopolists behave in this situation?

TABLE 16.1A
A's Profits

		columns		
		B1	B2	B3
	A1	2	8	1
rows	A2	4	3	9
	A3	5*	6	7

* saddle point

TABLE 16.1B
B's Profits

		columns		
		A1	A2	A3
	B1	8	6	5*
rows	B2	2	7	4
	B3	9	1	3

* saddle point

TABLE 16.2A
A's Profits

columns

	B1	B2	B3
A1	2	8	1
A2	4	3	9
A3	6	5	7

rows {

TABLE 16.2B
B's Profits

columns

	A1	A2	A3
B1	8	6	4
B2	2	7	5
B3	9	1	3

rows {

In simple game theory each player is presumed to follow the so-called minimax rule. That is,

A16.3 Each player will choose the strategy that promises to give him the greatest minimum payoff regardless of what the other players do.

Adhering to this rule, duopolist A will choose strategy A3. If duopolist B plays strategy B3, a strategy of A1 will bring duopolist A a profit payoff of 7. If duopolist B plays B2, duopolist A still collects 6 by playing A3. And if worst comes to worst and duopolist B plays B1, a strategy of A1 will still allow duopolist A to collect 5. Should strategies A1 or A2 be played by duopolist A, he may (not necessarily will) wind up with a payoff of less than 5.

Now consider duopolist B's behavior. Following the minimax rule, he will choose strategy B1. As table 16.1b shows, by playing B1 he assures himself a payoff of at least 5. With a strategy of B2 or B3 he could do worse.

If on the first move of the game strategies A3 and B1 are played, then the worst fears of both players are realized. A collects only 5 and B collects only 5. Should A and B be allowed to play again, they will, of course, retain their respective strategies, A3 and B1. In this game, there is an equilibrium strategy for both parties and hence a "stable solution."

Let us move on to another simple game. Table 16.2a gives the possible payoffs to duopolist A and table 16.2b gives the possible payoffs to duopolist B. Following the minimax rule, on the first move, A selects strategy A3 and B selects strategy B1. This time, however, the worst fears of duopolist A *are not* realized. He collects 6 because B played B1; whereas had B2 been played, he (A) could have collected but 5. On the first move, the worst fears of B are realized; he gains only 4.

What happens on the second move of this new game? If duopolist A thinks that he has learned from experience that B will always play strategy B1, then he (a) will stick to strategy A3. But now, duopolist B, believing that A3 will be repeated, switches from B1 to B2. The result is an unpleasant surprise for duopolist A. He expected to collect 6 but collects only 5.

And on the third move of this new game? If duopolist A thinks that B will stick with strategy B2, he (A) will switch to strategy A1, expecting to get 8. Duopolist B sticks with strategy B2. This time the result is an unpleasant surprise for B. He expected to collect 5 but collects only 2.

And so forth. In this second game, when each duopolist expects that the last move of the other will be repeated, there is no equilibrium strategy for either one and no "stable solution."

The "saddle point"

Why does the first game have a stable solution while the second game does not? In the language of game theory, the answer is that table 16.1a and table 16.1b each contains a "saddle point"; whereas tables 16.2a and 16.2b do not. By definition, a saddle point is present if, in a payoff table, one entry is both the highest of the row minima and the lowest of the column maxima.

Regard table 16.1a. Here the row minima reading from top to bottom are 1 from row #1; 3 from row #2; and 5 from row #3. The column maxima, reading from left to right, are 5 from column #1; 8 from column #2; and 9 from column #3. Thus, in table 16.1a, the payoff 5 is both the highest of the row minima and the lowest of the column maxima. Table 16.1a contains a saddle point.

Now regard table 16.1b. Here the saddle point is to be found in the upper northeast corner. The entry 5 is both the highest of the row minima (these minima being 5, 2, and 1) and the lowest of the column maxima (these maxima being 9, 7, and 5).

The economic significance of the saddle point has already been indicated. It is simply that when a player chooses a strategy designed to ensure the highest minimum payoff, the strategy chosen does exactly that. The player is never either pleasantly or unpleasantly surprised by the outcome of a move.

You can easily verify that the game described in tables 16.2a and 16.2b has no saddle points. In table 16.2a the highest of the row minima is 5; whereas the lowest of the column maxima is 6. In table 16.2b, the highest of the row minima is 4; whereas the lowest of the column maxima is 5.

The theory of games is much richer intellectual fare than the two simple games described above may suggest; indeed one mathematician has hailed game theory as one of the "major scientific achievements of the first half of the twentieth century." Games need not be confined to two players; coalitions between two or more players can be allowed; and players can be allowed to experiment with mixed strategies.

Still, while game theory may be a major development in mathematics, its usefulness for the study of real-world oligopoly would seem to be extremely limited. Businessmen have been charged with many crimes, vices, and follies. But not even their most implacable critics have accused them of the extreme timidity and inability to learn from experience that the minimax rule implies.

The dominant-firm model

In markets where sellers are few, it often happens that one seller is viewed by everybody as the dominant firm because his market share is far larger than that of his next largest rival. This situation is especially common in local markets because large firms in the same industry may concentrate their sales efforts in different regions of the country and because even a small firm may "dominate" a particular town or city.

Whenever great disparity in the size of firms is found, a blend of monopoly and competition is possible which can be analyzed with the domi-

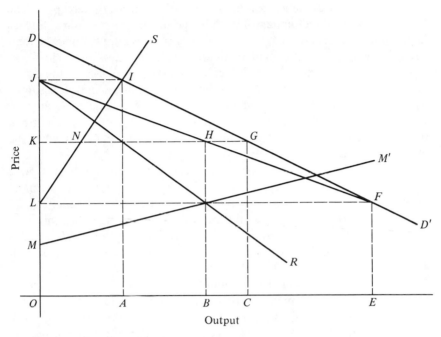

FIGURE 16.4

nant firm model of oligopoly. In this model, the dominant (biggest) firm selects a price and "allows" small firms to sell all that they wish at the selected price. In grateful return, all of the small firms tacitly agree not to seek a lower price. The dominant firm model is illustrated with the aid of figure 16.4.

Demand for the commodity is given by line *DD'*; that is, in figure 16.4 line *DD'* is an aggregate demand curve. Line *LS* is the supply curve of the small firms. It is drawn on the assumption that, behaving as perfect competitors when faced with the price set by the dominant firm, they equate price to marginal cost. Line *MM'* in figure 16.4 is the marginal cost curve of the dominant firm. Our first task is to discover the demand curve of the dominant firm; obviously it is not *DD'* since the sales of small firms must be taken into account at every possible price. Fortunately, the demand curve of the dominant firm is easily found.

Should the dominant firm set a price of *OJ* or higher, the small firms take over the market completely and it sells nothing. For at price *OJ* the small firms supply a total of OA units which is exactly what the market will take at price OJ. Hence point J is the vertical (price) intercept for the demand curve of the dominant firm. Now go to the other extreme. Should the dominant firm set a price of OL or lower, it takes over the market completely, having priced its small rivals out of the market. Since, in figure 16.4, $OL = EF$, point F must also lie on the demand curve of the dominant firm. To find the amount that it can sell at a given price we simply (i) calculate quantity demanded at that price; (ii) calculate the amount that small firms will supply at what price; and (iii) subtract the small firms' output from total quantity demanded. The difference is what the dominant firm can sell at the given price.

When the above computations have been performed for every price between OL and OJ, the result is line JF in figure 16.4. It is the demand curve of the dominant firm. The marginal revenue curve implied by JF is, of course, JR. Since the dominant firm is an income maximizer, it equates marginal cost to marginal revenue by charging price OK. At this price the dominant firm sells output OB; and the small firms sell output BC since (in figure 16.4), $BC = HG = KN$.

The dominant firm model of oligopoly has proved useful in the study of short-run pricing in many markets of the real world because, in the short run, both the number of firms and their plant capacities are fixed. However, in the long run this is not so. Firms can enter and leave the market and add or phase out plants; and, unless the antitrust agencies intervene, they can also merge with one another. Therefore, in figure 16.4, OJ is not a long-run equilibrium price unless (i) it is just sufficient to provide small firms with a normal rate of return on capital (and nothing more) and (ii) there are no economies to be gained by merging all firms in the industry in order to rationalize their production.[6]

Unhappiness with oligopoly models

For good and rather obvious reasons economists are not especially happy with the models of oligopoly discussed above and are even less happy with the less well-known models of oligopoly that we have not discussed.

6. In fact, the market share of the dominant firm will always decline in the long run (assuming no growth through merger) unless it is more efficient than its small rivals. This is true simply because the dominant firm accepts the burden of restricting output for the entire industry. Thus, when all firms are equally efficient, the dominant firm earns a lower rate of profit. See D. A. Worcester, "Why Dominant Firms Decline," *Journal of Political Economy*, 65 (1957), 338-46.

Cournot and Edgeworth are suspect because they assume that nobody learns from experience about his rival's behavior or that it pays to cooperate. The dominant firm model assumes some tacit cooperation on the part of the large firm and its small rivals but not enough to maximize joint profit in either the short run or the long run. Game theory is suspect because it posits businessmen who are both ignorant and exceedingly timid.

Still, we should not be disdainful of oligopoly models. In the real world oligopoly exists because business decisions must be made under conditions of uncertainty—that is, in a "dynamic" market setting. To the extent that oligopolists learn with the passing of time, uncertainty is removed and we move back toward the static setting. Should oligopolists ever gain complete information on one another's behavior, they will join together to replace oligopoly with something else. When entry into the industry by new firms is barred by Law or Nature, the something else is monopoly. When the entry of new firms is a possibility, the something else is a cartel or multiplant firm that practices stayout pricing. Either way, the uncertainty about the behavior of a rival that makes possible oligopoly disappears as the learning process goes forward.

Oligopoly can persist over time only so long as uncertainty persists. But clearly there can be no "one best way" to cope with uncertainty; otherwise everybody would adopt it and there could be no uncertainty. Hence there can never be a satisfactory all-purpose theory of oligopoly. In the real world, when sellers are few in a market, they always devise a method of co-existence that, most of the time, allows them to avoid the all-out price wars that are obviously unprofitable for everyone. These formulae for stabilizing the oligopoly markets of the real world are not to be confused with the joint profit maximization of a formal economic model; they are usually no more than crude aspirations in this direction. Some writers prefer to describe oligopoly as "incomplete collusion." This choice of words tacitly acknowledges the diverse character of real-world oligopoly. For while collusion can be complete in only one way, it can be incomplete in innumerable ways.

In the real world, every oligopoly employs a formula for limiting competition that is peculiarly its own. The detailed study of these formulae belongs to the industrial organization course. In this chapter we can only show why when sellers are few such formulae are necessary and indicate their rough-and-ready character. We will digress to consider one example of "oligopoly-in-action"—the market for metal cans. This example is chosen because it illustrates a type of price leadership very common in high concentration industries with homogeneous products.

Oligopoly-in-action: metal cans

In 1947 the production of metal cans could reasonably be described as "duopoly with a tail."[7] The American Can Company accounted for approximately 48.7 percent of total industry sales and the Continental Can Company for about 30.8 percent. The rest of the market was then divided among more than 50 small producers.

While the products of the metal can manufacturers (beer can, tomato can, etc.) were not, strictly speaking, homogeneous, they were highly standardized. And since most cans were sold to expert buyers—food processors, oil companies, and other industrial users—there was little point in trying to differentiate the products by advertising or styling. Any competition would have to be price competition.

Price competition, however, in the marketing of metal cans was (and is) extremely dangerous for can manufacturers since, in the short run, the demand for metal cans is price inelastic. This is because the demand for cans is derived from the demand for other products and the cost of cans is generally a small fraction of the cost of producing these other products. Hence, should a price war break out, total revenue is likely to decrease for all can manufacturers.

The main input in the production of metal cans in 1947 was tinplate and this fact presented the two leading producers—American and Continental—with a problem. The producers wished to keep the price of tinplate as low as possible "over the long run" in order to discourage the use of alternative containers such as cardboard and glass. However, they also wished to discourage frequent changes in the price of tinplate, fearing that such changes would trigger unprofitable price wars in the marketing of metal cans.

The United States Steel Corporation in the twenty years before 1947 was the leading supplier of tinplate. Each year the price of tinplate was set in a contract between American Can and United States Steel. Other tinplate manufacturers were prepared to accept the price leadership of the giant. Hence, there was a single, stable, "official" price for tinplate.

From 1925 and 1939—an era which saw prosperity, deep depression, and recovery—the official price of tinplate f.o.b. Pittsburgh varied from $4.25 to $5.50 per base box and never went up or down by more than 10 percent in any one year. In two intervals of three years, the official

7. For more details on oligopoly in can making, consult G. W. Stocking and M. W. Watkins, *Monopoly and Free Enterprise* (New York, 1951), pp. 166-81; and J. W. McKie, *Tin Cans and Tin Plate* (Cambridge, 1959).

price of tinplate did not change at all. Likewise the quoted prices of metal cans were very "sticky" in this period.

In a world of secret discounts and rebates, "official" prices are not always "true" prices and the price stability of the metal can industry before 1947 may have been less than the above account suggests. Nevertheless, it is reasonable to suppose (if only because it was regularly renewed) that the annual tinplate agreement between American Can and United States Steel did limit fluctuations in the "true" price of tinplate; and that this restriction did inhibit price cutting in the market for metal cans.

In this connection we might note that while the kind of price leadership that characterized the metal can industry in the past restrained rivalry among producers, it did not eliminate it completely. Can producers still had an incentive to get the jump on one another by introducing more efficient production techniques, expanding plant capacity, and developing new markets for their products.

If the can manufacturers had purchased their tinplate—their principal raw material—in a highly competitive market characterized by frequent price changes, they would, of course, have had to devise some other way of inhibiting price competition among themselves. There is no reason to believe that they would have been wanting in ingenuity. Does this mean that oligopolists are wicked men bent on undermining "free enterprise" or "our competitive economy"? (This view is widely held by economists and lawyers in the Antitrust Division of the Justice Department.) Of course not. Oligopolists are merely businessmen who find themselves in an oligopoly market situation. Given average intelligence, they will figure out some way to avoid the more obviously unprofitable forms of competition.

Oligopoly and rigid prices

In the metal can industry prices have often been "sticky" for months and sometimes years. This sort of price stability seems to characterize most oligopoly markets of the real world. There are at least three good reasons why this should be so.

    (i) Since oligopolists, at any moment in time, are usually not maximizing their joint profits anyway, a small random disturbance to supply or demand is as likely to increase industry profits as to decrease them.

    (ii) Price changes have a cost and so may not be worth making, especially if they must be rescinded in a short time. (We considered this possibility in connection with full-cost pricing.)

(iii) It takes time for oligopolists to agree upon the "correct" price change even when all agree that there should be some price change. No oligopolist dares to raise price on his own since he will lose part or all of his market if others do not follow suit. Usually no oligopolist will risk cutting price before securing the approval of his rivals because he fears to touch off a price war. Therefore, before actually changing price an oligopolist must "feel out the competition" or "feel out the market." This most often begins when he announces a price change to take effect in the future, e.g. a 10 percent price increase effective at the end of 30 days. He then sits back to await the reactions of his rivals. If they all announce the same increase, his 10 percent rise goes into effect at the end of 30 days. If the rivals all refuse to go along, it is canceled. By announcing future price changes which can be rescinded or modified, oligopolists exchange information with one another on what they believe the price change should be. This dance of the price change takes time. As it also agitates customers and may attract the attention of the antitrust agencies, it is not to be begun lightly, i.e. because of minor and possibly temporary changes in cost and revenue.

Some writers have tried to explain the observed stability of prices in oligopoly markets by surmising that the oligopolist's demand curve contains a kink at the point of market price.[8] The kink is said to be there because the oligopolist believes that if he cuts price his rivals will follow suit or cut even more; whereas if he raises price, they will raise by some lesser amount or not at all. As we know, a kink in the demand curve implies a discontinuous marginal revenue curve. Figure 16.5 describes such a possibility.

An oligopolist finds himself producing output *OA* and selling it at a price *OE*. For prices greater than *OE,* his demand curve is *DC* and his marginal revenue curve is *DF*. For prices less than *OE,* his demand curve is *CB* and his marginal revenue curve is *GH*. Thus, when his marginal cost curve is *MM'* (figure 16.5) the oligopolist cannot gain by changing price and indeed will be made worse off by either a price rise or a price cut.

On close examination the kinked demand curve so often imputed to the oligopolist turns out to be a pedagogical device of very limited value.

8. P. M. Sweezy, "Demand under Conditions of Oligopoly," *Journal of Political Economy,* 47 (1939), 568-73.

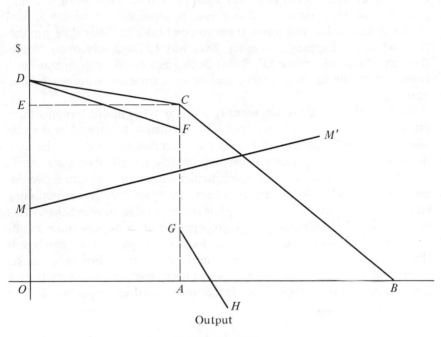

FIGURE 16.5

It does have the merit of suggesting that oligopoly prices frequently fail to respond to small changes in cost and revenue. But it offers a quite misleading explanation for this insensitivity. Oligopolists can (and do) eliminate the danger of kinks in their demand curves by announcing price changes in advance and then sitting back to await the reactions of rivals. At best, the kinked demand curve imputed to the oligopolist is an awkward way of indicating that (a) no single oligopolist is likely to change price on his own; (b) oligopolists must therefore usually negotiate price changes with one another; and (c) these negotiated price changes have a cost.

Summary

In this chapter we examined four formal models of oligopoly and one instance of oligopoly in the real world. We saw that the principal limitation of each of the formal models was basically the same. Each imposes a constraint on the capacity of oligopolists to learn from their experience. We noted that every model of oligopoly must place some limit on the learning process. For when no such limit exists, oligopolists will finally acquire the information that will allow them to combine and rationalize production. When this happens, oligopoly gives way to monopoly or to "something that looks like monopoly." But in the real world firms operate in a constantly changing environment and never learn enough to reach equilibrium.

In the real world there are literally as many types of oligopoly as there are markets where sellers are few. The distinctive feature of real-world oligopoly is an unspoken agreement on a formula that reduces the incidence of price cutting that can be unprofitable for all. Every real-world instance of oligopoly has its own particular formula for ensuring coexistence of firms. Some formulae, of course, are more effective in inhibiting competition than others. Moreover, it is never possible to prove that, of all the formulae for coexistence that are open to an oligopoly industry, its members have chosen the "best," i.e. most profitable. All we can say is that some formula will be employed most of the time. For in a market where sellers are few and price cuts promptly met, price instability is a sign not of "healthy competition" but of managerial incompetence and/or emotional instability.

REFERENCES

Cohen, K. J., and R. M. Cyert, *Theory of the Firm: Resource Allocation in a Market Economy* (Englewood Cliffs, N.J., 1965), chapter 12.

Fellner, W. J., *Competition among the Few* (New York, 1949).

Fisher, F. M., "The Stability of the Cournot Oligopoly Solution: The Effects of Speeds of Adjustment and Increasing Marginal Costs," *Review of Economic Studies,* 28 (2), (1961), 125-35.

Machlup, Fritz, *The Economics of Sellers' Competition: Model Analysis of Sellers' Conduct* (Baltimore, 1952).

Neumann, John von, and Oskar Morgenstern, *Theory of Games and Economic Behavior* (Princeton, 2nd ed., 1947).

Stigler, G. J., "A Theory of Oligopoly," *Journal of Political Economy,* 72 (1964), 44-61.

Vickrey, W. S., *Microstatics* (New York, 1964), chapter 8.

Worcester, D. A., *Monopoly, Big Business, Welfare in the Postwar United States* (Seattle, 1967), especially chapters 3 and 4.

17
General Equilibrium and Distribution

The limits of partial equilibrium analysis

So far in this book our concern has been mainly with what economists call partial equilibrium analysis. We have centered our attention on the actions of "firms" which comprise an "industry" and sell their outputs in a "market." And we have done so on the assumption that, in studying the determination of price and output in the industry, we can disregard the interactions between the industry and the other sectors of the economy. When the industry studied is itself only a small part of the larger economy—and equally important—when only the industry studied is presumed to vary its price and output—this assumption is reasonable enough. Does anybody want to worry about how a 10 percent increase in the output of paper clips will affect the level of prices and wages in the larger economy? But, of course, in the real world "everything depends upon everything else."

The effect of a 10 percent increase in the output of paper clips on the output of steel ingot may be so small that it can usefully be ignored when our object is to establish the connection between price and output changes in paper clip production. Nevertheless, a 10 percent increase in the output of paper clips *does* affect the output of steel ingot. And a change in the output of steel ingot *does* affect the demand for paper clips. Given "normal" supply and demand functions, an increase in the output of paper clips will lead to an increase in the output of steel ingot. Likewise, there will normally be a feedback effect. An increase in the output of steel ingot will lead to an increase in the demand for paper clips. The more orders for steel ingots, the more paperwork; the more paperwork, the more paper clips.

Almost inevitably, in economics, the development of partial equilibrium analysis raised the issue of a general equilibrium for all markets. That is, economists were led to the question: is it possible to construct an economic model of a competitive economy in which in every firm (i) price is equal to marginal cost and (ii) price is equal to average cost? You will recall why these two conditions are equilibrium conditions for a competitive economy. When price is equal to marginal cost, the firm has no incentive to alter its rate of output in the short run—the interval of time during which its plant capacity is fixed. When price is equal to average total cost, it has no incentive to alter its rate of output in the long run —the interval of time during which plant capacity can be increased by net investment or decreased by net disinvestment.

The simple Walrasian model

The French novelist and economist, Léon Walras (1834-1910) was the first investigator to offer a proof that a general equilibrium can exist.[1] In the present century, Walras's proof has sometimes been criticized as naïve equation counting, and there have been devised more rigorous mathematical demonstrations that a general equilibrium for all markets can exist.[2] Still, for making clear the economic content of the general equilibrium problem, the simple Walrasian system has never been surpassed. We shall consider it here. (One writer has suggested that Walras's achievement as an economist can be traced at least partly to the fact that he was a clumsy, though competent, mathematician; that his lack of mathematical elegance ensured that he never lost sight of general equilibrium as an economic problem.[3])

Three assumptions are central to Walras's general equilibrium model.

A17.1 All markets for commodities and factors are perfectly competitive.

A17.2 Consumer tastes, the state of technology, and the supplies of the factors are fixed and immutable; there is no technical progress, no fashion change, and neither investment nor disinvestment.

1. Léon Walras, *Éléments d'économie politique pure* (Lausanne, rev. 4th edition, 1926). Translated by William Jaffé as *Elements of Pure Economics: On the Theory of Social Wealth* (Homewood, Ill., 1954). The first edition of *Éléments* was published in 1874.
2. See, for example, Kelvin Lancaster, *Mathematical Economics* (New York, 1968), pp. 138-56.
3. Milton Friedman, "Léon Walras and His Economic System," *American Economic Review*, 45 (1955), 907.

A17.3 The coefficients of production are fixed and immutable. If the production of 1 unit of commodity x_2 requires an input of 2 units of factor y_1 and 3 units of factor y_2, then the production of n units of commodity x_2 requires an input of $2n$ units of factor y_1 and $3n$ units of factor y_2. (This is another case of "constant returns to scale.")

For notation we use the following:

$x_1, x_2, \ldots x_n$ denote the n commodities produced in the model.

$p_1, p_2, \ldots p_n$ denote the respective prices of the n commodities.

$y_1, y_2, \ldots y_m$ denote the m factors of production.

$w_1, w_2, \ldots w_m$ denote the respective prices of the m factors of production.

Walras quite correctly wished to avoid the complications, distractions, and irrelevancies of money. This can be done by picking one commodity—it does not matter which one—to serve as the *numeraire*. Thus prices can be expressed in terms of cigarettes, wheat, cattle, etc. For simplicity let us use commodity x_1 as the numeraire; so that $p_1 x_1 = x_1$, and $p_1 = 1$.

We can begin by writing down the individual's expenditure on each commodity. It is simply

$$x_1 p_1 + x_2 p_2 + \ldots + x_n p_n$$

or, since $p_1 = 1$,

$$x_1 + x_2 p_2 + \ldots + x_n p_n.$$

Continuing we can write down the sources of the individual's income. Since his income is obtained by renting out the factors of production (including himself) that he owns, we have

$$y_1 w_1 + y_2 w_2 + \ldots + y_m w_m$$

Assumption A17.2 rules out the possibility of saving (investment) and dissaving (disinvestment). Therefore, income equals expenditure for the individual; and

$$x_1 + x_2 p_2 + \ldots + x_n p_n = y_1 w_1 + y_2 w_2 + \ldots + y_m w_m \qquad (17.1)$$

Equation 17.1 is the *budget equation*. We shall meet it again very shortly.

Next we need a demand function for each of the n commodities that the individual buys. Obviously his demand for, say commodity x_2, depends upon the price of x_2 which is p_2. It also depends upon the prices of all other commodities that he can buy; and upon the prices that he obtains for the factors of production that he rents out to producers. These relationships we can express with the following set of equations.

$$x_2 = f_2(p_2, p_3, \ldots p_n, w_1, w_2, \ldots w_m)$$
$$x_3 = f_3(p_2, p_3, \ldots p_n, w_1, w_2, \ldots w_m)$$

$$\cdot$$
$$\cdot$$
$$\cdot$$

(I)

$$x_n = f_n(p_2, p_3, \ldots p_n, w_1, w_1, w_2, \ldots w_m)$$
$$x_1 = (y_1 w_1 + y_2 w_2 + \ldots + y_m w_m) - (x_2 p_2 + x_3 p_3 + \ldots + x_n p_n)$$

Does the last equation in set I bother you? It should not. It is the budget equation (17.1) that we have just met. Why is the notation of the demand equation commodity for x_1 different from the demand equations for the other commodities? It is different simply because commodity x_1 is our numeraire which means that, while the prices of other commodities may change, the price of x_1 cannot. By the definition of a numeraire, $p_1 = 1$.

We now have the information necessary in order to establish the requirements of general equilibrium. Let k designate the number of individuals in the model, every individual being both a consumer of commodities and a supplier of factors of production. Let X_1 designate the total amount of commodity x_1 consumed by all k individuals; let X_2 designate the total amount of commodity x_2 consumed by all k individuals. And so forth through all n commodities. Likewise, let Y_1 designate the total amount of factor y_1 owned by all k individuals, Y_2 the total amount of factor y_2 owned by all k individuals, etc. Thus.

$$X_n = x_{n1} + x_{n2} + \ldots + x_{nk}$$

(II)

and

$$Y_m = y_{m1} + y_{m2} + \ldots + y_{mk}$$

We can now write down the set of aggregate demand functions for all n commodities.

$$X_2 = F_2(p_2, p_3 \ldots p_n, w_1, w_2, \ldots w_m)$$
$$X_3 = F_3(p_2, p_3 \ldots p_n, w_1, w_2, \ldots w_m)$$

$$\cdot$$
$$\cdot$$
$$\cdot$$

(III)

$$X_n = F_n(p_2, p_3 \ldots p_n, w_1, w_2, \ldots w_m)$$
$$X_1 = (Y_1 w_1 + Y_2 w_2 + \ldots + Y_n w_m) - (X_2 p_2 + X_3 p_3 + \ldots + X_n p_n)$$

We now have a set of n demand equations for n commodities. Our next task is to construct a set of supply equations. This is easily done. Since all factor and commodity markets are perfectly competitive (assumption A17.1), all factors must be fully employed in equilibrium. For if a factor is not fully employed, there can be no equilibrium; its price must fall until it is fully employed. Let the amount of factor y_1 needed to produce 1 unit of commodity x_1 be designated a_{11}. And so forth through all n commodities and all m factors.

$$a_{11}w_1 + a_{12}w_2 + \ldots + a_{1m}w_m = p_1 = 1$$
$$a_{21}w_1 + a_{22}w_2 + \ldots + a_{2m}w_m = p_2$$
$$\cdot \qquad\qquad\qquad \cdot$$
$$\cdot \qquad\qquad\qquad \cdot \qquad\qquad\qquad\qquad (IV)$$
$$\cdot \qquad\qquad\qquad \cdot$$
$$a_{n1}w_1 + a_{n2}w_2 + \ldots + a_{nm}w_n = p_n$$

and

$$a_{11}X_1 + a_{21}X_2 + \ldots + a_{n1}X_n = Y_1$$
$$a_{12}X_1 + a_{22}X_2 + \ldots + a_{n2}X_n = Y_2$$
$$\cdot \qquad\qquad\qquad \cdot$$
$$\cdot \qquad\qquad\qquad \cdot \qquad\qquad\qquad\qquad (V)$$
$$\cdot \qquad\qquad\qquad \cdot$$
$$a_{1n}X_1 + a_{2n}X_2 + \ldots + a_{nm}X_n = Y_m$$

Let us now pause to take an inventory of the equations that have proliferated all over the place. We now have n demand equations for n commodities in set III. We have n commodities in set IV. And we have m supply equations for m factors in set V.

Here we meet a minor complication. Our total number of equations from sets III, IV, and V is $2n + m$. Yet we have only $2n - 1 + m$ unknowns. And, as you recall from your basic algebra, a necessary condition for the solution of a set of simultaneous equations is that the number of independent equations be equal to the number of unknowns. How did we lose an unknown? We lost it when we selected commodity x_1 to serve as our numeraire. We set the price of x_1 equal to unity and wrote $p_1 = 1$. Hence the equations in sets III and IV contain only $(n - 1)$ unknown prices.

To get back on the road to general equilibrium we must eliminate one equation. We perform this feat in the following steps.

Step 1 Multiply the first equation in set IV by X_1, the second equation in set IV by X_2, and so forth through all n equations in set IV. Call the equations that result from this multiplication set IV.A.

Step 2 Multiply the first equation in set V by w_1, the second equation in set V by w_2, and so forth through all m equations. Call the equations that result from this multiplication set V.A.

Step 3 Note that when the above multiplications have been performed, the left-hand side of set IV.A contains the same terms as the left-hand side of set V.A. Hence the sum of the right-hand terms in set IV.A must be equal to the sum of the right-hand terms in set V.A. That is,

$$X_1 + X_2p_2 + \ldots + X_np_n = Y_1w_1 + Y_2w_2 + \ldots + Y_mw_m \quad (17.2)$$

or

$$X_1 = (Y_1w_1 + Y_2w_2 + \ldots + Y_mw_m) - (X_2p_2 + X_3p_3 + \ldots + X_np_n)$$
$$(17.2a)$$

But equation 17.2a is the same as the last equation in set III (being derived from the budget equation), and is not an independent equation. Thus we have established that there *may* be a solution to our system of equations. What was the economic significance of eliminating one equation? Simply this. Suppose that we know the prices of all commodities and that price is equal to average total cost for all commodities; suppose also that we know the output of every commodity except one. Then we can deduce the equilibrium output of this remaining commodity. This is analogous to saying that if we can manage to fit all pieces of a jigsaw puzzle into place save one piece, we can deduce the shape of this piece even though it is missing.

Walras not perfect

Over the years a number of criticisms have been made of the simple Walrasian system of general equilibrium described above. For our purposes, the most important of these criticisms is that the existence of n equations in n unknowns does not guarantee a solution that is both unique and economically meaningful. For example, a system of general equilibrium which requires that $X_n = -7$ has no economic meaning. Suffice it to say that the work of later writers put the finishing touches to the Walrasian system. It is "all in the literature" for those who wish to consult it.

Let us accept that a unique system of general equilibrium can exist for a model of perfect competition. Does it follow that, beginning in a state of disequilibrium, movement will be toward such an equilibrium? Here we encounter some unfinished business in the history of economics. As yet, no economist or mathematician has succeeded in describing the path by which general equilibrium will be approached even though its existence can be demonstrated. By the same token, no economist or mathematician has yet proved that there is no way by which an economy can move from disequilibrium to general equilibrium.

What of the economic system that is not perfectly competitive in all commodity and factor markets? The general equilibrium problem of such an economy is almost entirely unexplored territory in economics. It has often been conjectured that the presence of monopoly elements precludes the existence of general equilibruim. But nobody knows for sure.

Input-output analysis and general equilibrium

In conclusion we might note that the study of general equilibrium provides a good example of the impossibility of predicting the practical consequences of arm-chair reflection. For more than fifty years following the publication of Walras's general equilibrium results, his work was regarded as a theoretical curiosity with no discernible empirical application. Indeed the most popular history of economic theory published in the first half of this century completely ignored the work of Walras.[4] Then in the 1930's Wassily Leontief showed how it could be used as a basis for constructing detailed input-output tables showing the interactions of the industries that comprise an economic system.[5] Indeed no capitalist economy can afford to do battle with the business cycle without input-output analysis; and no socialist economy can afford to attempt the "planning of production" without it. Is it really surprising that not a few economists regard Léon Walras as the greatest name of all in economics?

The adding-up problem

We have found that it is possible to construct a general equilibrium model of a perfectly competitive economy; and that in such a model price is equal to average total cost for every commodity produced. In the history of economics the search for a general equilibrium model has been closely related to the "adding-up" problem of factor shares. As we shall see, economists had to settle this last problem (shortly to be defined) before they could construct a logically consistent theory of how income is divided among the factors that produce it.

4. Alexander Gray, *The Development of Economics Doctrine* (London, 1931).
5. W. W. Leontief, *The Structure of the American Economy, 1919-1939: An Empirical Application of Equilibrium Analysis* (New York, 2nd ed., 1951).

Beginning with Adam Smith (1723-90), economists sought to gain a clear view of the principle (or principles) that governed the division of income into factor shares. Smith's economics recognized three factors of production—land, labor, and capital. The great Scotsman had no well-developed theory of factor shares. He clearly grasped that in a perfectly competitive labor market, labor would be hired until the wage rate is equal to the value of its marginal product. But he had no precise idea of how the rest of the income is divided between capital and land.

During the nineteenth century Smith's treatment of factor shares underwent two major modifications (and improvements). First, it was gradually recognized that the tripartite division of the factors of production—what Frank Knight was later to call the "Unholy Trinity"—was certainly arbitrary and possibly unsatisfactory. There is, for example, no reason why management, risk-bearing, skilled labor, semi-skilled labor, and un-skilled labor should not be treated as separate factors of production. Second, during the nineteenth century, the principle that a factor of production will be hired until its price becomes equal to the value of its marginal product was gradually applied to all factors. In the soporific prose of Alfred Marshall:

> Every agent of production, land, machinery, skilled labour, unskilled labour, etc., tends to be applied in production as far as it profitably can be. If employers, and other business men, think that they can get a better result by using a little more of any one agent they will do so. They estimate the net product (that is the net increase of the money value of their total output after allowing for incidental expenses) that will be got by a little more outlay in this direction, or a little more outlay in that; and if they can gain by shifting a little of their outlay from one direction to another, they will do so.[6]

Consider one instance of how the marginal productivity principle was gradually honed and refined. Adam Smith made no distinction between interest on capital and the profits of entrepreneurs. Both of these elements of income were lumped together as "the profits of stock." Some years later in the work of Nassau Senior (1790-1864) these two elements are clearly distinguished; and Senior is clear that in a competitive capital market the marginal productivity of capital is equal to the rate of interest.[7] The idea that the rent of land is a surplus that remains after every other factor has been paid its marginal product died very hard (so great was

6. Alfred Marshall, *Principles of Economics* (London, 8th ed., 1920), p. 521.
7. Nassau Senior, *An Outline of the Science of Political Economy* (London, 1836).

the hostility to landlords). Nevertheless, in the end the rent of land also yielded to marginalism. For J. B. Clark (1847-1938) showed that, when the market for land is perfectly competitive, land too has a marginal product; and land will be hired until rent per unit is equal to land's marginal product.[8]

Once it was accepted that in a competitive factor market a factor is paid its marginal product, a problem analogous to that of general equilibrium had to be faced. Is it possible to show that, when every factor employed in the production process is paid its marginal product, then "payments to the factors exhaust the product"? This is the venerable adding-up problem of economics.

Let us go back a little. In a simple Walrasian model of general equilibrium, payments to the factors do unmistakably exhaust the product. The only incomes that an individual receives are obtained by hiring out the factors that he owns; and, for every commodity, price is equal to average total cost. The trouble is that, in a simple Walrasian model, there is, strictly speaking, no such thing as the marginal product of a factor. This is so because, in such a model, production is governed by fixed factor coefficients.

Suppose that the production of a unit of a commodity x always requires 1 unit of factor y and 2 units of factor z. The one cannot increase the output of commodity x by keeping the input of factor y constant and increasing the input of factor z. To raise the output of commodity x, one must simultaneously increase the inputs of both factor y *and* factor z. To attack the adding-up problem, we have to discard the assumption that factor coefficients of production are fixed.

Let the production function be of the form

$$x = \phi(y_1, y_2, \ldots y_m) \tag{17.3}$$

where x designates commodity output ("product") and $y_1, y_2 \ldots y_m$ the input of m different factors.

The marginal (physical) product of factor y_1 is the first partial derivative of x with respect to y_1. And so forth through all m factors.

Let us further assume that there are no fixed coefficients of production so that a set of partial derivatives exists for all positive values of $y_1, y_2, \ldots y_m$.

In order for "payments to the factors to exhaust the product" it is necessary that

8. J. B. Clark, *The Distribution of Wealth* (New York, 1899), pp. 354-72.

$$x = \frac{\partial x}{\partial y_1} y_1 + \frac{\partial x}{\partial y_2} y_2 + \ldots + \frac{\partial x}{\partial y_m} y_m \tag{17.4}$$

To solve the adding-up problem we need a production function, which, when differentiated, will yield a set of partial derivatives that satisfies equation 17.4. The English economist Philip Wicksteed (1844-1927) is usually regarded as the first investigator to have cracked the adding-up problem.[9] With the aid of awkward mathematics acquired by self-education, Wicksteed was able to show that any production function that was homogeneous of the first degree will yield partial derivatives that satisfy equation 17.4. (An equation is homogeneous if the sums of the exponents in all terms are equal; it is of the first degree if the sum of the exponents in every term is unity.) The most important economic property of this class of production functions is that they imply constant returns to scale. Double the amount of each factor input simultaneously and you double the amount of commodity output.

We will not stop to work through a rigorous proof of the proposition that when (a) each factor is paid a price equal to its marginal product and (b) the production function is homogeneous of the first degree, then payments to the factors exhaust the product. This cannot be done without proving a theorem on homogeneous equations (Euler's) which is encountered nowadays only in advanced calculus courses (and not always there).

We will settle for an illustration. Let the production function for a commodity x which is produced by using factors y and z be given by

$$x = ky^a z^{1-a} \tag{17.5}$$

subject to $k > 0$, $y > 0$, $z > 0$, and $0 < a < 1$.
Then

$$\frac{\partial x}{\partial y} = kay^{a-1} z^{1-a} \tag{17.6}$$

And

$$\frac{\partial x}{\partial z} = \frac{k(1-a)y^a}{z^a} \tag{17.7}$$

Now

$$\frac{\partial x}{\partial y} y + \frac{\partial x}{\partial z} z = y(kay^{a-1} z^{1-a}) + z(\frac{k(1-a)y^a}{z^a}) \tag{17.8}$$

9. Philip Wicksteed, *Co-ordination of the Laws of Distribution* (London, 1894).

or

$$\frac{\partial x}{\partial y} y + \frac{\partial x}{\partial z} z = k y^a z^{1-a} \qquad (17.8a)$$

Since the right-hand side of equation 17.8a is the same as the right-hand side of equation 17.5, payments to the factors exhaust the product. What happens when the production function is of the form

$$x = k y^a z^b \qquad (17.9)$$

where $a + b \neq 1$?

There are two possibilities. If $a + b > 1$, then $\frac{\partial x}{\partial y} y + \frac{\partial x}{\partial z} z > x$. In this case, it is economically impossible to pay each factor its marginal product. This is the case of increasing returns to scale where "competition breaks down." Competition here breaks down because one can always get more output from a given quantity of inputs by giving the inputs to a large production unit ("firm") rather than dividing them between two or more smaller production units.

Alternatively, when $0 < (a+b) < 1$, then

$$\frac{\partial x}{\partial y} y + \frac{\partial x}{\partial z} z < x.$$

In this case, a surplus remains after each factor has received its marginal product. This is the case of "decreasing returns to scale" where production is organized in microscopically small units. The study of these non-linear production functions still lies on the unexplored frontier of economic analysis and need not concern us in this book.

One final comment on the adding-up problem is in order. A production function of the first degree can be used to solve this problem. But it is, strictly speaking, incompatible with the U-shaped curve of average total cost in the plant on which (almost) all microeconomic analysis is founded. For if the production function of the plant is of the first degree, then there can be no optimum size of plant. A pygmy plant is as efficient as a giant operation. This difficulty once caused economists much discomfort. Happily, there is a way out.

If the firm can always expand output by increasing the number of optimum size plants that it operates (and without causing average total cost to rise), then the production function *of the firm* can usefully be viewed as approximated by an equation of the first degree. Average total cost for the firm will be minimized whenever some multiple of the output of the optimum size plant is produced. And, even if there is some finite number of plants at which average total cost in the firm is minimized, the production *of the industry* can be described by an equation of the first degree provided that the industry can expand production by increasing the number of optimum size firms.

Barber shops are a case in point. As population increases—and with it the demand for haircuts—barber shops do not get bigger and multishop firms do not emerge. The economy simply adds more barber shops of existing size. In short, the production function of the first degree that we use to solve the adding-up problem can reasonably be regarded as an "aggregate production function"—the production function of a multiplant firm or of a multifirm industry.

Modern dissent

Walras's system of general equilibrium and Wicksteed's solution to the adding-up problem were both intellectual products of the nineteenth century, and in recent years they have come to be regarded by many economists as unacceptably primitive. One feature of this discontent might well provide these two great economists with some wry amusement. Walras has often been criticized because his production function has fixed factor coefficients while Wicksteed has often been criticized for exactly the opposite reason. Still, there is a strong presumption that any bit of economic analysis more than seventy years old can be improved upon. Two efforts to go beyond Walras and Wicksteed are considered in the appendices to this chapter.

Summary

Microeconomics is, for the most part, partial equilibrium analysis. It assumes that the activities of the set of firms that comprise the industry can be studied without attention to the interactions beween the industry and the larger economic system. For many—indeed most—purposes, this assumption is useful. However, since these interactions do exist, economists have felt it necessary to say something about them. We have now examined two famous efforts to widen the perspective of economic analysis. We have seen that it is possible, with the aid of carefully chosen assumptions, to prove the existence of general equilibrium in the model of a perfectly competitive economy. And we noted that this demonstration, the essential ingredients of which were supplied in the nineteenth century by Léon Walras, provides the basis for modern input-output analysis. We also saw that, in the case of a perfectly competitive economy, it is possible to solve the adding-up problem again provided that the appropriate assumptions are employed. That is, it can be shown that when every factor is paid its marginal product, payments to the factors exhaust the product.

REFERENCES

Arrow, K. J., and F. H. Hahn, *General Competitive Analysis* (Edinburgh, 1971), especially chapters 1 and 2.
Dewey, Donald, *Modern Capital Theory* (New York, 1965), chapter 8.
Ferguson, C. E., *Microeconomic Theory* (Homewood, Ill., 3rd ed., 1972), chapters 13, 14, and 15.
Nicholson, Walter, *Microeconomic Theory: Basic Principles and Extensions* (Hinsdale, 1972), pp. 463-74.
Stigler, G. J., *Production and Distribution Theories: The Formative Period* (New York, 1946), especially chapter 12.
Stonier, A. W., and D. C. Hague, *A Textbook of Economic Theory* (New York, 3rd ed., 1964), chapter 16.

APPENDIX A
A CRITICISM OF MARGINAL PRODUCTIVITY

An alternative model

The marginal productivity theory of income distribution has never been without its critics. This is not surprising. Provided that the basic assumptions of welfare economics are accepted, it implies that general equilibrium is a Pareto optimum—that once it has been reached, nothing can be changed without making at least one person worse off. Many economists are unwilling to accept the theory because, rightly or wrongly, they believe that it creates a presumption that any interference by the State with market prices is likely to reduce economic welfare. One can argue that the theory *per se* creates no such presumption since the real world is always in disequilibrium; but it is true that many uncritical admirers of marginal productivity theory have viewed State interference with real-world prices as somehow immoral. Therefore, it is not surprising that a counterattack has been mounted not only against the uses to which the theory is put but also against the theory itself. In recent years, a number of economists in Cambridge (England) have promoted the following alternative model of income distribution.[1]

1. The model described in this appendix is, with very minor modifications, a model first presented by Piero Sraffa, *Production of Commodities by Means of Commodities: Prelude to a Critique of Economic Theory* (Cambridge, 1960), pp. 9-11.

Suppose that commodities a, b, . . . k are to be produced; and that the production of a commodity requires the use of (i) other commodities and (ii) labor. Thus the production of one unit of commodity a requires the sum of inputs $A_a + B_a + \ldots K_a + L_a$. Here A_a denotes amount of commodity a needed to produce one unit of commodity a. Likewise B_a denotes the amount of commodity B needed to produce one unit of commodity a. And so forth. The labor input of the model is given by L and, of course, L_a gives the amount of labor needed to produce one unit of commodity a. (Note that we have returned to a model of fixed factor coefficients in the production function.)

Suppose further that "production is profitable" in the sense that:

$$A_a + B_a + \ldots + K_a < A$$
$$A_b + B_b + \ldots + K_b < B$$
$$\begin{array}{cccc} \cdot & \cdot & & \cdot & \cdot \\ \cdot & \cdot & & \cdot & \cdot \\ \cdot & \cdot & & \cdot & \cdot \end{array}$$
$$A_k + B_k + \ldots + K_k < K$$

On the premise that all labor is fully employed we can write:

$$L_a + L_b + \ldots + L_k = 1$$

We define the net output of commodity a during the period of production to be:

$$A - (A_a + B_a + \ldots + K_b) = \bar{A}$$

Generalizing, we define the net output of all commodities during the period of production to be:

$$\bar{A} + \bar{B} + \ldots + \bar{K} = \phi$$

Thus ϕ designates a composite commodity produced during the period of production. As always, we need a numeraire. This time we obtain it by setting the value of the composite commodity ϕ equal to unity. Thus we can write:

$$\bar{A} p_a + \bar{B} p_b + \ldots + \bar{K} p_k = 1 \qquad (17.10)$$

where p_a is the price of commodity a; p_b is the price of commodity b. And so forth through p_k.

Since the composite commodity ϕ is greater than zero, there is a net output to be divided in each production period. Commodities have been used to replace themselves and create a surplus. Presumably, two claimant groups exist—workers and capitalists. A capitalist, by definition, is a person who supplies commodities used in production. The same person can, of course, be both a worker and a capitalist.

Given perfect competition, the wage w must be the same in all industries. We can write:

$$(A_a p_a + B_a p_b + \ldots K_a p_k)\,(1 + r) + L_a w = A p_a$$
$$(A_b p_a + B_b p_b + \ldots K_b p_k)\,(1 + r) + L_b w = B p_b \qquad (17.11)$$
$$\cdot$$
$$\cdot$$
$$\cdot$$
$$(A_k p_a + B_k p_b + \ldots K_k p_k)\,(1 + r) + L_k w = K p_k$$

Now we have a set of $k + 1$ equations and $k + 2$ unknowns (these unknowns being k prices, the wage w, and the rate of profit r). Note that since $\overline{A} = A - (A_a + B_a + \ldots K_a)$ etc., equation 17.10 contains no unknown that does not appear in equations 17.11. (The converse is not true.) In order to obtain a system of equations that can be solved we must arbitrarily specify the value of either the wage w or the rate of profit r.

One implication of this Cambridge view of income distribution is clear; the division of income between workers and capitalists *is not* determined by competition. Rather competition merely ensures that the wage w will be the same in all industries; and that the rate of profit r will be the same in all industries. This result implies a rather drastic reduction in the importance of the role assigned to competition in economic activity. Presumably "forces exogenous to the economic system"—custom, institutions, laws, trade union pressure, etc.—determine the division between wages and profits. Presumably too the distribution of income can be changed by altering these exogenous forces.

Within limits (which we will not pause to identify), the higher the rate of profit, the lower the wage rate. And vice versa. Moreover—again within limits—wages can be increased at the expense of profits without any reduction of total income.

Labor as a Unique Commodity

On its face, the Cambridge criticism of the marginal productivity theory of distribution appears to be rather formidable. But its force really stands or falls on one feature—its treatment of labor. In equations 17.11, labor appears only as an input in the production process. If labor were viewed as having a production function like commodities a, b, . . . k, then we would be able to add another equation to the set of equations 17.11. And we would now have $k + 2$ equations, $k + 2$ unknowns and hence the possibility of a determinate system. In such a system there would be one, and only one, division of income between workers and capitalists consistent with equilibrium.

That labor (or more accurately human capital) is a commodity with a cost of production is a truth that should be self-evident to anyone who has gotten this far in economics. However, in a modern industrial economy, it takes a minimum of sixteen years to "produce" a member of the labor force. Hence it is not unreasonable to assume, in analyzing problems of the short run that (a) labor is an input in the production process but not an output and (b) all other commodities are both inputs and outputs.

Since the real world is characterized by both never-ending disequilibrium and imperfect competition, a model which explains the division of income on the assumption that equilibrium and perfect competition exist is obviously of limited usefulness. And these limitations characterize both the Cambridge model and the marginal productivity model. The question, as always, is simply: which model will allow us most accurately to predict those events that we wish to predict. For example, suppose that we wish to estimate the effect on the employment of inexperienced teen-age workers of a 25 percent rise in the minimum wage prescribed by federal law. Here there is no doubt that the superiority of marginal productivity theory. It says that such a rise in the minimum wage will cause unemployment of teen-agers to increase. Our experience with previous jumps in the legal minimum wage indicates that the result will, in fact, be more unemployment for teen-agers.

But suppose the question is: what will happen to employment in the next 18 months if a limitation is placed upon profits which may be retained or paid out to stockholders by business firms? Then, given the complexities of the savings and investment process, it is not clear that marginal productivity theory is the best predictor. Economics still has room for more than one theory of income distribution.

APPENDIX B
AN ALTERNATIVE APPROACH TO
GENERAL EQUILIBRIUM

In recent years economists have found more rigorous and elegant ways to show the possibility of general equilibrium under perfect competition than were attainable by Walras. Since these proofs draw upon mathematics not found in introductory university courses (and use an unfamiliar notation) we shall not work through them in detail. However, the modern approach to general equilibrium can be indicated by considering the special case of a pure exchange economy—one in which the stock of commodities to be traded is fixed for each time period and there is no cost of production for any commodity. The following demonstration is mainly useful as an example of how modern mathematics has been applied to one very old problem in economics.

Suppose that on market day n different commodities are brought into a perfectly competitive market to be exchanged for one another. Let q_i $(i = 1, 2, \ldots n)$ denote the quantity of the ith commodity and p_i the price of the ith commodity. The set that consists of the prices of all n commodities we write simply as p. Excess demand for the ith commodity we write as z_i. (Strictly speaking, we should write $z_i(p_i)$ instead of z_i, but no confusion will result from the use of the simpler notation.) The set of excess demands for all n commodities we denote z. Excess demand may, of course, be positive, negative, or zero. By definition, the ith market is in equilibrium when

$$p_i z_i = 0, z_i \leqq 0, p_i \geqq 0$$

Thus, for the ith market to be in equilibrium either $p_i > 0$ and $z_i = 0$ or $p_i = 0$ and $z_i \leqq 0$. The economic meaning of $z_i < 0$ for $p_i = 0$ is simply that some part of the stock of the ith commodity will not be demanded at a zero price, i.e. when it is a free good.

Our definition of market equilibrium in the ith market can be generalized to cover all n commodities. General equilibrium exists if, and only if,

$$pz = 0, z \leqq 0, p \geqq 0$$

We can prove the existence of general equilibrium in a pure exchange economy with the aid of a definition and a theorem (Brouwer's fixed-point theorem) provided by mathematicians.

We define the fundamental simplex in n-space to be

$$S_n = \left\{ p | p \geqq 0, \sum_{i=1}^{n} p_i = 1 \right\} \qquad (17.12)$$

Do not be intimidated by the above notation. Suppose that p stands for the price of a commodity. Then the above definition is merely a statement that S_n is the set of every combination of n prices that are (i) non-negative and (ii) sum up to 1.

Brouwer's fixed-point theorem states:

Let $x = f(p)$ be a continuous mapping of the fundamental simplex into itself. That is, to every p in S_n the mapping gives an x in S_n such that as p moves about in S_n, x always moves smoothly and never jumps discontinuously from one point to another. Then there exists a point p^* in n-space such that $f(p^*) = p^*$.

In order to make use of Brouwer's fixed-point theorem we must first provide ourselves with a set of commodity prices that form a fundamental simplex.[1] This we can easily do by normalizing a set of prices of the n commodities which are traded in the market. It does not matter which particular set of prices is chosen for normalization so long as the set includes only non-negative prices.

When p_i is the non-normalized price of the ith commodity and p_i' its nomalized price, we have

$$p_i' = \frac{p_i}{\sum\limits_{i=1}^{n} p_i}$$

Normalization does not alter the ratio of any pair of prices. That is, $p_i' / p_j' = p_i / p_j$. And, of course,

$$\sum_{i=1}^{n} p_i' = 1$$

The set of n normalized prices now forms a fundamental simplex. For every normalized price p_i', there exists another price $f(p_i')$ such that

$$f(p_i') = p_i' + z_i \tag{17.13}$$

Here we meet two minor complications. Since z_i can be negative, $f(p_i')$ can be negative; yet our definition of market equilibrium ruled out negative prices. We eliminate this complication by writing $f(p_i') = \max [p_i + z_i, 0]$ where "max" merely means that $f(p_i')$ must be either positive or 0. In effect, we adopt the rule: replace every $f(p_i') < 0$ with $f(p_i') = 0$.

The second minor complication is that the $f(p_i')$'s may not sum up to 1. But this is no real problem. We can normalize them in the same way that we normalized the original p_i's.

1. Brouwer's fixed-point theorem is proved in S. S. Cairns, *Introductory Topology* (Urbana, Ill., revised printing, 1968), pp. 137-39.

When all prices have been normalized, and all negative prices have been eliminated, we have

$$f(p) = [\max p + z, \ 0] \tag{17.14}$$

Now, provided that $f(p)$ is continuous, the fundamental simplex contains both $f(p)$ and p. Hence the fundamental simplex is mapped into itself by equation 17.14. And by Brouwer's fixed-point theorem there is a set of prices p^* such that

$$f(p^*) = \max [p^* + z^*, \ 0]. \tag{17.15}$$

Now if $f(p^*) > 0$, then $f(p_i{}^*) = p_i{}^*$ implies $z_i{}^* = 0$. If $f(p_i{}^*) = 0$, then $f(p_i{}^*) = p_i{}^*$ implies $z_i{}^* \leqq 0$. In any event, we can write $p^*z^* = 0$, $p^* \geqq 0$, $z^* \leqq 0$, and so satisfy the conditions of general equilibrium.

As yet, the modern treatments of general equilibrium have provided no tools that are useful in empirical work or in the analysis of economic policy. But patience would seem to be advisable. After all, over seventy years elapsed between the first appearance of Walras's formulation of general equilibrium and its use in Leontief's construction of statistical input-output tables.

18

Linear Programming

The production function of linear programming

For most of our work in this book we have founded our analysis squarely on production functions that are consistent with the U-shaped curve of average total cost in the plant. All such production functions have two features in common: (i) they require the use of specialized, indivisible ("lumpy") factor inputs; (ii) the factor input coefficients of these production functions are not completely fixed—within limits they allow the substitution of one factor input for another.

Nobody in his right mind will doubt the realism of the assumption that the curve of average total cost in the plant is U-shaped. However, as we have learned, in economic analysis realism is nice but not essential; the important criterion for judging a bit of scientific apparatus is utility. And often we can increase our stock of useful results by switching to a less realistic assumption. We have already made this substitution on occasion. Recall that in Chapter 17 we made use of a linear production function with fixed factor coefficients in order to prove the possibility of general economic equilibrium under conditions of perfect competition.

The linear production function with fixed factor coefficients has other uses as well. Indeed it provides the basis for the set of analytical techniques which are generally called linear programming. In recent years the sister subject of non-linear programming has also developed but because it has, as yet, achieved far fewer applications and is considerably more complicated, we shall confine our attention to linear programming. The details of linear programming are more appropriate to a course in industrial management than to a course in economics. Still, there are at least two good reasons why we should make the acquaintance of the subject.

First, linear programming allows us to deal succinctly and rigorously with certain problems of microeconomics that would otherwise be worse handled. For example, in this book most of the time we have simply assumed that the "best" production function has already been chosen by the firm. With the aid of linear programming we can be more precise about how the production function is selected in the first place. Again, we have usually assumed that the plant or firm produces only one commodity. The techniques of linear programming permit us to describe, in a compact way, the activities of the multicommodity plant and multicommodity firm.

Second, many businessmen, engineers, and management consultants have found that linear programming can profitably be applied to a wide range of strictly practical problems. In fact, it was originally developed,

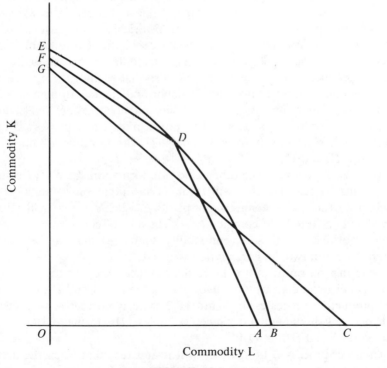

FIGURE 18.1

shortly after World War II, in the course of an effort to make less inefficient the procurement activities of the United States Air Force. The production functions of the real world may not "really" exhibit constant returns to scale and fixed factor coefficients. But the assumption that they do have these features has often proved to be an immensely useful one. This is not surprising. After all, any non-linear relationship can be approximated by a series of linear functions. Consider figure 18.1.

In figure 18.1 the non-linear curve *EDB* can be taken as representing the "true" terms on which commodity K can be exchanged for commodity L when resources are shifted from the production of commodity K to commodity L. That is, *EDB* is a production transformation curve of the sort you met in the Principles course. In figure 18.1, line *CG* is a "rough" approximation to curve *EDB,* and line segments *FD* and *DA* together form a less rough approximation to curve *EDB*. Clearly, by increasing the number of line segments, we can approximate curve *EDB* as closely as we wish in figure 18.1.

The nature of the production function in linear programming is illustrated by figure 18.2. In the language of linear programmers what economists call a production function is, for historical reasons, usually termed a "process." Beginning now, we shall respect this convention. Assume that the state of technology is such that three different processes are available to produce commodity A. Assume also that each of these three processes requires the use of two factors—labor and capital. In figure 18.2 the quantity of labor input is measured along the horizontal axis and the quantity of capital input along the vertical axis. Each process is represented by a ray from the origin (point *O*), the three possibilities being labeled I, II, and III.

Figure 18.2 conveys one other kind of information. Line *VV'* connects the points on each ray that will result in an output of 20 units of commodity A. Line *WW'* connects the points on each ray that will result in an output of 40 units of commodity A. There is, of course, no limit to the number of lines of this sort (commodity isoquants) that can be drawn in figure 18.2. But two lines are all that we need.

Note that on ray I, *OW* is twice the distance *OV;* and that on ray III, *OW'* is twice the distance *OV'*. However, since rays I and II depict different production processes, in figure 18.2 there is no reason why distance *OV* on ray I should equal distance *OV'* on ray III. In figure 18.2, in fact, *OV* ≠ *OV';* and *OW* ≠ *OW'*.

Consider process I. In figure 18.2 it is apparent that when the decision is made to produce commodity A with process I, an input of 1 unit of labor must always be matched with an input of 2 units of capital. When 4

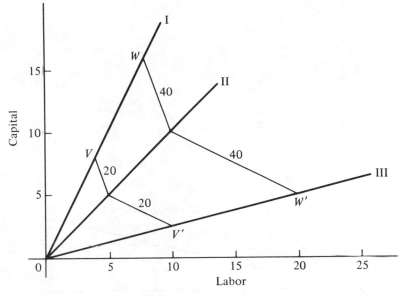

FIGURE 18.2

units of labor are combined with 8 units of capital, the use of process I results in an output of 20 units of commodity A. When 8 units of labor are combined with 16 units of capital, the result is an output of 40 units of commodity A.

Now consider process II in figure 18.2. We see that 1 unit of labor must be used for every 1 unit of capital. When, using process II, 5 units of capital are combined with 5 units of labor, the result is an output of 20 units of commodity A. When, using process II, 10 units of capital are combined with 10 units of labor, the result is an output of 40 units of commodity A. You should by similar reasoning interpret the economic meaning of ray III in figure 18.2.

Selecting the best process

Assuming that the firm wishes to produce commodity A, which of the three processes available to it should it adopt? And, when the "right" process has been selected, how much of commodity A should be produced? We cannot answer these questions with the aid of figure 18.2 alone. We must have additional information on (i) the firm's budget—how much it can afford to spend on factor inputs—and (ii) the prices of the two factor inputs (capital and labor) that it must use. Turn now to figure 18.3.

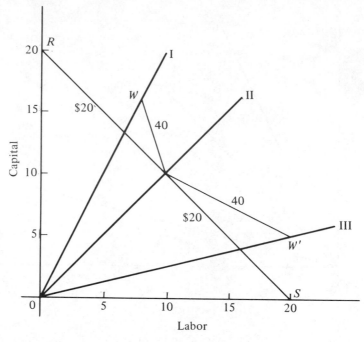

FIGURE 18.3

Figure 18.3 is constructed on the assumptions that the firm can spend the sum of $20 (per hour) on its factor inputs; that the price of a capital input is $1; and that the price of a labor input is also $1. With this budget, the firm can, of course, purchase various combinations of capital and labor. At one extreme, it can hire 20 units of capital and zero units of labor. At the other extreme, it can buy 20 units of.labor and zero units of capital. Any point on the budget line *RS* in figure 18.3 depicts a feasible combination of factor inputs (given the budget constraint that the firm can spend only $20 per hour).

The firm, as an income maximizer, wishes to obtain the greatest output of commodity A consistent with an expenditure of $20 per hour on factor inputs. As figure 18.3 indicates, this goal is achieved when the firm (i) uses process II; (ii) spends $10 on capital and $10 on labor; and (iii) produces an output of 40 units of commodity A. If the firm could spend more than $20 per hour on factor inputs, obviously it could move up to a higher commodity isoquant by making greater use of process II. If it used one of the other two processes, and spent $20 on factor inputs, it would have an output of less than 40 units of commodity A.

An unusual case

Will process II always be the "best" way of producing commodity A? Clearly not. In figure 18.3, process II is best because the input prices of both capital and labor are $1. If the price of a labor input were to fall to zero, the price of a capital input remaining unchanged at $1, the firm would obviously prefer process III (since it is the most labor intensive process). Conversely, if the price of a capital input were to fall to zero, the price of a labor input remaining unchanged at $1, the firm would prefer process I (since it is the most capital intensive process).

For every set of factor prices, is there one "best" production process in linear programming? The answer is: "usually but not always." Consider figure 18.4. Here it is assumed that four processes are available to pro- duce commodity A; that *MM'* connects the points on each process ray that will yield an output of 70 units; and that the firm's budget line is given by *BB'*. In figure 18.4, between points *a* and *b,* the budget line coin-

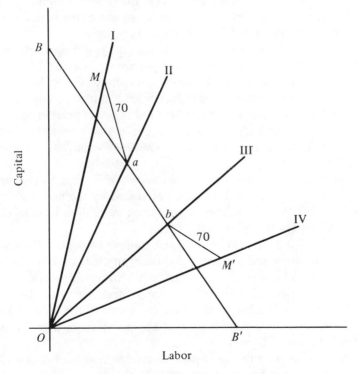

FIGURE 18.4

cides with the commodity isoquant *MM'* thanks to the factor price ratios that are implied by the slope of *BB'*. Hence it is a matter of indifference to the firm whether 70 units of commodity A are produced with process II or process III or, indeed, with some combination of processes II and III. In the "normal" case, however, the budget line and the highest commodity isoquant have only a single point of contact (which must be an extreme point or "kink" in the commodity isoquant).

A tougher problem

We are now in a position to move on to a more complicated (though still quite manageable) problem in linear programming. In the real world the firm generally produces more than one commodity or provides more than one service. Likewise, in the real world the firm, especially in the short run, is subject to more than a single production constraint. There are likely to be production ceilings in the form of some maximum amount of warehouse space or some maximum number of hours that workers will accept. Suppose that the firm faces the following problem.

The firm may hire up to 14 units of labor (L) and up to 12 units of capital (K). It may use its capital and labor to produce two commodities, X_1 and X_2. The production of 1 unit of commodity X_1 requires 1 unit of labor and 3 units of capital. The production of 1 unit of commodity X_2 requires 2 units of labor and 1 unit of capital. The production and sale of every unit of X_1 adds \$6 to the firm's net profit. Every unit of X_2 adds \$4 to net profit. What output mix of commodities X_1 and X_2 will maximize the firm's net profit?

Let us begin by identifying the combinations of X_1 and X_2 that are feasible, i.e. the combinations that can be produced by the firm given that it can hire no more than 14 units of labor and no more than 12 units of capital. This we do with the aid of figure 18.5.

In figure 18.5, line AD shows all combinations of commodities X_1 and X_2 which require 14 units of labor for their production. Line EB shows all combinations of commodities X_1 and X_2 which require 12 units of capital for their production. The perimeter and shaded area of the polygon $OACE$ includes all feasible combinations of commodities X_1 and X_2, that is, all combinations that can be produced using no more than 14 units of labor and 12 units of capital.

We note at once that the most profitable combination of X_1 and X_2 for the firm must lie on the perimeter ACE. If the firm were producing the

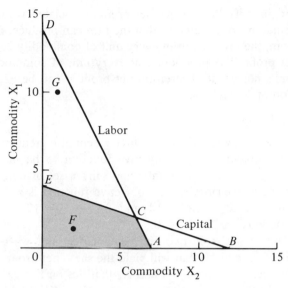

FIGURE 18.5

combination of X_1 and X_2 represented by point F in figure 18.5, it would be using neither all of its available labor nor all of its available capital. Hence by putting idle labor and capital to work, the firm could produce more of X_1 and X_2 (or more of X_1 or X_2) and so increase its net profit.

Point G denotes a combination of 10 units of X_1 and 1 unit of X_2. It lies outside the shaded area in figure 18.5 and so does not represent a feasible combination. There is enough labor available to the firm to produce this combination but not enough capital.

Mathematically then, the perimeter and shaded area $OACE$ in figure 18.5 is defined by the set of inequalities

$$X_1 + 2X_2 \leqq 14 \tag{18.1a}$$
$$3X_1 + X_2 \leqq 12$$
$$X_1, X_2 \geqq 0 \tag{18.1b}$$

The labor constraint, which is line AD in figure 18.5, is defined by the equality

$$X_1 + 2X_2 = 14 \tag{18.2a}$$

The capital constraint, which is line BE in figure 18.5, is defined by the equality

$$3X_1 + X_2 = 12 \tag{18.2b}$$

Let us now identify the various net profits associated with the various output combinations of X_1 and X_2 that the firm can produce. By the terms of our problem, the production of every unit of commodity X_1 adds \$6 to the firm's net profit. The production of every unit of commodity X_2 adds \$4 to the firm's net profit. Therefore, net profit π can be expressed as a linear function of X_1 and X_2.

$$\pi = 6X_1 + 4X_2 \tag{18.3}$$

Indeed we have now identified the three essential ingredients of a linear programming problem: (i) an objective function to be maximized (or minimized); (ii) a set of constraints; and (iii) a set of non-negative restrictions. In the above problem the objective function is $\pi = 6X_1 + 4X_2$; the constraints are $X_1 + 2X_2 \leqslant 14$ and $3X_1 + X_2 \leqslant 12$; and the non-negative restrictions are $X_1, X_2 \geqq 0$.

With the aid of a simple two-dimensional diagram, we can show all combinations of X_1 and X_2 that will yield the same net profit. Thus in figure 18.6 every combination of X_1 and X_2 that lies on line JJ' yields a net profit of \$24. Every combination that lies on line KK' yields a total net profit of \$36. And every combination that lies on line LL' yields a net profit of \$48. There is, of course, no limit to the number of "iso-profit" lines that could be drawn in figure 18.6.

To find the feasible combination of X_1 and X_2 that is also the most profitable combination for the firm we need only (i) impose the set of iso-profit lines in figure 18.6 on the production possibility set of figure

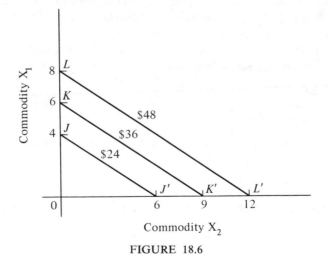

FIGURE 18.6

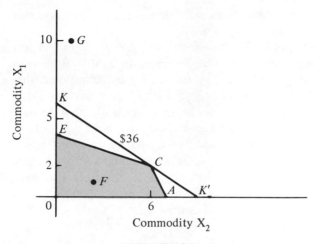

FIGURE 18.7

18.5 and (ii) note the feasible combination of X_1 and X_2 that yields the greatest net profit. This is done in figure 18.7.

Clearly, the greatest net profit that the firm can earn is $36. It is gained when the firm produces 2 units of X_1 and 6 units of X_2. This combination is represented by point C in figure 18.7. Every other combination of X_1 and X_2 is either not feasible (because not enough labor or capital is available to produce it) or, if feasible, yields a net profit that is less than $36.

Beyond geometry

A linear programming problem that allows the firm to produce no more than two commodities can be solved with the simple geometric technique described above. And a 3-commodity problem can be handled with the aid of horrible three-dimensional diagrams. But, of course, when the problem involves the possible production of more than 3 commodities, a solution can only be obtained by using more elaborate mathematical techniques. It is these techniques that receive most of the attention in the standard books on linear programming. Here we will limit ourselves to showing the difficulties that these techniques are designed to surmount.

Consider figure 18.7 once more. It is clear that, for most sets of prices, the most profitable combination of commodities X_1 and X_2 for the firm is given by one of the extreme points, *A, C,* or *E.* In this simple example, instead of taking the trouble to construct iso-profit lines for different combinations of X_1 and X_2, we could have simply computed net profit for each of these three combinations and selected the combination that yielded the greatest net profit.

Since in figure 18.7 there are only two commodities and two constraints, the extreme points A, C, and E can be located by inspection. We need, however, an algebraic method of locating extreme points that can be applied to linear programming problems that contain more than a very small number of variables. In order to apply such a method to our problem we must first convert the mathematical inequalities of system 18.1a into mathematical equalities. This we do by introducing *slack* variables.

Let L^* denote the amount of labor available to the firm that *is not* used to produce either X_1 or X_2. Let K^* denote the amount of capital available to the firm that *is not* used to produce either X_1 or X_2.

Our problem is now to maximize

$$\pi = 6X_1 + 4X_2 \tag{18.3}$$

subject to

$$\begin{aligned} X_1 + 2X_2 + L^* &= 14 \\ 3X_1 + X_2 + K^* &= 12 \\ X_1, X_2, L^*, K^* &\geq 0 \end{aligned} \tag{18.4}$$

Here we encounter an obvious difficulty. System 18.4 contains 4 unknowns (X_1, X_2, L^*, K^*) but only two equations containing these 4 unknowns. Since system 18.4 contains more unknowns than equations, it has no unique solution. To obtain a unique solution, we must revise the system in a way that will eliminate 2 of the 4 unknowns.

Suppose that we arbitrarily eliminate X_1 and X_2. This we do by writing $X_1 = 0$ and $X_2 = 0$. Then clearly the equations in 18.4 are satisfied if, and only if, $L^* = 14$ and $K^* = 12$. You can easily verify that this solution is represented by the origin (point O) in figure 18.7. In the language of linear programming we have "formed a basis" with the variables L^* and K^*. The variables X_1 and X_2 were relegated to the status of *non-basic* variables when we set them equal to zero. L^* and K^* then became the *basic* variables.

Since the firm's profit π is zero when $X_1 = 0$ and $X_2 = 0$ (that is, when nothing is produced because no capital or labor is used), point O perforce represents a sub-optimal combination of X_1 and X_2. Nevertheless, point O is a good place from which to begin the search for the most profitable combination. One thing we do know. The most profitable combination of X_1 and X_2 must lie at one of the extreme points A, C, or E. If we start at point O and systematically check out the profitability of the combinations represented by these three points we are sure to get the correct answer. In this problem the correct answer is, of course, the combination of commodities X_1 and X_2 that will yield the firm its greatest profit.

Note again that we have no interest in moving from point O to any point other than A, C, or E in figure 18.7. As we previously noted, point F would represent a feasible but sub-optimal combination of X_1 and X_2. Point F is a feasible combination because there is enough capital and labor available to produce it; but point F is a sub-optimal combination because there is also capital and labor available to produce more of both X_1 and X_2. Point G is a more profitable and hence more desirable combination but it is not feasible. There is not enough labor available to produce it.

Suppose that we wish to move from point O to point E in figure 18.7. To do this, it is only necessary to write $K^* = 0$ and $X_2 = 0$. In the language of linear programming, we have formed a new basis with the variables L^* and X_1. In this new basis, the basic variables are now L^* and X_1; and the non-basic variables are K^* and X_2. The variable X_1 replaces K^* in the basis.

The equations that we must solve have now become

$$X_1 + L^* = 14$$
$$3X_1 = 12$$

The solution is, of course, $X_1 = 4$ and $L^* = 10$. Substituting for X_1 and X_2 in the objective function, $\pi = 6X_1 + 4X_2$, gives $\pi = 24$. (Remember that we have $X_2 = 0$.) A glance at figure 18.7 will confirm that we have reached extreme point E which is the combination consisting of 4 units of X_1 and zero units of X_2.

To get from point E to point C in figure 18.7, we form yet another basis. This time we replace $X_2 = 0$ with $L^* = 0$ so that now our basic variables are X_1 and X_2 and our non-basic variables are L^* and K^*. This time we decree that all available labor and capital shall be employed. The equations that we must solve have become

$$X_1 + 2X_2 = 14$$
$$3X_1 + X_2 = 12$$

Solving, we obtain $X_1 = 2$ and $X_2 = 6$. Substituting in the objective function, $\pi = 6X_1 + 4X_2$, gives $\pi = 36$.

One more time. Let us move from point C to point A in figure 18.7. This time we replace $L^* = 0$ with $X_1 = 0$ so that now our basic variables are X_2 and K^* and our non-basic variables are X_1 and L^*. The equations to be solved become

$$2X_2 = 14$$
$$X_2 + K^* = 12$$

TABLE 18.1[a]

	Point O	Point E	Point C[b]	Point A
X_1	0	4	2	0
X_2	0	0	6	7
L^*	14	10	0	0
K^*	12	0	0	5
π	0	24	36	28

[a] table 18.1 refers to figure 18.7
[b] most profitable combinations of X_1 and X_2

Solving, we obtain $X_2 = 7$, $K^* = 5$ and, from the objective function, $\pi = 28$.

We can summarize the results of our search, via algebra, for the most profitable combination of commodities X_1 and X_2 in table 18.1. It confirms what we have already established via geometry. The combination of commodities X_1 and X_2 given by point C in figure 18.7 provides a total profit of $36; and neither of the other extreme points (which are E and A in figure 18.7) will yield so great a total profit. We emphasize again that the most profitable combination of activities in a linear programming problem is always found at an extreme point.

The great merit of linear programming techniques is that they permit us to locate the optimal combination of activities with a reasonable expenditure of time and energy. For with their aid we are able to concentrate on extreme points and ignore all others. They also provide us with a number of shortcuts for reaching the optimal combination of activities without checking out all of the extreme points. For details see any standard work on linear programming. It is also an immense advantage of linear programming that all of its problems can be turned over to computers. Since they are stated in terms of equations of the first degree, they contain none of the exponents or derivatives that defeat the present state of computer technology. While a linear programming problem is often messy (because of the large number of variables involved), it is always, in principle, quite simple.

Shadow pricing

So far we have considered linear programming as a set of techniques for maximizing the firm's profit with profit being written as the dependent variable in objective function. However, linear programming has another important role in the planning of production that should be noted. It can be used to find the value that the firm should place upon every unit of factor input that it employs.

Suppose that a firm is considering adding to its capital stock. How does it go about calculating the value of an additional machine? It could, of course, add the additional machine and observe the amount by which its total revenue increases. This is the way that elementary textbooks in economics sometimes view businessmen as deciding upon their factor combinations. But juggling the factor combination is a cumbersome and expensive way to determine the economic productivity of factor inputs. With the aid of linear programming, the amount of trial and error needed to select the optimum factor combination can sometimes be greatly reduced. At this point we need to introduce the idea of the dual problem in linear programming.

For every problem in linear programming there is a corresponding *dual* problem, the original problem being called the *primal*. (Some writers prefer to say that every problem in linear programming has two forms—the primal and the dual.) When the primal is a maximization problem, the dual is a minimization problem. Conversely, when the primal is a minimization problem, the dual is a maximization problem.

Suppose, for example, that the primal problem is to maximize the output of a commodity that can be produced with a given outlay on costs. Then the corresponding dual problem is to minimize the cost of producing a given quantity of commodity output. If the primal problem is to minimize the cost of a given output, the dual problem is to maximize output with a given outlay.

Should a problem in linear programming be set up and solved in its primal form or in its dual form? No fixed rule applies here. The form chosen depends (i) upon the information that the programmer seeks and (ii) which form can be most easily programmed.

Let us take another look at the simple problem involving commodities X_1 and X_2 that we have already solved both geometrically and algebraically in this chapter. We know the maximum profit ($36) that can be obtained by producing X_1 and X_2. Suppose that we wish to impute a part of this maximum profit to each unit of capital and labor that is used in production. We may wish to make this imputation because we have some ill-defined ethical commitment to paying each factor "what it contributes to production." Then again, we may simply want to know what each factor "really" contributes to production regardless of what is being paid. We solve this imputation problem by translating the primal problem (which was a profit-maximization problem) into its dual form. But first we need additional notation. Recall that the production of 1 unit of commodity X_1 requires the use of 1 unit of labor and 3 units of capital; and that the production of 1 unit of commodity X_2 requires the use of 2 units of labor and 1 unit of capital.

Let π' denote the total cost of producing commodities X_1 and X_2. Let W denote the value imputed to a unit of labor and R the value imputed to a unit of capital. The imputed value W is sometimes called the shadow price of labor and the imputed value R the shadow price of capital. For the record, we emphasize that W indicates the amount by which total revenue would be increased if 1 more unit of labor were hired; and R indicates the amount by which total revenue would be increased if 1 more unit of capital were hired. Thus W is a measure of the opportunity cost of not using labor to produce commodities X_1 and X_2, and R is a measure of the opportunity cost of not using capital to produce them.

We can now write the two forms of our linear programming problem side by side.

Primal	Dual
Maximize	Minimize
$\pi = 6X_1 + 4X_2$	$\pi' = 14W + 12R$
subject to	subject to
$X_1 + 2X_2 \leq 14$	$W + 3R \geq 6$
$3X_1 + X_2 \leq 12$	$2W + R \geq 4$
$X_1, X_2 \geq 0$	$W, R, \geq 0$

Comparing the primal and dual forms of the problem we note the following. The numerical constants, 14 and 12, on the right-hand side of the constraints in the primal form become the numerical coefficients of the variables W and R in the objective function to be minimized in the dual form. Likewise, the numerical coefficients, 6 and 4, in the objective function of the primal form become the numerical constants on the right-hand side of the constraints in the dual form.

Is this reformulation of our linear programming problem confusing? If so, take it very slowly. Consider. The inequality $X_1 + 2X_2 \leq 14$ in the primal form merely says that the amount of labor used to produce X_1 and X_2 cannot exceed the amount of labor available, namely, 14 units. The inequality $W + 3R \geq 6$ in the dual form merely says that the expenditure on inputs of labor and capital used to produce 1 unit of commodity X_1 cannot be less than 6. This is the dollar amount by which total revenue is increased when 1 additional unit of commodity X_1 is produced. This constraint is perfectly sensible. Obviously we need some constraint in the dual; otherwise the firm minimizes total cost by producing nothing. So long as $W + 3R < 6$, it is always possible that the firm can increase its profit by producing an additional unit of commodity X_1.

Again, the inequality $3X_1 + X_2 \leq 12$ in the primal form says that the amount of capital used to produce commodities X_1 and X_2 must not exceed the amount of capital available, namely 12 units. The inequality $2W + R \geq 4$ in the dual form says that the combined expenditures on labor and capital used to produce 1 unit of commodity X_2 cannot be less than 4. This is the dollar amount by which total revenue is increased when 1 additional unit of X_2 is produced.

To find the values for W and R that minimize total cost π' we convert the inequalities of the dual form into equalities and write

$$W + 3R = 6$$
$$2W + R = 4. \qquad (18.5)$$

Solving this exceedingly simple set of linear equations, we get $W = 1.2$, and $R = 1.6$.

Note that in linear programming the process of imputing shadow prices to factor inputs "exhausts the product." In our problem you can easily verify that

$$WL + RK = \pi$$

since $W = 1.2, L = 14, R = 1.6, K = 12$
and $\pi = 36$.

The method of reckoning shadow prices of factor inputs illustrated by our example is especially useful in those situations where there is no market in existence that places a price tag on factor inputs.

We can imagine the case where the members of an isolated community in the South Pacific form a producers' cooperative enterprise to produce commodities X_1 and X_2 for the world market. Three sorts of people join the cooperative—those who contribute only labor, those who contribute only capital, and those who contribute both capital and labor. Inevitably, the problem will arise as to how the income obtained from the sale of commodities X_1 and X_2 is to be divided among the members of the cooperative. One solution is to calculate shadow prices for labor and capital inputs and use them as a basis for compensating the members. But even if the decision is reached to divide the cooperative's income equally among the members, disregarding the contribution of each, shadow prices for labor and capital inputs should be calculated. Otherwise, the cooperative has no way of telling whether, in any effort to increase its income, the first priority should be given to increasing its stock of capital or its supply of labor.

In the interest of uncomplicated exposition we have cast our production problem of linear programming in the ultra-simple case of the firm that uses two factor inputs to produce two commodities. But the reasoning that we have employed is, of course, independent of the number of factor inputs and commodities assumed.

Summary

Linear programming is a set of techniques that allows the firm to solve maximization and minimization problems subject to specified constraints. It assumes a production function which is (a) linear in that there are constant returns to scale and (b) characterized by fixed factor coefficients.

Linear programming assumes that the prices at which the firm sells its outputs are fixed and immutable. This assumption can be interpreted to mean either that the firm operates only in perfectly competitive commodity markets, or that, for purposes of short-run planning, it chooses to behave "as if" it operates in such markets. For example, in planning the production of a commodity for the next month, the firm may choose to assume that every unit produced can be sold for a $1 price even though its managers know that at a $1 price some part of the month's output may have to be stockpiled in inventory. The managers choose to behave in this way simply because some assumption must be made about demand. And the assumption that all planned output can be sold at a $1 price may seem to be as useful as any other.

We considered two simple applications of linear programming. In the first, we used it to find the "best" process open to a firm for producing a commodity when its budget was limited and the prices of its factor inputs were given. In the second case, we used it to determine the most profitable mix of two commodities that the firm was tooled up to produce.

For every problem in linear programming there is a corresponding dual problem. As we noted, when the original or primal problem is a maximization problem, the dual is a minimization problem. When the primal problem is one of minimizing, the dual is one of maximizing. By casting a maximizing problem of linear programming in its dual form, we can place a shadow price on each of the factor inputs, a shadow price being the amount by which the firm's total revenue would be increased if one additional unit of the factor were used. Shadow prices are extremely useful in those situations when there is no organized market for factor inputs in existence that places a price tag on each factor input.

REFERENCES

Baumol, W. J., "Activity Analysis in One Lesson," *American Economic Review*, 47 (1958), 837-73.

Dorfman, Robert, P. A. Samuelson, and R. M. Solow, *Linear Programming and Economic Analysis* (New York, 1958), especially pp. 1-38.

Ferguson, C. E., *Microeconomic Theory* (Homewood, Ill., 3rd ed., 1972), chapter 12.

Lancaster, Kelvin, *Mathematical Economics* (New York, 1968), chapter 3.

Leftwich, R. H., *The Price System and Resource Allocation* (Hinsdale, Ill., 5th ed., 1973), chapter 19.

Spivey, W. A., *Linear Programming: An Introduction* (New York, 1963).

Throsby, C. D., *Elementary Linear Programming* (New York, 1970).

Tisdell, C. A., *Microeconomics: The Theory of Economic Allocation* (Sidney, 1972), chapter 15.

19
Last Words

Looking back

In this book we have examined the foundations of microeconomics and explored certain topics that lie in the borderlands between microeconomics and the rest of economics. The subject matter of microeconomics we have defined as the study of markets with particular attention to the activities of households, firms, labor unions, and industries.

At the outset of our survey, we accepted that the study of markets is by no means the whole of economics. The market, however, is the principal method by which economic activity is organized in a predominantly private enterprise economy. It is also extensively employed by all avowedly socialist economies. And, given the vast number of decisions that must be made every hour in a modern industrial economy whether called capitalist, socialist, or mixed, it is difficult (if not impossible) to imagine economic activity being carried on without a very great reliance on markets.

Most of the time, we have proceeded by the method of formal, self-conscious abstraction—the method that is sometimes called model-building. The choice of this method was justified in our opening chapter with the assertion that it was the experience of economists that since real-world markets with very different institutional frameworks have a great deal in common, "little explains much." At the very least, you are now in a position to check this assertion against your own experience.

Throughout most (but not all) of this book we were mainly concerned with positive economics. Our goal was to get from useful assumptions to useful conclusions according to the accepted rules of logic. We did not pause to speculate at great length about the implications of our results for the good life or man's spiritual condition. The justification offered for the emphasis on positive economics was a simple one. It is quite impossible to make intelligent normative (welfare) judgments about economic policies or arrangements without a solid grounding in positive economics. For us to give our support to a proposed economic change simply because its backers have their hearts in the right place would be plain silly. Before we can pass judgment on the desirability of the proposal for change, we must be able to form some idea of the economic consequences which will follow. And to say the obvious for one last time: in an immensely complicated real world that is coordinated by markets of varying degrees of imperfection, things are not always what they seem.

In the pursuit of positive microeconomics, we began by deriving the individual's demand curve for a commodity on the assumption that his income and consumption tastes were given. We summed up the demand curves of individuals to obtain the market demand curve for the commodity. Then, turning to the supply side of the market, we examined the nature of a production function. We showed that every production function which requires the use of specialized factor inputs must give rise to a U-shaped curve of average total cost in the plant, and that for every plant embodying a production function, there is an output or range of outputs at which average total cost is minimized. Next, we proceeded to construct a set of cost curves for the multiplant firm and found a most important difference between plant and firm. The need to employ specialized factor inputs in the production function dictates that there is always an optimum size of plant. But when the size of a firm can be varied by changing the number of optimum size plants that it operates, then there need be no optimum size of firm.

Armed with a set of revenue and cost functions for the firm, we traced the determination of price and output under conditions of undoubted monopoly, psuedo-monopoly, perfect competition, stayout pricing, and simple oligopoly. Moving on, we examined some of the complications that arise when economic decisions are made in a world of compound interest. We noted that, in such a world, all economic rents are ultimately transformed by the capitalization process into higher bookkeeping costs; so that, in the long run, price will always seem to the unwary observer to equal average total cost. Our survey of static microeconomics concluded with a look at the distinctive features of the markets for factor inputs.

While this book was mainly concerned with positive economics, Chapters 13 and 14 examined the set of value judgments and analytical techniques that constitute modern "welfare economics." We noted that the touchstone for assigning praise or censure in modern welfare economics is the compensation test: Can people who benefit from an economic change fully compensate those who are injured by it and still be better off? In Chapter 13 we considered how the tools of welfare economics have been applied to the problems of public utility pricing, selection criteria for public works, and the social costs of production. In Chapter 14 we expanded our view to consider the conditions that must be satisfied before the whole economic system can achieve a Pareto optimum—the happy state where the economy cannot increase its economic welfare by altering the distribution of economic resources.

The economic decisions of the real world must be made under conditions of uncertainty. Therefore, all static models have their limitations and, our survey of such models completed, we moved on to consider certain complications that arise when a model is not completely static, i.e. when economic decisions are made on the basis of incomplete information. Chapter 15 examined the meaning of "profit," "profit maximization," and "economic rationality" in the context of uncertainty. Chapter 16 considered the behavior of the firm under a particular kind of uncertainty: that which is present because firms are few and the reaction of a rival to one's own moves is not wholly predictable. This is "oligopoly with limited information."

Finally, we concluded our survey of microeconomics by broadening our viewpoint to include a complete economic system. In Chapter 17 we found that, by the careful specification of assumptions, it is possible to prove that for a perfectly competitive economic system, there exists a general equilibrium set of prices and outputs; and that payments to the factors exhaust the product.

Looking forward

It is hardly necessary to say that, since time and space were limited, we have dealt rather cavalierly with some very important matters in microeconomics. Fortunately, there is a wealth of information and wisdom in your faculty and your library which can make good the deficiencies in coverage of this book.

In every generation, a few students who meet economic theory for the first time will be fascinated—not to say mesmerized—by its order and elegance. But for most of us economic theory is a collection of tools whose cost of acquisition is justified only to the extent that they have a positive payoff when applied to real-world problems. You now have the basic equipment needed for "the study of markets by the method of formal, self-conscious abstraction." The next move is up to you.

Subject Index

Author Index